FLINTLOCK AND TOMAHAWK

New England in King Philip's War

To my parents,
Saidee Raybold and Arthur Edward Leach,
whose sacrifice and encouragement
made this book possible

ISBN 978-0-88150-885-7

Library of Congress Cataloging-in-Publication Data
has been applied for.

Published by The Countryman Press,
P.O. Box 748, Woodstock, VT 05091

Distributed by W. W. Norton & Company, Inc.,
500 Fifth Avenue, New York, NY 10110

Printed in the United States of America

10 9 8 7 6 5 4 3 2 1

Preface

MY interest in King Philip's War was first aroused during my boyhood in Rhode Island when I began to browse in the chapters written by the "Rhode Island Historian," Mr. John W. Haley. There I read of the desperate fight in the Great Swamp and of the Queen's Fort with its legendary hidden chamber. Curiosity impelled me to visit these storied spots, and I recall searching in vain, as hundreds of others have done, for the hidden chamber. Some years later I undertook the serious study of American History at Harvard, where I encountered the subject again, this time in the seminar of Professor Samuel Eliot Morison. It was he who convinced me that this book should be written; his inspiration and example lie behind every page.

Little has been written about King Philip's War in more than half a century. The subject was one which fascinated earlier generations, but most of the available accounts tend to be uncritical and otherwise limited in scope. None presents a fully rounded picture of a whole society in travail—the true picture of New England in 1675–1676. The Indians who fought the war and lost it left behind them no records to tell us their side of the story, a fact which makes a complete and impartial reconstruction of the events especially difficult for the modern historian. I set out to learn all I could about the war by carefully studying the scattered and sometimes fragmentary records which have survived, and by visiting most of the scenes of action. The trail has led me back and forth over southern New England, with stops to consult not only the more important archives, but also the many local records still tucked away in town clerks' offices. It has been a fascinating quest.

vii

King Philip's War was the first major test for the budding civilization which had been planted in New England in the seventeenth century. It was a crisis of staggering proportions, threatening to undo much of the careful work that had been accomplished. No society can pass through such a crisis without experiencing deep and abiding changes. Similarly, the Indians were hurling themselves, for better or for worse, into a new stage of existence. They too would never be the same again. The story of New England in this crisis, with all its attendant heroism, bloodshed, and suffering, is the story that I have tried to tell within these covers.

In one respect, at least, I have had the advantage of my predecessors. Today we are able to view the long and bloody strife between Indians and Europeans with much greater detachment than was possible even as recently as fifty years ago. Equally important, our experience with savagery in World War II has reacquainted us with the passions that underlie cruel and relentless "total war." We can have a real "feeling" for the seventeenth-century situation without being unduly favorable to either side. Furthermore, recent advances in the fields of anthropology and sociology enable us to understand more correctly the deeper meanings of the struggle. Throughout our contemplation of this subject the eternal yardstick of Christian love continues to remind us of another great opportunity lost.

Professor Morison's valuable suggestions and his encouragement over a period of years deserve special mention with heartfelt thanks. The maps drawn by Robert L. Williams are a valuable supplement to the text. Other people, too, have given generous assistance in a variety of ways, among them W. Wallace Austin, Richard LeBaron Bowen, Clarence S. Brigham, William R. Carlton, Marjorie E. Case, Clarkson A. Collins 3rd, Professor Roy P. Fairfield, Leo Flaherty, Zoltán Haraszti, Professor and Mrs. Robert H. Hardie, Edith E. Hazelton, William Foy Lisenby, Clifford P. Monahon, Marshall Morgan, Florence M. Osborne, Mary T. Quinn, Stephen T. Riley, Marvin Sadik, Clifford K. Shipton, Wilcomb E. Washburn, Walter Muir Whitehill, and Harry A. Wright. My wife, Brenda Mason Leach, has been a faithful helper and supporter through every stage of the work. I cannot begin my story without a word of loving appreciation to her.

DOUGLAS EDWARD LEACH

Introduction

SAMUEL ELIOT MORISON

MY friend Dr. Leach has written the first comprehensive history of King Philip's War to appear since the seventeenth century. Most historians, including myself, believe that it was the most severe of all the colonial Indian wars, subsequent to the 1622 massacre in Virginia. In view of our recent experiences of warfare, and of the many instances today of backward peoples getting enlarged notions of nationalism and turning ferociously on Europeans who have attempted to civilize them, this early conflict of the same nature cannot help but be of interest. It was an intensely dramatic struggle, decisive for the survival of the English race in New England, and the eventual disappearance of the Algonkian Indians.

Behind King Philip's War was the clash of a relatively advanced race with savages, an occurrence not uncommon in history. The conquering race (and this is as true of the Moslems and Hindus as of Christians) always feels duty-bound to impose its culture upon the native; the native in the process of absorbing it acquires the conqueror's vices and diseases as well, and in the end is either absorbed or annihilated, the only compromise being a miserable existence on a "reservation." The Algonkian Indians of New England, notably King Philip's father Massasoit, welcomed the Englishman as an ally against their Indian neighbors and appreciated his tools and firearms; but the Englishman expected them to take the whole of his culture, including Puritan theology, in one package. That was like expecting a Stone Age savage to be at home in a modern skyscraper

ix

apartment. The New England colonists tried hard to be fair and just to the natives; but their best was not good enough to absorb them without a conflict.

Dr. Leach has told how and why this particular war happened; he has related the story of it, with all its desperate massacres, battles, and stratagems. He gives a vivid picture of the conditions under which it was fought, and of the protagonists—Governor Winslow, Captain Church, Captain Moseley, Ninigret, Weetamoo the Squaw Sachem, Pomham, Monoco, and King Philip himself. He has described the tactics and the logistics by which the redskin was finally conquered. He has pulled no punches in his story of cruelty and vengeance on both sides; and the modern reader will discern many analogies to recent events. The treatment of the converted "praying" Indians was no worse than that of the United States to Japanese-Americans in World War II. The Reverend John Eliot pointed out that the harsh policy of killing prisoners or selling them into slavery would prolong the Indian war—an early instance of "unconditional surrender." When emotions are stimulated to the boiling point, as they are in desperate wars, Christians forget their religion and descend to the level of the brute fighting for his life.

This is not only a military but a political and social history. The tactics and the weapons of 1675 are of historical interest; but the policies and attitudes of Puritan and Indian are just as alive today, and as relevant, as those of World War II, or of the Peloponnesian War as described by Thucydides.

Contents

New England in
King Philip's War
1675-1676

○ English Settlement   ● INDIAN VILLAGE

------- Trail (Conjectural)

PENNACOOK

Northfield (Squakeag)

Dunsta

PESKEOMPSCUT

PAQUOAG

Deerfield

Mount Wachusett

Bloody Brook

Lancaster

Hopewell Swamp

N I P M U C K S

Hatfield

WASHACCUM

Hadley

Northampton

MENAMESET

Quinsigamond

To Albany

(Quabaug)
Brookfield

HASSAN

ASHQUOASH

Westfield

Springfield

MANCHAGE

CHABANAKONGKOMUN

Suffield

SENECKSIG

WABAQUASSET

Nipsachuck ×

Simsbury

Windsor

Hartford

Farmington

Wethersfield

NARRAGANSETTS

W

QUINEBAUG

Middletown

Connecticut River

MOHEGANS

Norwich

PEQUOTS

Pettaqu

Haddam

Wallingford

Powcatuck River

New London

Stonington

NIANTI

Killingworth

Westerly

New Haven

Branford Guilford

Saybrook

Lyme

Long Island Sound

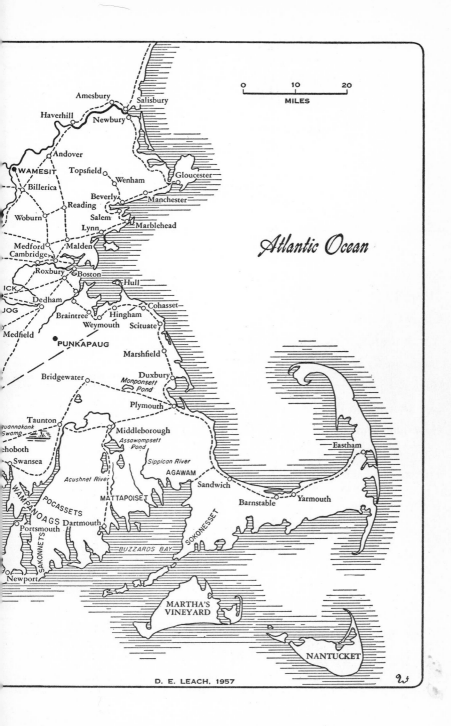

MILES
0   10   20

Amesbury
Salisbury
Haverhill   Newbury
Andover
WAMESIT   Topsfield
Billerica   Wenham
Gloucester
Beverly
Reading   Manchester
Woburn
Salem
Lynn   Marblehead
Medford   Malden
Cambridge
Roxbury   Boston
ICK   Hull
Dedham
JOG   Cohasset
Braintree   Hingham
Weymouth   Scituate
Medfield   PUNKAPAUG
Marshfield
Bridgewater   Duxbury
Monponsett
Pond
Plymouth
Taunton
quannakonk
Swamp   Middleborough
Assawompsett
Pond   Eastham
ehoboth   Sippican River
Swansea   AGAWAM
Acushnet River   Sandwich
POCASSETS   MATTAPOISET   Barnstable   Yarmouth
WAMPANOAGS   Dartmouth
Portsmouth   SOKONESSET
SAKONNETS
BUZZARDS BAY
Newport

Atlantic Ocean

MARTHA'S
VINEYARD

NANTUCKET

D. E. LEACH, 1957

Illustrations

CHAPTER I

The Land and the People

FROM the day when the first English settlers landed on New England shores and built permanent homes there, King Philip's War became virtually inevitable. Here in the wilderness two mutually incompatible ways of life confronted each other, and one of the two would have to prevail. At first the Indians, in their primitive ignorance, failed to realize the size and strength of the invading movement, and so for a time were even willing to welcome the first waves of newcomers. But in 1637 the ominous drumbeats of large-scale organized Indian resistance were heard in Connecticut as the enraged Pequots rose up against the English settlers. Prompt and ruthless retaliation by colonial military forces ended the Pequot War, and ushered in a new era of uneasy peace, a peace which was to last until a fateful June day in the year 1675.

The Indians of southern New England belonged to the Algonkian language group, as contrasted to the Iroquoian tribes of upper New York, which meant that the members of the various tribes in the area could understand each other readily. The actual strength of these tribes in the early 1670's was difficult to measure, since neither their numbers nor their intentions could be accurately determined. In all likelihood the total Indian population of southern New England was around 20,000, or about half the number of English settlers in the same area. Of these 20,000 Indians, about 4,000 were Narragansetts, perhaps 3,000 were Nipmucks, something over 1,000 were Wampanoags, while the remainder included Mohegans, Pequots, Pocomtucks, Massachusetts, Cape Cods, and other assorted groups. Theoretically, one could wander through the forest for days with-

1

out encountering a single Indian; the Nipmuck country, for example, contained only about 3,000 Indians in more than 1,500 square miles.

In appearance as well as in mode of life the Indians differed sharply from the fair-skinned English colonists. Physically well-formed and agile, they possessed a native toughness derived from centuries of wilderness experience. In complexion they were dark, the skin being reddish coppery in color, the eyes black and piercing. The men wore their straight black hair closely cropped except for a tuft along the center line of the head; the women usually allowed their hair to grow long. In warm weather the men often went naked except for a deerskin breechclout and moccasins, while the women wore a simple skirt of the same material. Feathers were used to adorn the head. Colder weather would require the addition of other garments such as leggings, jackets, and cloaks. By the middle of the century the native Indian costume of animal skins was increasingly supplemented by clothing of colonial or English manufacture such as stockings, trousers, coats or jackets, and woolen blankets. In fact, these became important articles of trade between the two races, along with such items as tools and other utensils.

Usually Indian families lived congregated in villages, each consisting of a cluster of huts. The typical Algonkian dwelling was made by planting a circle or oval of flexible green poles in the ground and bending their tops together to form a dome-like framework. This was then covered with bark or mats, leaving a doorway on one or two sides. In the center of the wigwam was located a simple hearth for the cooking fire. Around the interior perimeter was a low platform used as a bench and common bed for the inhabitants. If the Indians considered this kind of habitation cozy, the English were more likely to find it dark, smoky, and ill-smelling. Certainly by current English standards the Indians were a dirty and indelicate people.

Near the village were located the cleared fields where the Indians raised their maize or corn, squashes, beans, and pumpkins. Generally speaking, all land was held in common by the group, the Indians having originally no concept of personal and perpetual title. Each family had temporary possession of its own campsite, but it is likely that the village fields were farmed on a communal basis. Most of the routine work in the fields was performed by the squaws, who were the drudges of the community. They tended the crops, cared for the children, cleaned and dressed the animal skins which they made into clothing, and cooked the meals. The men led a more leisurely life in which the principal business was hunting and fishing, or preparation for these activities. At certain seasons the whole village might move to another location to hunt or fish, or just the men might go. Fish were taken in streams and coastal waters with bone hooks, nets, and weirs. Springtime in particular was looked upon as the fishing season, and in April large groups of Indians would congregate at the falls of the rivers to take advantage of the upstream runs. Along the seashore at low tide during the summer months the Indians were able to gather a variety of shellfish such as clams, mussels, quahaugs, and oysters. Game animals and fowl were secured with cleverly contrived traps and snares as well as bows and spears. Venison in particular was a common meat, for the woodlands of southern New England were wonderful deer country in the seventeenth century. The deerskins, of course, were utilized by the squaws for the manufacture of clothing. The corn was harvested in September, at which time the surplus might be carefully stored underground in covered pits against the day when it would be needed.[1] With the coming of cold weather the village would be dismantled, and the entire community would trek to some preferred winter site, where the huts would be reconstructed. These winter camps were usually located deep in the woods in some sheltered valley where the cold north winds would be less punishing.

Anyone dropping in on an Indian camp might expect to receive an invitation to dinner, for the Indians usually were a hospitable people, especially if they had enough food to share. Entering the dark interior of the hut, one would find the assembled inhabitants lounging on the skin-covered platform that formed the perimeter. Their eyes were on the great pot simmering above the campfire, a pot whose exterior was black and crusty from long hard usage. Bubbling within the pot was the most common of all Indian fare, a sort of corn-meal mush fortified by almost anything edible that could be thrown into it—beans and pieces of flesh being most usual. Depending on the season, the meal might include also broiled venison, fish, fowl, birds' eggs, chestnuts, berries, groundnuts (a tuberous plant occupying the place of the potato in the Indian diet), and acorns. In serving and eating the meal the Indians made no artificial show of good manners, but all dug in with a will, using fingers rather than knives and forks. Each one ate from a wooden bowl which, when scraped clean, might be quickly dipped into the steaming pot for a second helping. The only beverage available, was water, for the Indians normally did not have milk cattle, nor did they brew alcoholic beverages.

As forest dwellers the Indians were a resourceful and practical people. They had learned much about the ways of nature and how to live in nature's domain. They understood that nature was both kindly and harsh, sometimes favoring them with abundance and easy living, at other times afflicting them with disease, famine, bitter cold, and lashing storms which tore down their shelters and even sent the great trees of the forest crashing to the ground. Of supernatural forces, in the modern sense of the term, the Indians seem to have had only the most primitive concept. Attempts to show that they had a body of religious beliefs are based on the most dubious of evidence. They did seem to have some notion of a spirit world, for their medicine men or *powaws* claimed to be able to consult the spirits and propitiate those whose mood was hostile. Doubtless the *powaws* also functioned as healers of the sick and wounded. If the New England Indians had a concept of survival after death, it probably was an extremely vague one. Mostly they lived for the present and the immediate future. Ceremonials such as solemn councils and dances on special occasions were an important part of Indian life, and helped reinforce the group or tribal spirit. Similarly, athletic games were a much-enjoyed community activity which helped satisfy the combative instinct in times of peace.

Government and law, like religion, seem to have been no more than vague concepts among these Indians. Since land was held in common and personal possessions were few, there was little need for litigation. Most personal disputes could be settled by reference to a third party, usually the recognized leader of the community, who was known as the sagamore or sachem. Monogamy was customary, and the family was the basic unit in Indian society. The husband and father was the head of the family and the supreme authority within it. The sachem, together with his council of leading men, ruled the community, although probably not as a despot. Indians were not prone to regimentation, and every sachem needed the continued good will of his people in order to rule effectively. The sachemship normally remained within the same family from generation to generation, although the actual line of succession might be quite flexible. It was not unusual for a woman to be a sachem, as in the case of the Wampanoag squaw sachems Weetamoo of the Pocassets and Awashonks of the Sakonnets, or Quaiapen, the Old Queen or "saunk squaw" of the Narragansetts. Above all, the people demanded a sachem whom they could respect and follow.

Each village of Indians belonged to a larger unit—the tribe, and each tribe was ruled or at least led by a chief sachem and his council of lesser sachems and sagamores. Sometimes within a large and scattered tribe the lines of allegiance and command were rather indefinite, and it is sometimes difficult to tell which sachem, if any, was the supreme leader. Whenever some difficult problem arose within the village, the local sachem and his advisers would meet to discuss it. Larger issues affecting the entire tribe would be considered by a great council of all the sachems, some of whom might travel for miles along forest trails to attend the meeting.

Normally the tribe was sovereign. It possessed extensive territory upon which other tribes were not allowed to encroach. Strong tribes sometimes dominated weaker ones, exacting tribute from them. Tribes might enter into alliances with each other, usually to augment their strength against enemies. Indian warfare tended to be sporadic and poorly organized. For the most part it consisted of raiding activity by small parties of warriors against a village or similar party of the enemy. Before taking the warpath the braves would engage in frenzied dancing around the village campfire to conjure up their full measure of ferocity, and demonstrate their reckless courage to the assembled onlookers. With their faces painted and their naked limbs glistening with sweat, they must have resembled fiends in Hell as they performed their gyrations to the insistent beating of drums. For weapons they carried bows and arrows, or muskets which they had acquired from traders, plus knives and stone-headed hatchets or tomahawks. In skirmishes it was every man for himself—planned tactics seem to have been rudimentary at best. The individual warrior relied heavily upon stealth and agility in approaching the enemy, preferring to fight from behind cover if possible. Arrows would fly, and then at the climax of the action the more aggressive of the two groups, uttering hideous yells, would rush to grapple with the foe in hand-to-hand combat. Whenever possible the individual victor would stoop over a fallen enemy, swiftly cutting and peeling the scalplock from the victim's head, sometimes even before death had made good its claim upon him. Back in the village these bloody trophies of war would be dried out and displayed as symbols of courage and might. Sometimes prisoners were taken and held for later torture, or in some cases they might be spared and even adopted into the tribe. Daring in battle and contempt for pain were traits much admired.

Obviously, the New England Indians were a primitive people, occupying a much lower level of civilization than that of the English settlers who moved in upon them during the seventeenth century. Most of the colonists held the Indians in contempt, looking down upon them as complete savages, little better than wild beasts, perhaps even children of the Devil.[2] Even those few colonists who may be considered real friends and benefactors of the Indians were emphatic in their criticism. Daniel Gookin wrote that "these poor, brutish barbarians . . . are like unto the wild ass's colt, and not many degrees above beasts in matters of fact." John Eliot called them the dregs and ruins of mankind. Even Roger Williams, who was as tolerant of the Indians as anyone in the colonies, described them as the "barbarous scum and offscourings of mankinde." [3] Clearly there was no great amount of natural affection between the English settlers and their more primitive neighbors. This attitude was constantly being reinforced by what appeared to be unwarranted deception and other delinquencies on the part of the Indians in their relations with the white men.

Whenever the English thought of the possibility of converting and redeeming the savages, it was always in terms of bringing them into conformity with the higher civilization at the expense of the native way of life, a concept fraught with difficulty and danger. The usual policy of the missionaries was to gather the converts into villages of their own as quickly as possible in order to remove them from the harmful influence of the unconverted heathen. By 1675 there were several thousand "Praying Indians" in New England, many of them living in these special villages which were organized in accordance with colonial patterns and under close colonial supervision. The

Indian town of Natick, located on the Charles River a few miles above Watertown, was the most advanced of these communities, and served as a model for the rest. Here the converted Indians built their shelters, tilled their fields, conducted town business, and worshiped in their own church. To the settlers, the Christian Indians represented both a hope and a problem. Many a pioneering farmer whose home lay near a community of such Indians growled his doubt that the conversion experience was really stronger than Indian blood, and pessimistically concluded that in case of a general Indian uprising the Praying Indians would be on the warpath with the rest of the bloody fiends.

*   *   *

Had it been possible in 1675 for an observer to view New England from the air, he would have been most vividly impressed by the almost unbroken expanse of forest which lay over all the land like a shaggy carpet. Here and there the monotonous wilderness was broken by a few acres of cleared land and a small cluster of houses— a village set down in the midst of the forest. New England was a land of isolated villages and occasional towns, interconnected by a network of woodland paths which served as virtually the only means of access to most of the inland settlements. Along all of these routes, and up and down the rivers which laced the interior, moved the products of New England's economy—grain and other crops from the agricultural villages, valuable furs from the wilderness, manufactured goods imported from Europe. A fleet of small but sturdy cargo vessels from ports such as New Haven, New London, Newport, Marblehead, and Boston plied their trade along the coast and ventured beyond to the Southern plantation colonies and the West Indies.

Practically all of New England's leaders during the seventeenth century, and probably also the major part of the general population, were Puritans by conviction or at least were heavily endowed with Puritan attitudes. As such they were primarily interested in two things—worldly prosperity achieved by wise and diligent stewardship of God's blessings, and eternal salvation granted by God to His chosen few. In pursuit of the first objective they devoted their lives to hard work, valuing industry and scorning indolence. They proved themselves to be excellent husbandmen, tradesmen, and entrepreneurs. They started businesses, developed commerce, and speculated in real estate. When time and personal finances permitted, they made or purchased additional furniture and equipment, enlarged their houses to accommodate their growing families, and added to their holdings, oftentimes by shrewd deals. They were extremely community-minded, and began to develop in their town meetings democratic habits which were to have a lasting influence in American life.

The religious concepts of these people centered upon an all-powerful, all-knowing God who was a completely righteous judge. God was like a typical Puritan father, who loved his children, and in his love severely punished their wrongdoing, while rewarding their virtues. Salvation was preordained; a fiery Hell awaited the doomed sinner. This was a grim concept of existence, which served very well a people living in a harsh and dangerous world. The Puritans never expected life to be easy, nor did they imagine that salvation was to be lightly achieved. Satan was constantly at work seeking to trip up the godly in order to foil God's benevolent purposes. Hence every evidence of Satan's work must be carefully examined, and every appearance of personal or community sin must be stamped out. This is why the Puritans insisted upon such close supervision of personal behavior, thereby acquiring their everlasting reputation for prying.

In Puritan New England the church congregation was the community at worship. Normally everyone was expected to attend the periodic services in the meetinghouse and contribute to the support of the church, but only a choice few were admitted to full membership, the main requirement being proof of a personal experience of God's grace. The congregation was led by a pastor together with elders from the congregation. In Puritan society the pastors collectively constituted a most influential group, for not only were they the best-educated men in the colonies, but, even more important, they were the interpreters of God's will for the whole community.

The organized township, governed by an elected board of "selectmen" and certain other officials, was the basic political unit. Towns were organized into counties, each of which had a county court, and the counties, in turn, made up the colony. Typically, a New England colony was governed by an elected governor and deputy governor together with a bicameral legislature whose upper house served also as the governor's council and the supreme court for the colony. Members of this house—known as Assistants in Massachusetts—also functioned as magistrates in their own local communities. This relatively simple structure of government, evolved from the practices of English trading corporations, proved to be entirely suitable for the young and growing society which was occupying more and more of New England's wilderness area. Against all who opposed their advance, whether other Europeans or Indians, the New Englanders were ready to direct the full force of their strength and authority, for they knew themselves to be God's people, and they were determined to uphold and further His divine purposes in this corner of the world.

In the short half-century since the Pilgrims had first set foot upon New England's coast the basic elements of European civilization, somewhat modified by New World conditions, had been reproduced here by the unceasing labor and care of the settlers, so that by 1675, at least in the older and more firmly established communities, men were able to live their lives in comparative comfort and security. Flourishing towns with streets, well-built homes, meetinghouses, and places of business, were to be found at various points along the coast and the larger rivers. Men farmed, engaged in business, and raised their families with all the assurance of a people living in a well-established society, as indeed they were. The beckoning future stretched endlessly before them, and they knew that under God they were the masters of the land. Yet always there was the nagging fear of the Indians, and what they might do together if sufficiently aroused.

Included in the area of southern New England were four separate colonies, each with its own government and laws. Quarrels among these neighboring states over such issues as land and trade were not uncommon, and the Indians were sometimes able to exploit such rivalries for their own advantage. On the other hand, the three Puritan colonies of Massachusetts Bay, Plymouth, and Connecticut remained loosely bound together through an organization known as the New England Confederation, which had served since 1643 as a useful means of consultation about mutual problems, and occasionally common action. Meetings were held periodically at the three capital towns of Boston, Plymouth, and Hartford in rotation, with two delegates in attendance from each of the member colonies. These six men were known as the Commissioners of the United Colonies, and from their deliberations emerged whatever policies or actions the member colonies were obliged to support in common. However, the concurrence of at least five of the Commissioners was necessary for passage of a proposal, which meant that every colony held the power of veto over the others.

The dominant member of the Confederation was undoubtedly Massachusetts, whose population of some 17,000 people living in more than fifty separate towns and villages far surpassed that of its nearest rival.[4] Massachusetts was still rigidly Puritan in policy, ruled by strong-willed men who were determined to maintain the strength, independence, and purity of God's commonwealth. Boston was in a very real sense the hub of Massachusetts, for around this bustling seaport and center of government were grouped in a series of concentric rings the great majority of the colony's townships. The outermost ring consisted of Dunstable, Groton, Lancaster, Marlborough, Mendon, and Wrentham. Beyond these, in the very midst of the Nipmuck country, lay two isolated outposts of civilization—Quinsigamond (Worcester) and Brookfield (Quabaug). Along the Connecticut River where it passed through Massachusetts territory was a string of pioneering settlements of which the most important was Springfield, whose busy mills and bulging barns amply testified to the richness of the valley soil.

Connecticut also was a Puritan colony, with an English population numbering some 10,000. The importance of good water transportation in the growth of a pioneering state is well demonstrated by the fact that most of Connecticut's towns were located along the shore of Long Island Sound and up the length of the Connecticut River as far as the border of Massachusetts. Inland from the great river for many miles in both directions were vast stretches of wilderness through which passed only occasional wandering groups of Indians following the age-old trails which threaded their way from river and seashore to the interior.   .

Plymouth Colony, with a population of about 5,000, included all of what is now southeastern Massachusetts. The original township of this colony, the home of the Pilgrim Fathers, was still the capital, but many other towns had grown up around it, some of them surpassing the parent community in size and strength. Most of these were situated along the curving arm of Massachusetts Bay and Cape Cod, but there were also a few inland farming villages such as Bridgewater and Taunton, and three even more distant outpost settlements—Dartmouth, Swansea, and Rehoboth. Generally speaking, the colony was Puritan in attitude and policy, although somewhat less rigid in this respect than either Connecticut or Massachusetts.

The fourth state in New England was Rhode Island, which differed in many ways from its neighbors, and hence tended to stand alone. Among orthodox Puritans Rhode Island had the reputation of being the resort of heretics and other outcasts from godly society, a veritable sink of iniquity, not worthy of membership in the New England Confederation. Secretly the surrounding Puritan colonies, especially Massachusetts and Connecticut, longed for a chance to end Rhode Island's independent existence in order to set things right in that corner of God's New England. In addition, it may be said, they longed to acquire the valuable lands on the western side of Narragansett Bay. It is true that the Rhode Islanders, numbering altogether no more than perhaps three or four thousand people, were a factious lot with a strong tradition of individualism. Among them, especially at Newport, the capital, were a large number of Quakers, a sect feared and hated by the Puritans. In fact, by 1675 the Quakers were actually dominant in the colony government. Providence, at the head of Narragansett Bay, was still the home of the venerable Roger Williams, who continued active in the life of town and colony, while maintaining at the same time his excellent reputation with the neighboring Indians.

Ever since the English had first settled in New England they had maintained a posture of military preparedness based largely upon the old militia system of the mother country.[5] In theory every ablebodied man of military age was required to be a member of a local militia company, or "trainband," as it was called, the unit around which all military preparedness was built. The company officers also were local men, in most cases elected to their positions. Some of them could boast of previous military experience in Europe or the New World, but many knew their tactics only from well-thumbed military manuals and the periodic training sessions required by law.

The men were trained to maneuver in a body and fire their weapons upon command, in accordance with the accepted practices of European armies.

At the head of every full-sized company was a captain, who was directly responsible to the colony government for the training and discipline of his command. Below him were a lieutenant, an ensign, a clerk, and several sergeants. All the rest of the men were privates, serving as either pikemen or musketeers. Some companies bore a strong resemblance to fraternal organizations, and not only subjected candidates to a process of election, but also charged regular dues. Just how a candidate who had been "blackballed" would be able to fulfill his military obligation to the state is not clear. As new towns sprang up new companies were formed, and eventually the colonial governments organized these scattered units into regiments, usually by counties, placing a major in command of each regiment.

Weapons were apt to be miscellaneous, for the militiamen were expected to furnish their own firearms. The law required that these weapons conform to certain standards of size and type, but beyond this there was little uniformity. Until about 1675 the most common type of firearm was the matchlock musket, a weighty, cumbersome weapon usually requiring the use of a *fourquette* or forked pole upon which the barrel was rested when in firing position. The gun was fired by releasing a mechanism which brought the lighted end of a piece of cotton string called "match" into contact with the powder. The rate of fire of such a weapon was extremely slow, and the matchlock ignition system was unreliable in wet weather. Moreover, the match had to be kept lighted in order to be ready for instant use, a nuisance under most conditions. Gradually more and more of the colonists had been acquiring the newer, faster firing, more reliable weapons known as snaphance and firelock, or flintlock, muskets. Although the principle of loading was the same as in the matchlock musket, the propelling charge was ignited by causing a piece of flint to strike against a piece of steel just over the pan, thereby sending a spark down into the powder. This type of mechanism was also widely used on pistols and carbines. In addition to firearms, the soldiers of the New England colonies were equipped with swords and cutlasses for hand-to-hand fighting, but the long sharp pikes so common in Elizabethan and early Stuart armies were found to be impractical under the peculiar conditions of forest warfare, and so were largely abandoned by New England forces in 1675.

In the general scheme of military defense, the town trainbands had a dual function. First of all, they existed in order to defend their own communities against attack. In those days of poor communications and slow transportation it was imperative that each community have an organized group of soldiers always ready to spring to arms. But in addition to this vital function, the trainbands also assured the colonial governments of a large reservoir of trained men for any military need. Obviously, it would be impractical to fight a war simply by committing the defense of each town to its own trainband. Expeditions for offensive operations would have to be organized, and for this purpose the colony governments intended to draw men out of the local companies by a system of town quotas. Such expeditions, then, would normally consist of newly organized companies made up of volunteers or conscripts from a number of different towns. Because there was no regular standing army in any of the colonies, the military security of New England depended entirely upon the system of universal training in peacetime.

The average male citizen of Plymouth Colony, Massachusetts, or Connecticut was a man who had to work hard to make a decent living for his large family. All his life he had lived under the strict discipline of church and state, and he knew his rank in society. Yet thrusting up through this solidified crust of tradition and social discipline was a growing spirit of personal independence. Out here in the New World a man was to a considerable extent master of his own destiny. If he wasn't afraid of the forest, he could always find good land somewhere, and perhaps be a first-comer in a new community. The typical New Englander took an active part in local town affairs, and knew how to stand on his feet and speak his mind. Owning his own gun, he was naturally familiar with its use; loving his home and family, he was ready to defend them with his life if necessary. Men like this were the citizen-soldiers upon whom New England would have to depend in its hour of extreme peril.

CHAPTER II

Gathering Clouds

TIME and again after 1637 the black clouds of Indian war seemed to be gathering over New England, only to be temporarily dispersed by a new agreement or treaty. What the settlers feared most of all was a general and simultaneous uprising, hatched in a well-planned conspiracy, which would send the aroused warriors burning and killing through every village in the colonies. Such an attack might well mean the total destruction of the English settlements in this part of the New World. Fortunately for the English, however, a perfect conspiracy would be extremely difficult for the Indians to organize. Long-standing rivalries among the various tribes kept the Indians divided, and helped the English maintain a dominant position. Only a masterful leader, able to perform a near miracle, would be able to unite all the tribes in a common effort.

During these years friction of various sorts between English and Indians was almost constant, a not surprising fact in view of the close proximity and the divergent interests of the two peoples. On both sides there were cases of trespass, assault, theft, and even murder, all of which served as a continual irritant. The Indians, moreover, felt a gnawing concern over the mounting indications that their own culture and way of life were being slowly but surely undermined by the white men.

Basic to the whole problem of interracial friction, of course, was the fact that the English were gaining control over more and more land which had formerly belonged to the various tribes, thereby pushing the Indians into an ever-decreasing extent of territory. Many men who later became prominent leaders in King Philip's War were financially interested in land grants and speculation. Governor John Winthrop of Connecticut was not so busy directing affairs of state that he could not take a personal interest in promoting a new plantation at Quinebaug. Benjamin Church, Josiah Winslow, and Constant Southworth were interested in land at Sakonnet. Daniel Gookin, Ephraim Curtis, Daniel Henchman, and Thomas Prentice had a financial stake in the new plantation at Quinsigamond. John Winthrop, Richard Smith, Josiah Winslow, George Denison, and Edward Hutchinson were associated with a company which was busy acquiring land in the Narragansett country.[1] And the list could be extended. Inevitably the attitudes and actions of these men during the crisis of 1675–1676 would be shaped to some extent by their financial interests.

The way in which friction was produced as a result of land transactions is well demonstrated by the following case. The domain of the Wampanoag sachem Philip had formerly included an area known as Wollomonuppoag, in what is now Wrentham, Massachusetts. This land having been purchased by some Dedham people who intended to begin a settlement there, the town of Dedham now claimed jurisdiction in the area. In the early spring of 1668 the owners of the property, still living some fifteen miles away in Dedham, were disturbed by reports that the Indians were occupying their land at Wollomonuppoag, cutting wood there, and preparing to plant crops. Accordingly, the selectmen of the town sent a message to the intruders, demanding that they remove themselves, but the Indians only sneered at the message, and announced that they intended to proceed with their planting. Outraged at this defiance, the English owners appealed to Philip through Captain Thomas Willett of Rehoboth. Philip apparently questioned the title to the property, claiming that the land at Wollomonuppoag still belonged to him, but in August, 1669, he offered to grant a clear title to the property in exchange for a down payment of £5. This offer seemed acceptable to the Dedham people, who resolved to comply with Philip's demand. In November further negotiations were carried on with a view to purchasing all land still claimed by Philip within Dedham bounds. Over a year later the Dedham records still described the situation as a "problem," and as late as 1672 some Indians were still making use of English land at Wollomonuppoag.[2] The hard feelings engendered by this long-drawn-out land controversy were not likely to be soon forgotten by either side.

It would appear that Indians often did not fully grasp the meaning of landownership as understood by the English. To the Indians, the mere signing of a paper did not transfer exclusive right to a piece of uncultivated land. If the English owners failed to occupy the land and use it, the natives saw no reason why they should not continue their usual activities there. Even after the English had arrived on a piece of property and constructed houses upon it, the Indians often clung to their old rights of fishing and hunting. In short, the natives of New England seemed to believe that, generally speaking, the forest belonged to him who was able to make use of it.

The most tumultuous and highly publicized case of land controversy occurred in the Narragansett country, an area claimed by at least two colonies, but fully controlled by none. Down to 1659 the struggle for control of that region was sporadic and rather petty, but suddenly in that year there broke out a storm of activity which ushered in a new and more violent phase of the controversy. A powerful group of prominent Massachusetts and Connecticut men, in alliance with the Richard Smiths who owned a trading post on the western shore of the bay, concluded in rapid succession two big deals with the Narragansett sachems, thereby gaining title to a large extent of territory in the eastern part of the Narragansett country. Early in the following year the holdings of this so-called Atherton Company were still further enlarged. The government of Rhode Island, of course, was bitterly opposed to these transactions which might well serve as the entering wedge for political control of the area by hostile neighboring colonies.[3]

Later, when Indians caused trouble in the vicinity of several Connecticut plantations, the Commissioners of the United Colonies ordered the Narragansetts to pay 595 fathoms of wampum in compensation, with the further stipulation that unless the required payment were completed within four months, the entire Narragansett country would be forfeit. Not being able to make the payment, the angry but helpless Indians grasped at what appeared to be a last chance to save their lands by exchanging the four-month mortgage for a six-month mortgage held by the Atherton Company. Of course, the six-month period also proved insufficient, and soon the jubilant

Atherton partners found themselves nominal owners of the entire Narragansett country.[4] Soon after this the situation was further complicated when both Connecticut and Rhode Island obtained royal charters which contradicted each other by awarding to each of the two colonies exclusive jurisdiction over the Narragansett country. From this time on, both colonies tried to rule the area, thereby irritating and confusing the settlers and the Indians who lived there.

In 1665 the royal commissioners sent by Charles II to investigate matters in New England looked into the boiling Narragansett situation, and ruled that full jurisdiction over the area should be lodged in the hands of the Rhode Island government until the King himself could make a final decision. Moreover, the commissioners took an ax to the entire complicated structure of Atherton land claims. They summarily canceled the two big purchases of 1659, and ordered the purchasers to quit the premises as soon as the sachems had paid 300 fathoms of wampum in compensation. At the same time the commissioners ruled that the Narragansetts could void the mortgage on the rest of their territory at any time by paying 735 fathoms of wampum to any one of the claimants. Finally, they declared all grants made in the area by Massachusetts or by "that usurped authority called the United Colonies" to be void.[5]

These drastic rulings evoked a howl of protest from Connecticut and Massachusetts. The government of the Bay Colony later claimed that the removal of strong Massachusetts authority from the Narragansett country immediately caused the Indians there to become more insolent, since the Narragansetts knew the Rhode Island government to be weak and pacifistic, and since they could now assume that even the King of England was their ally.[6] This argument has much evidence to support it, and may offer an additional clue to the actions of the Narragansetts in the crisis of 1675.

During the next ten years the quarrel continued with full vigor. Connecticut refused to accept the adverse decision as final, with the consequence that both Rhode Island and Connecticut continued their attempts to exercise exclusive jurisdiction in the disputed area. Several attempts were made to settle the matter by negotiation, but without success. As might be expected, the Indians were again caught between the two antagonists, sometimes to their own disadvantage. Furthermore, the disorder and lawlessness which accompanied the struggle for control not only set a bad example for the Indians, but also revealed the lack of unity among the English. These lessons were not lost upon the Narragansetts.[7]

There is a common impression that the New England Indians were cheated out of their land by fraud. Generally speaking, this was not true, but occasionally some unscrupulous promoter, by plying the natives with liquor and enticing them with certain much-desired articles of clothing and hardware, did manage to acquire Indian lands at an amazingly low price. A smart trader named Samuel Marshfield once induced the Indians at Springfield to mortgage so much of their land to him that when he took over the property the poor natives found themselves without enough land even to plant on.[8]

One of the most notable cases of possible fraud in the acquisition of Indian land occurred in Rhode Island. When the town of Providence was still in its infancy, the Narragansett sachems Canonicus and Miantonomi granted to Roger Williams a large tract of land lying between the Pawtucket and the Pawtuxet rivers. Shortly thereafter a settler named William Harris persuaded Williams to turn the southern part of this tract over to a group of thirteen proprietors of whom Harris was the leader. Henceforth there was a fundamental division in the Providence lands. Every townsman, as such, held an interest in the northern part of the tract, but only Harris and his group had title to the southern part. In 1640 a line of division was agreed upon to separate the "Providence Purchase" from the "Pawtuxet Purchase." The real trouble began when the colonial assembly in 1659 authorized the town of Providence to make an additional purchase from the Indians. Harris quickly seized this opportunity by proceeding to obtain three so-called "confirmation deeds" from the brothers of Miantonomi and the grandsons of Canonicus. These documents purported to confirm the original grant, but actually were so worded as to imply that the grantees had right to all the land lying between the Pawtucket and Pawtuxet rivers, extending upstream *without limits*. Thus, in effect, the holdings of the town of Providence were extended to include a vast tract in northern and western Rhode Island. Harris and his partners were in a position to make a pretty penny on the deal, for the Pawtuxet Purchase, of which they had absolute ownership, was expanded along with that section of the tract which belonged to the town of Providence itself. When Williams charged Harris with having defrauded the Indians, Harris, of course, loudly proclaimed his innocence. Regardless of who was deceiving whom in this very complicated case, there can be no doubt that the Indians felt aggrieved.[9]

Fortunately, the Harris Case is not typical of the methods used by the English in their acquisition of Indian land. The Puritan colonies, especially, tried to protect the natives by forbidding anyone to purchase land from the Indians without prior permission from authority. Indeed, the colonial governments even sought to bring as much Indian land as possible under their direct jurisdiction so that they might have complete control over its distribution, reserving for the natives that which was necessary for their existence, and arranging for the remainder to be purchased and occupied by the English. While this policy reduced actual fraud to a minimum, it did little to check the tide of English expansionism which was the great underlying cause of Indian unrest.

English jurisdiction meant English justice, and this too was a sore point with the Indians. In many ways the natives were totally unprepared to embrace those concepts of right and justice which to an Englishman seemed fundamental and beyond question. Yet the colonial authorities apparently expected the Indians, when on English land, to act in complete conformity with the elaborate body of law under which the settlers themselves lived, and the Indian who violated the law in some way soon found himself facing a colonial court. On the whole, the courts seem to have made an honest attempt to render true justice to Indians in both civil and criminal cases, although Indian testimony was given relatively little weight, and until about 1673 Indians were seldom if ever called to be jurymen, even in cases involving other Indians. The important question here is not so much whether the Indians actually did receive justice at the hands of the authorities as whether they *thought* they did. When Indian lawbreakers were seized by an English constable, dragged off to an English jail, examined by a stern-faced English tribunal, and punished in a humiliating way before a crowd of jeering English townspeople, they naturally felt abused. To the English, the law was the one thing that stood between them and anarchy; therefore it must be maintained at all costs. The Indians, on the other hand, had lived for generations without the benefit of English law, and were quite

ready to reject it the moment it seemed to be contrary to their interests. But at this point they encountered the factor of compulsion,
and learned that once under the law they would be forced to remain
there. The result was the slow but steady accumulation of resentment
by the Indians, resentment which was enlarged by every adverse
decision of the English courts.

Liquor was a constant cause of trouble for the Indians, who
seemed constitutionally unable to absorb it in moderate amounts and
with moderate effects. For years shortsighted settlers who thought
only of the attractive profits to be made had been selling firewater to
the natives, and for years the colonial governments had been trying to
stamp out the dangerous traffic. Drunken Indians were always getting
into difficulty with the colonists, and at the same time the Indians
resented being punished for using a product which many white men
were so eager to sell.[10] Had the authorities been able to deal with this
problem more effectively, they could have done much to lessen the
tensions which were leading toward war. All attempts to prevent the
sale of firearms and ammunition to the natives were equally unsuccessful, with the result that by 1675 the Indians were fairly well
equipped with modern guns, and knew how to use them.

Ever since the coming of the white men, there had been economic
intercourse between Indians and English traders. At first it had
seemed that the flourishing trade in furs, tools, cloth, and foodstuffs
was as beneficial to the Indians as to the colonists, but as time went
on and the English extended their activities the Indians grew more
and more dissatisfied with the situation. It became apparent that
they were gradually sinking into a position of complete economic
subservience. Indian villages which once had enjoyed almost total
self-sufficiency were now increasingly dependent upon products of
English manufacture. Individual Indians became enmeshed in debt,
which degraded them still further in the eyes of the English. The
wiser leaders among the Indians saw that if the trend were not
reversed, the time would soon come when the natives of New England would be completely stripped of their independence.

In the meantime, some of the Indians were exchanging their forest
ways for the security and comfort of English habitations by engaging
themselves as servants or laborers to the settlers, whose ambitious
expansionism was fostering a continual shortage of labor. This meant

that members of the two races were now being brought into frequent contact with each other on the streets of colonial villages, producing still more interracial friction. Furthermore, the migration of individual Indians to the English plantations was disturbing to the other Indians who chose to cling to their old independence, and who saw with dismay the weakening of tribal and family bonds.

In like fashion the efforts of Christian missionaries to convert the natives were viewed by many Indians as a divisive force threatening their own way of life. The sachems feared the loss of their own authority within the tribe, and many of them, including Philip, maintained a generally hostile attitude toward Christianity. Even more obstructive were the *powaws*, who stood to lose great power and influence if the Indians adopted the white men's religion. Thus the preaching of the gospel tended to divide Indian society, and confirmed the pagan elements in the belief that their own native culture was being undermined by the English.

Even those Indians who resisted all attempts to convert them to Christianity sometimes could not escape its influence entirely, as the colonial authorities imposed upon them a Puritanical code of behavior. In 1646, for example, Massachusetts decreed that Indians as well as colonists could be executed for blasphemy, a crime which was interpreted to include denial or cursing of the true God, and derogation of the Christian religion. At Plymouth the Indians were forbidden to fish, hunt, plant, or carry burdens on the Sabbath. In the spring of 1675 the government of Connecticut sponsored a great meeting of the subject Pequot Indians, at which time the authorities introduced to the assembled natives a new code of laws which they must obey, a code which specifically prohibited such offenses as Sabbath breaking, the practice of heathen rites, adultery, and drunkenness. Interestingly enough, the "Old Queen" of the Narragansetts, Quaiapen, and her council were also present at this meeting. One can easily imagine her secret thoughts as she watched the power of the English exert itself over the docile Pequots.[11]

More and more the Indians as a people were becoming aware of a disagreeable fact, that at every point where their own way of life came into conflict with the white men's civilization the latter always revealed an aggressive and usually predominant strength. Even the possibility of retreat was denied them, for to the west beyond the

Hudson River dwelt the hostile Mohawks, one of the Five Nations
of the Iroquois Confederacy. Thus the New England Indians found
themselves caught between Iroquois power on the one side and the
aggressive force of an expanding English civilization on the other.
It was a situation from which there seemed to be no escape except
by violence.

At the same time, the English colonists were being hardened in the
conviction that the Indians were a graceless and savage people, dirty
and slothful in their personal habits, treacherous in their relations
with the superior race. To put it bluntly, they were fit only to be
pushed aside and subordinated, so that the land could be occupied
and made productive by those for whom it had been destined by
God. If the Indians could be made to fit into a humble niche in the
edifice of colonial religion, economy, and government, very well, but
if not, sooner or later they would have to be driven away or crushed.

*   *   *

One of the first things learned by the English colonists when they
arrived in New England was that the various Indian tribes confronting them were often bitterly hostile toward one another, which
prevented the savages from uniting against the new arrivals. In fact,
the weaker tribes sometimes tried to gain an advantage over their
stronger enemies by striking up a friendship with the English. This
was one reason why the Wampanoag sachem Osamequin (Massasoit)
had entered into alliance with the Pilgrims, for he saw in their guns
the effective answer to the powerful Narragansetts. If some of the
tribes were willing to seek the friendship and protection of the
settlers, the English were equally willing to fall in with the scheme.
To them it became a lever which could be used to break the resistance of the more powerful and unfriendly tribes. However, once
started, the system could have no foreseeable end. Year by year the
English became ever more deeply enmeshed in the web of Indian
rivalries, and year by year the store of Indian resentment grew.

Soon after the defeat of the Pequots in 1637 new trouble broke
out between the Narragansetts and the Mohegans, quickly developing into open warfare. When Miantonomi, the great sachem of the
Narragansetts, was taken prisoner by the Mohegans, the English
advised that he be put to death, which was accordingly done. This,

of course, not only embittered the Narragansetts against the Mohegans, but also increased their enmity toward the English. As the apparently endless quarrel between the two tribes dragged on, the Commissioners of the United Colonies continued to show a decided favoritism toward sachem Uncas and the Mohegans at the expense of the Narragansetts. Roger Williams more than most other men of his time saw the danger in this policy, but his pleas for a more fair-minded attitude fell upon deaf ears, or at least ears which were not attuned to any arguments from the direction of Providence.[12] Probably the Commissioners were attempting to be judicious, but their own interests and the interests of their respective colonies were too strong. Especially after the adverse decision made by the royal commissioners in 1665 in the matter of the Atherton land claims, the Narragansetts could expect little but hostility from the Puritan colonies. Thus a pattern was gradually becoming clear. The Pequots and Mohegans were looked upon as satellites of the New England Confederation, while the Narragansetts were classified as inveterate troublemakers and potential enemies. These alignments, although somewhat flexible, underwent no drastic changes in the next ten years, and later played an important part in the development and outcome of King Philip's War.

Meanwhile, on the western fringes of Plymouth Colony the old Wampanoag sachem Osamequin, long-time friend of the English, had died, and had been succeeded by Wamsutta, his eldest son. Upon this young sachem and his younger brother, Metacomet, the English now conferred classical names—Alexander and Philip respectively—as a mark of friendship.[13] But the good will and mutual respect suggested by this episode soon withered as the Wampanoags became noticeably bolder and more independent under their new leader. Younger ideas were coming to prevail at the council fires; the caution of old age was less evident. There came a day in 1662 when the English summoned Alexander to Duxbury to be questioned concerning a suspected plot against the colony. After submitting to this interrogation, the young sachem went to nearby Marshfield as a guest of Josiah Winslow, where he was taken ill with a fever. Some writers have surmised that the illness was brought on by Alexander's violent anger at being treated so rudely by the English. Indians later spread the story that he had been poisoned by his hosts. Actually, there is no reason to credit either of these rumors. So far as we can tell, Alexander was reasonably well treated during his stay at Duxbury and Marshfield. At the time when he was suddenly taken ill he had already been dismissed by the authorities, and was planning a trip into the Bay Colony. The attack forced a change of plan, however, and the failing sachem was carried toward his home at Mount Hope. Within a few days Alexander was dead.[14]

The younger brother, Philip, now became the supreme ruler of the Wampanoags. Soon after his accession he formally renewed the ancient covenant which his father had made with the men of Plymouth, promising to keep the peace.[15] But Philip was a man of firm will, ambitious, proud-spirited, quick to resent an affront to his dignity. Within his breast there burned a sullen spark of dissatisfaction fed by the ever-growing power of the white men, who were slowly but relentlessly squeezing the Indians to death, while rebuking them for their savage ways. As sachem Philip looked out over the land of his fathers from his vantage point at Mount Hope, brooding on that which was past, and trying to surmise that which was ahead, he was gradually brought face to face with the awful alternatives— total submission to the English and their way of life, or a bloody war to clear them from the country and restore the land to its rightful masters, the Indians.

For a while Philip continued to follow the traditional Wampanoag policy of hostility toward the Narragansetts, and so, like Uncas, was looked upon with some degree of favor by the United Colonies. During these years Ninigret, the crafty sachem of the southern Narragansetts, or Niantics, was a prominent object of English suspicion, a fact which his Indian enemies were quick to exploit at every opportunity. So it was that we find Philip in 1666 dictating a letter to one of the English officials on Long Island, warning him that Ninigret was planning to exact tribute from the Indians there. This little-known letter from Philip reveals not only his malice toward Ninigret and the Narragansetts, but also his forwardness in trying to play an influential role in the affairs of the day.[16]

Then in 1667 came another war scare in Plymouth Colony, based upon a rumor that Philip was ready to cooperate with the Dutch and the French in a campaign against the English settlers. When questioned about the alleged plot, Philip "stifly deneyed it," and suggested that Ninigret was deliberately stirring up these false rumors against him.[17] Nevertheless, he was ordered to appear at the June session of the General Court for further questioning. In due time Philip appeared bearing a letter which he claimed had been written by a certain Narragansett sachem, substantiating his claim that Ninigret was the originator of the false rumor. Being suspicious of this evidence, however, the Court sent a party of men to interview the supposed author of the letter, a move which Philip apparently had not foreseen. Soon the news came back that the Indian in question denied having made such a statement, thereby cutting the ground from under Philip's defense. Nevertheless, the embarrassed Wampanoag sachem continued to profess his innocence, and it is possible that he was speaking the truth. He may even have been the victim of an Indian double cross. At any rate, because the Court had no desire to press matters to extremes at this time a settlement was reached. Philip consented to pay £40 toward the expenses incurred by the government in the case, whereupon the authorities restored the Wampanoag guns which had been confiscated at the start of the trouble. Peace settled down upon the land once more.[18]

The next big Indian scare occurred in 1669, but this time the tables were turned, and it was Ninigret who was the principal object of suspicion. Apparently the English first became uneasy when they learned that both Uncas and Ninigret had been present at a great Indian dance the previous winter. Considering the usual enmity of these two sachems, their joint participation in such an affair seemed to bode no good for the English. Soon other hints of impending hostilities began to accumulate, and the Rhode Island government, exercising its right of jurisdiction over the Narragansett country, summoned Ninigret to Newport for questioning. The wily sachem proved to be more than a match for his questioners; for every previous suspicious action on his part he had a logical explanation. Apparently convinced that the suspected Indian conspiracy had no basis in fact, the authorities sent Ninigret back to his own domain. A few days later there occurred in the Narragansett country some sort of drunken brawl between English and Indians, with the result that Ninigret, along with Pessacus, another prominent Narragansett sachem, was returned to Newport for further questioning. Again the evidence seemed to indicate that there was no real plot against the English, and again the stolid sachem was released, no doubt inwardly amused at the apprehensiveness of the white men.[19]

One thing which increasingly disturbed the English during these years was the thought that the French in Canada might be stirring up the New England tribes against them. There were frequent rumors of French traders selling guns and ammunition to the savages, and stories of sinister Jesuit missionaries going into the Indian villages with a message of death to the English Protestants. One of the matters upon which Ninigret was questioned in 1669 was his alleged connection with the French, but the Niantic sachem flatly denied the charge, and sealed his denial with the hearty boast that he didn't even know in what part of the world the Frenchmen lived. There is, to be sure, considerable evidence to indicate that French traders were selling munitions to the New England Indians during these years, but so were the English. Beyond this, there is no justification for charging that the French authorities at Quebec were deliberately trying to start an Indian war in New England, even though that was to become their policy later on.

The war scares of 1667 and 1669 passed away without major damage, and the next great crisis developed in the spring of 1671. Like the others, it began with reports of unusual activity among the Indians. Early in March, Hugh Cole of Swansea informed the authorities at Plymouth that during a recent visit to Mount Hope he had seen a number of Narragansett Indians there busily repairing guns and making other weapons. There was also a report that groups of Wampanoag warriors had been seen armed and deployed as though for combat. Plymouth quickly passed the word on to the authorities at Boston, and New England girded itself for trouble. Philip seemed to be as worried as the English. Even if he was plotting mischief for some future date, the time was not yet here, and he wanted no premature showdown with the white men. Therefore, he agreed to appear at Taunton in April for the purpose of ironing out his differences with the English. The proud chieftain and his solemn counselors, making their way past the curious stares and unfriendly glances of the villagers, entered the meeting chamber, and found themselves in the presence of Plymouth officialdom. This time the English were flint-hard in their determination to set things right. Confronted by the facts of the case, and conscious of his own military weakness, Philip was forced to swallow his pride and admit his own culpability. Although inwardly seething, he maintained his composure, and even acquiesced in the demand that his people surrender their guns to the English as a guarantee of future fidelity. For the moment Philip was out-faced, out-talked, and beaten. After signing a new treaty with the English, he and his retinue stalked back to Mount Hope weaponless, like little boys deprived of their slingshots at school.[20]

The Taunton Agreement of April, 1671, proved to be a failure. Many Indians who were nominally under Philip's control refused to surrender their arms, and Philip himself was believed to be active in trying to foil any attempts at confiscation. Samuel G. Drake has offered the suggestion that when Philip agreed at Taunton to surrender the guns of the Wampanoags, he meant only the guns of his immediate retinue then present, not of his entire people.[21] This may or may not be true. Certainly it would not be the first time that trouble between white men and Indians was caused by misunderstanding of a word or phrase. But the government of Plymouth had no doubts in the matter, and as soon as it became clear that the Wampanoags were retaining their firearms the General Court declared the guns previously surrendered at Taunton to be forfeit.

During the early summer attention was temporarily shifted to the extreme southwestern corner of Plymouth Colony, where the squaw sachem Awashonks, ruler of the Sakonnets, began to defy the English. Under the threat of military action, however, Awashonks quickly saw the futility of further resistance, and signed a treaty with the government. Now the authorities were free once more to concentrate most of their attention upon Philip and the main body of the Wampanoags.[22] Declaring that Philip had violated the Taunton Agreement by his recent actions, the Council of War decided to force him to come and "make his purgation," and laid tentative plans for a punitive expedition in case he should prove obstinate. In addition, Plymouth appealed to the governments of Massachusetts and Rhode Island for support.[23] The authorities at Newport, quickly expressing their willingness to cooperate, prepared for war. Massachusetts, meanwhile, sought to play the role of peacemaker by entering into direct negotiations with Philip at Boston. The Wampanoag sachem was clever enough to see the possibilities in this situation, and adopted the tactic of trying to prejudice the Massachusetts leaders against their Plymouth colleagues, not without some success. At least he was able to make headway in persuading a number of important people in Boston that Plymouth was treating him with undeserved severity. As a result, some attempt was made by certain well-intentioned individuals to moderate the stern course of action being planned by the Plymouth authorities. The thin wedge which Philip had so cunningly inserted at Boston was beginning to have its effect.

Plymouth, unwilling to plunge into war without the full backing of her sister colonies, agreed to a new plan for resolving the crisis. The Commissioners from Connecticut and Massachusetts were invited to come to Plymouth, hear the arguments of both sides, and try to reach a decision. In this way responsibility for whatever was done would be shared by the colonies, and Philip's attempt to exploit any differences among them would be foiled. So it was that on September 24, 1671, the town of Plymouth witnessed one of the most important gatherings of notables in its history. The highest officials of the colony played host to such distinguished Commissioners as Governor John Leverett of Massachusetts and Governor John Winthrop of Connecticut. Before them appeared Philip and his counselors in their colorful regalia. All those present showed by the grave aspect of their faces the seriousness of the occasion. War might well be the outcome.

The meeting was conducted almost as though it were a criminal trial, with Philip at the bar of justice. He tried to justify his past actions, but his arguments were overwhelmed by the weight of evidence introduced by the English, who of course had every advantage in this situation. As might have been expected, the Commissioners decided that the Wampanoag sachem was clearly in the wrong. Once more the grim-faced Indians had to stifle their wrath, for they realized that obstinate resistance was useless, at least for the present. What private resolves they made at this time will, of course, never be known. Again Philip forced himself to utter words of confession, and expressed his eagerness for reconciliation. Penance followed.

On September 29, 1671, Philip formally accepted a new covenant between the Wampanoags and Plymouth Colony. By its terms he promised to pay £100 worth of goods to the colony treasury, and henceforth to follow the government's advice in matters of war and the disposal of Indian land. He also admitted that he and his people were subject both to the royal government and to the colony government, and bound by their laws. This was almost complete surrender. Secretly Philip must have sneered, even as he took the pen and scratched his mark at the bottom of the page.[24]

This document was certainly a slim reed upon which to fasten the future security of the English colonies. The men who knew Philip well must have realized that fact when they considered the fate of all previous agreements made with the Wampanoag sachem since the death of Alexander. Yet the Plymouth authorities could take satisfaction from the role played by Connecticut and Massachusetts in creating the new covenant. If Philip should ever rise up against Plymouth in the future, the other colonies which had helped arrange the settlement of 1671 would certainly feel some obligation to help suppress him. Henceforth there was to be a shared responsibility with respect to the troublesome Wampanoags.

Philip spent the next few years brooding over the degradation of his race. Well aware of the bitter rivalries among the various tribes, nevertheless he must have allowed his sullen mind to dwell frequently upon the possibility of uniting the Indians for a desperate last attempt to crush the encroaching English. He knew it would be folly for the Wampanoags to rise up alone. Hence there must be developed an intertribal understanding, a secret plan, and that would require much patience and effort to accomplish. Messengers must be sent far and wide along the trails of New England; parleys must be held at council fires all over the lands of the Algonkins. And all of this must be kept a close secret until the tribes were ready. Then would come the appointed day, the fateful hour. Painted warriors, yelling in exultation, would fall upon the surprised English, overwhelming them in the first shock of the attack. Blood would flow freely, and great billowing clouds of flame and smoke would roar to the skies in testimony to the power of Philip and his victorious followers. In that hour would be righted a half-century of wrongs, and the green hunting grounds of New England would be restored to their rightful occupants. Then would the spirits of great sachems long dead smile upon Philip and praise his deeds, he, the liberator of his people. So dreamed the son of Osamequin in his bitterness and humiliation; and, dreaming, he acted.

CHAPTER III

The Outbreak of War

AT the beginning of June, 1675, the usually placid town of Plymouth was alive with excitement as the authorities made preparations for one of the most important murder trials in the colony's history. Wherever the people gathered in little groups—at the meetinghouse, at the waterfront, on the streets—they constantly mentioned such names as Sassamon, Patuckson, and Philip, for this was to be no ordinary trial dealing with ordinary crime. Rather, it was concerned with a matter of Indian tribal vengeance, and bore directly upon the already strained relations between the government of Plymouth Colony and the Wampanoag Indians. Well might the good people of Plymouth ponder the outcome of this unusual and dangerous case.

At the appointed hour the members of the court, sitting in the wooden town house which the settlers had constructed on the slopes above Plymouth harbor, watched with keen attention as the three alleged murderers, all Wampanoags, were brought in to be tried for their lives. Identified as Tobias, one of Philip's own counselors; Wampapaquan, son of Tobias; and Mattashunnamo, the three defendants denied their guilt, and the government proceeded to present its evidence in the case.

Several miles due south of the tiny inland settlement of Middleborough and about fifteen miles southwest of Plymouth itself lay a sizable body of water known as Assawompsett Pond. Here on the preceding 29th of January the Christian Indian John Sassamon had met a violent death. Later, a group of local Indians happening by noticed Sassamon's hat and gun lying on the surface of the frozen pond, and beneath the ice they found his body. Hauling the dripping corpse from the water, they saw that the head was badly bruised; nevertheless they buried the body on shore, and went on their way.

In time word had come to the ears of the authorities at Plymouth concerning the possibility of foul play in connection with Sassamon's death. The body was exhumed and subjected to careful examination, which revealed suspicious injuries. Not only was the head extremely swollen, but the neck itself seemed to be broken as though by a violent twisting motion. Witnesses had testified that when the body was first pulled from the pond no water issued from it, "which argued that the body was not drowned, but dead before it came into the Water." [1] Apparently the victim had been struck in some way before entering the water. Murder became a probability.

The suspicion of murder was greatly strengthened by the known facts of Sassamon's life. He had been raised under the Christian influence of Massachusetts Puritanism, and had even studied at Harvard, but later fled from civilized ways and the white men's faith. He returned to the wilderness, and became a valuable aide to Philip, serving as the sachem's secretary. One contemporary later described him as "a very cunning and plausible Indian, well skilled in the English Language." [2] Such a person would be invaluable to the uneducated Philip, whose knowledge of English must have been rudimentary. In time, however, Sassamon felt the pull of his earlier background, returned like the Prodigal Son, and was readmitted to the Christian Indian community at Natick. From this time on, Sassamon seems to have been a model convert, for he maintained his good standing in the church, and was even given the responsibility of instructing the other Indians. When a native preacher was needed by the Indians at Nemasket near Middleborough, Sassamon was chosen for the position, and there he had subsequently resided, apparently respected both by the Indians and by the English of the vicinity.[3]

Not many days before his death Sassamon had informed the government of Plymouth Colony that the Wampanoags were organizing a general conspiracy against the English, a warning which Governor Josiah Winslow and his colleagues seem to have taken rather lightly at the time. Sassamon, however, was in dead earnest, and even expressed the fear that his warning to the government might cost him his life. Thus when his death at Assawompsett Pond did occur a short time later, the authorities had every reason to be suspicious, and drew the obvious conclusion that Philip was the power behind this brutal crime.

It was easy enough to conjecture about the details of Sassamon's murder, but how could the actual killers be discovered? What evidence justified the hailing of these three Indian defendants before the bar? Admittedly the evidence so far was inconclusive, but now the government introduced its star witness, an Indian by the name of Patuckson. His testimony proved to be of the utmost importance, and indeed was the very foundation of the government's case, for Patuckson claimed to have seen the murder committed, and was ready to identify the murderers. According to his story, he was standing unseen on a hill near the shore of the pond at the time of the attack upon Sassamon. From his vantage point he was able to see the men who carried out the vicious assault and shoved their victim's body beneath the ice to give the appearance of accidental death. Those killers were the very three Indians now on trial.

The jury of twelve Englishmen plus the smaller auxiliary jury made up of some of the "most indifferentest, gravest, and sage Indians" of the colony heard this testimony with great interest, and then began their deliberations.[4] When the verdict was announced, every man in the courtroom knew that Philip and the Wampanoags would burn with resentment at the conviction of their fellows. The record states that the auxiliary jury of Indians fully concurred with the decision of their white colleagues; therefore from the point of view of the Plymouth government complete justice was rendered. Accordingly, the three murderers, still stoutly maintaining their innocence, were sentenced to be hanged on the 8th day of June.

It is now impossible to tell whether the accused were actually guilty of the crime. They were convicted largely on the testimony of a single Indian at a time when public feeling against the Wampanoags was running high. We shall probably never know for certain if passion and prejudice did gain the upper hand over justice in this case. Philip's deep interest in the matter is readily understandable. If Sassamon spoke the truth, Philip himself was guilty of conspiring against the government and people of Plymouth Colony contrary to his previous commitments, and would naturally be suspected of having ordered Sassamon killed for having revealed the plot. Thus, in effect, Philip himself might be considered guilty of the murder and subject to the same penalty as his agents who carried out the order. But if, on the other hand, Philip and his three men actually had no connection with the death of Sassamon, then the anger of the Wampanoags at the arrest and conviction of their fellows is also understandable. Wherever the truth may lie in this case, it is certain that the prosecution of the three Wampanoags by the Plymouth authorities had the effect of bringing Philip and his followers to the boiling point.

Something unusual happened at the scene of the executions. Two of the condemned Indians died as scheduled, but when Wampapaquan was swung into the air, the rope broke or slipped, and he fell to the ground with a thud. In the terror of the moment the gasping Indian chose to talk. Perhaps he first gained the promise of a reprieve, for he now completely abandoned the claim of innocence which had been maintained by his father and Mattashunnamo to the very end, and confessed that he and his two companions were indeed the agents by whose hands Sassamon had died at Assawompsett Pond. He insisted, however, that the actual killing was done by the other two, and that he himself was only a bystander. Despite this story, Wampapaquan was later hanged again, this time successfully.

Even before the trial, the Wampanoags had begun to show signs of their seething anger against the white men. Observers noticed that they were increasingly hostile in their attitude and actions. The inhabitants of Swansea and vicinity occasionally sighted armed groups of Indians near their houses, and no-one knew what was intended or planned by the angry Philip. Many who followed these developments at the time believed that Philip was alarmed by the active prosecution in the Sassamon Case, fearing that his own role as instigator of the crime would be revealed. Perhaps the Wampanoags were warning the English against attempting Philip's arrest. But what if these excitable savages should take it into their heads to swarm out of the Mount Hope peninsula and attack the nearest settlements? What if Sassamon's story of a great secret Indian conspiracy were true? These were burning questions of the hour.

After the execution of the convicted murderers events moved

quickly toward a crisis. On June 11th Lieutenant John Brown reported from Swansea that the Wampanoags were in arms and had sent their women across the bay to take refuge with the Narrragansetts. Worse yet, Brown had heard that Indian warriors were coming in from Narragansett, Cowesit, Pocasset, and other areas to join Philip, and that the route between Swansea and Taunton, one important avenue of reinforcement and retreat for the English in case of trouble, was already under close surveillance by the Indians.[5] This was the sharpest warning yet received by the Plymouth government. By the 14th the authorities were convinced that some attempt to pour oil on the troubled waters was urgently needed, but they still failed to comprehend how serious the situation really was. Messengers were dispatched with soothing letters from Governor Winslow to both Philip and Weetamoo, squaw sachem of the Pocassets, who, like Awashonks, was nominally subject to Philip.[6] These late attempts at peacemaking seem to have had little of the desired effect, and the Wampanoags continued to behave more like enemies than like loyal subjects or friendly neighbors.

It was about this time that Deputy Governor John Easton and a few other prominent men of Rhode Island made a serious attempt to avert the impending conflict by mediation. They were able to arrange a conference with Philip on his own territory. According to Easton's account, the white men and the Indians talked very rationally together, and Easton's party advanced the novel proposal that the differences between the Wampanoags and Plymouth Colony be referred to a board of arbitration consisting of the Governor of New York and a sachem chosen by the Wampanoags themselves.[7] Although this idea seemed to interest the Indians, they preferred to talk about their many grievances which, of course, the Rhode Islanders could do little to cure, so the conference broke up without significant results.

Also about the middle of June, Awashonks held a dance to which she invited Benjamin Church, the pioneer settler in the Sakonnet country. Church, who at this time was a vigorous and aggressive man in his mid-thirties, had established a farm in what is now Little Compton, and had managed to win the friendship and respect of the neighboring squaw sachem. At the dance Church found not only a large number of Sakonnets, but also six of Philip's own Indians, their faces smeared with war paint. It soon became clear that these six were there for the purpose of persuading the Sakonnets to join Philip in resisting the English. After hearing their arguments, Awashonks turned to her friend Church, and while the six painted Wampanoags glowered fiercely at him he boldly urged the wavering squaw sachem to remain loyal to the Plymouth government. Seemingly successful in his appeal, Church left the Sakonnets and headed for the Pocasset country and Plymouth. En route he talked with Peter Nunnuit, the husband of Weetamoo, who gave him to understand that Philip was actually bent on war, and that other Indians were even now flocking in to his support. Early on the morning of June 16th Church hastened into the presence of Governor Winslow, and related his experiences of the past few days. Added to what the authorities already suspected, this report was grim news indeed.

The temper of the Wampanoags was again displayed about the 17th of June when some English settlers advanced into Philip's country in search of horses which had strayed away from their owners. The men were seized by Wampanoags, but then released upon orders from higher authority, presumably Philip himself.[8] The episode seems to indicate that the Wampanoag sachem, unlike his young warriors, was still hesitant about resorting to open violence. If true, this is a fact of major significance in our story.

*   *   *

In any all-out attack by the Wampanoags the frontier village of Swansea would be the first to suffer, for Swansea stood like a sentinel at the very entrance to Philip's peninsula of Mount Hope, barring his way to the rest of Plymouth Colony and Massachusetts. So long as Swansea remained in English hands Philip's Indians could never feel completely secure on the peninsula. Furthermore, Swansea was a tempting target for attack. The town consisted of only a few dozen families at most, living in homes which were scattered rather than clustered. A small subsidiary settlement of about eighteen houses was located some distance to the south of the main settlement, actually within the narrow neck of land leading to Mount Hope. The few families here were living almost under the very shadows of their enemies. There was also an outlying settlement to the eastward on what is now called Gardner's Neck, but which was known in the seventeenth century as Mattapoiset. One can readily understand why every word and sign of increasing Wampanoag truculence, especially the reported gathering of strange Indians from other parts, the insistent throbbing of drums, and the occasional glimpses of armed warriors moving in bands, produced an ever-rising level of tension and fear among the inhabitants of Swansea. Other nearby towns, especially Rehoboth, also began to feel apprehensive as the indications of approaching trouble increased with each passing day. At Plymouth itself the authorities took some precautionary measures, and watched the situation closely.

The events of the next few days cause one to doubt that any mastermind was directing a well-planned and well-coordinated conspiracy against the English. Rather, it almost seems as though Philip's eager and hot-blooded young warriors were dragging him, reluctant, into open violence and hostilities. Tradition, indeed, supports this latter view, although positive documentary proof is lacking.[9] From threatening words and movements the Wampanoags next turned to looting. The house of Job Winslow at Swansea was reportedly the first victim of this new activity about the 18th or 19th of June, but it was on Sunday the 20th that the real trouble began. Philip's warriors either were unleashed at this time, or managed to slip their leash, and moved in force toward the neck of land which joined their peninsula to the mainland. They appeared in the vicinity of the English farms there on the neck, and began to act like hoodlums and bandits. A number of the English houses had already been deserted, which gave the excited Indians a splendid opportunity to loot and plunder. In their eagerness to destroy, they set two of the houses on fire. In the meantime the terrified settlers were hastening northward toward the main part of Swansea to spread the alarm and take refuge. These were the first people in King Philip's War to leave homes and worldly goods behind in a flight for life itself. They were not to be the last.

The villagers received the refugees and their tidings with the utmost apprehension, for now their worst fears seemed to be confirmed. The Indian uprising which had been dreaded for so long now appeared to be an immediate and terrible fact. English property was being wantonly attacked in complete defiance of authority, and who could even hope that the Indians would stop short of mass murder? The outlying southern section of Swansea was in the hands of Philip's men; the other parts of the town would be next. Knowing that every minute was precious, the people of Swansea dispatched a mounted messenger to the governor, and threw themselves into a posture of defense. If the messenger could get through in time, they might yet be saved.

People along the way in Taunton and Bridgewater heard the news with deep concern, and stared after the rider as he disappeared down the trail which led to the coastal settlements. As day was breaking over the sea at Marshfield on June 21st the weary horseman drew reins at Governor Winslow's door, hurried into the governor's presence, and made his report. Winslow recognized at once that the situation was now extremely critical.

The first and most urgent need was to send help to Swansea. Not only were the people there in immediate danger, but a resolute opposition to the Indians at that point might put an end to Philip's insolencies, and smother a general conspiracy before it could gain momentum. Winslow therefore sent orders to Bridgewater and Taunton for the immediate raising of seventy men to leave that very day for Swansea. Additional orders provided for a second force of about twice that size to march on the 22nd.

Word of these developments must be sent to Boston so that the Bay Colony might be ready to send aid if needed. Winslow hastily penned a letter to Governor Leverett, informing him of the occurrences at Swansea on the preceding day and the countermeasures being initiated by the Plymouth government. Both the Narragansetts and the Nipmucks, Winslow stated, were believed to be ready to join Philip, and since both of those groups were supposedly under Massachusetts jurisdiction, Winslow particularly requested Leverett to take some steps to prevent their participation in the uprising. While recognizing the potential danger in Philip's attack, Winslow presented the matter as more or less of a localized problem, and made no immediate attempt to draw the other colonies into the quarrel. "If wee can have faire play with our owne," Winslow optimistically stated, "wee hope with the help of god wee shall give a good accompt of it in a few dayes." [10] Leverett received Winslow's urgent message about four o'clock that afternoon, immediately called for a meeting of the Council, and at five o'clock wrote a reply promising the cooperation of his colony.

At Swansea, in the meantime, the frightened settlers had been anxiously waiting for encouragement and aid from Plymouth. Surely their government would not leave them to their own devices in this terrible crisis. After the looting and burning raid of the 20th the Wampanoags had recoiled into their lair, but no-one knew when they would once again sally forth to plunder and destroy, and perhaps kill. The settlers who lived on outlying farms had abandoned their homes, with the result that the population of the town was now concentrated at a relatively few defensible points such as the Bourne garrison house at Mattapoiset, and the Miles garrison house just to the north of the Mount Hope peninsula. The abandoned homes would be easy pickings for any Wampanoag raiding party, but human lives were what counted now. Queasy with tension, the people of Swansea stood guard, and waited.

The first reinforcements, coming from Bridgewater and Taunton in response to Winslow's order, tramped into Swansea in the late afternoon or evening of the 21st. This welcome addition of strength encouraged the local populace, and it might well give Philip cause to reflect before he allowed his men to act rashly again. Meanwhile Taunton, designated as the assembly point for the second and larger relief force, was the scene of bustling activity as still more men poured into the town. Major William Bradford, son of the first Governor Bradford, was there supervising the formation of the additional force. The audacious Benjamin Church was also at Taunton, and to him was given a task much to his liking—leadership of the advance guard which was to scout ahead of the second force en route to Swansea. Church, never bashful about blowing his own horn, later recalled that his mixed unit of English and friendly Indian scouts proceeded so far ahead of the main force that he and his men were able to kill, cook, and feast on a deer before the rest of the army caught up with them. Perhaps Church would not have thought himself so clever if the enemy had laid an ambush between him and the main force which he was supposed to be shielding. Fortunately, the army arrived at Swansea without serious mishap. The troops were posted at the several garrison houses to protect the

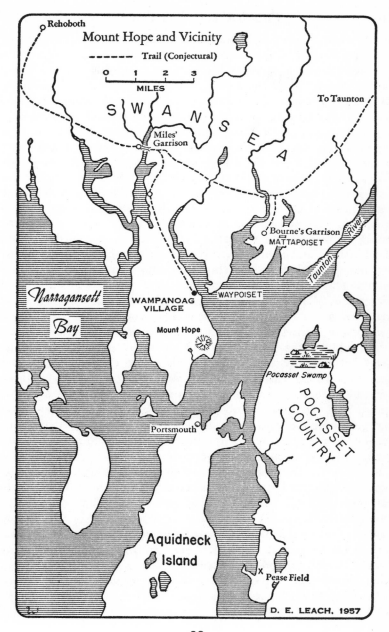

Mount Hope and Vicinity

- - - - - - Trail (Conjectural)

0   1   2   3
MILES

Rehoboth

SWANSEA

To Taunton

Miles' Garrison

Bourne's Garrison
MATTAPOISET

Taunton River

WAYPOISET

Narragansett Bay

WAMPANOAG VILLAGE

Mount Hope

Pocasset Swamp

POCASSET COUNTRY

Portsmouth

Aquidneck Island

X Pease Field

D. E. LEACH, 1957

people who had assembled there, and it began to look as though the English were getting matters well in hand.

Both Governor Leverett of Massachusetts and Governor Coddington of Rhode Island wrote to Winslow on the 23rd, promising wholehearted cooperation with Plymouth in her difficulties.[11] Leverett gave assurance that troops and munitions were available in his colony, and Coddington told of his intention to establish a boat patrol in nearby waters. Shortly thereafter the Rhode Island governor wrote to the commander of the Plymouth army in the field, the elderly James Cudworth, and reported that the boats were alerted to prevent the enemy's escape from the Mount Hope peninsula by water. Cudworth, in turn, felt free to send further instructions to Rhode Island concerning the best means of employing these boats. This correspondence reveals the friendly relations which prevailed between Rhode Island and Plymouth in the early days of the war. Probably Benjamin Church, who had close connections in both colonies, was instrumental in furthering the much-desired liaison between the two governments. The vital importance of Rhode Island's fleet of small boats becomes evident when we look at the map. Philip and his followers were located on a southward-jutting peninsula whose narrow neck could be effectively blocked by a small army, so that if he could be prevented from escaping by water to the Narragansett country or to the eastern shore of Mount Hope Bay, his uprising could be confined and crushed. None of the Plymouth towns in the vicinity had any great number of boats, but nearby Rhode Island was well furnished with small craft, and these constituted the only possible fleet which could be quickly assembled to form an effective blockade of the Mount Hope peninsula.[12]

It will be recalled that on the 21st of June Winslow had urgently requested the government of Massachusetts to use its influence with the Nipmucks and Narragansetts to keep those tribes from joining Philip. Leverett and his council were heartily in favor of this project, and to it they added another—an attempt to mediate between Plymouth Colony and Philip himself. Thus it was that the authorities in Boston decided to send three separate missions to the Indians of the three colonies as part of an over-all plan to prevent the general Indian war which seemed to be impending.

The small party sent to the Nipmuck country east of Springfield spent its time interviewing the rulers of the various villages there, extracting from them solemn promises of fidelity to the English. Most of these rulers denied that any of their men had gone to aid Philip, and those who did have men away on such business promised that they would be recalled.[13] This was reasonably encouraging to the English, and gave some assurance that the frontier towns of Massachusetts would be safe.

The important mission to the Narragansett country, entrusted to Captain Edward Hutchinson, Seth Perry, and William Powers, was a more difficult one because of the greater spirit of independence and the more hostile temper of the Narragansetts. In accordance with their instructions, the three emissaries proceeded to Providence, where they called upon Roger Williams and requested his assistance. Certainly nobody would be more valuable than Williams on such a mission. For years he had been instrumental in preserving peace between the two races, and perhaps he could succeed again in this latest crisis. Williams readily consented to join Hutchinson and his party, and the four men started at once for Richard Smith's trading post at Wickford on the western shore of Narragansett Bay.[14]

Williams hoped that the sachems would agree to meet with them at Smith's, but the Narragansetts were either timid or sullen or both, and insisted that the white men come farther into the Narragansett country if they wished to hold a meeting. Preferring not to quibble at this point, Williams and his companions agreed to meet the sachems near Worden's Pond, which lay some twelve or fifteen miles southwest of Smith's along the old Pequot Path. Here in conference with the highest rulers of the powerful Narragansetts —Pessacus, Ninigret, Quinnapin, and the Old Queen, Quaiapen— the four white men discussed the current crisis. They told the sachems that it would be foolish for them to become involved with Philip, since the English were determined to crush any uprising with thousands of troops if necessary. After hearing this scarcely veiled threat, the Narragansetts gave complete assurances that they would have no hand in Philip's rebellion, so Williams and his party were able to come away with some feeling of encouragement, although they remained deeply suspicious of Narragansett intentions. On the

morning of June 25th the three Massachusetts men said their fare-
wells to Roger Williams at Wickford, and continued on their way
to Boston to make their report.[15]

Of the three missions sent out by the government of Massachusetts
about June 23rd, the one to the Wampanoags would naturally be
the most difficult. But Massachusetts remembered its successful role
as mediator between Philip and the people of Plymouth Colony in
1671, and now hoped that the same good office might be useful again.
The matter was put in the hands of Captains Thomas Savage, James
Oliver, and Thomas Brattle. Perhaps these worthy men had high
hopes of success as they journeyed on horseback down the trails
toward Swansea. Approaching their destination on June 25th, they
were suddenly struck with horror when they saw sprawled on the
ground before them the corpses of two men. The victims were
Englishmen, slain by Indians, terribly mutilated, and left lying in
their own blood. Briefly, in shocked silence, the three would-be
peacemakers contemplated the grisly results of Indian savagery, and
then continued on their way, their hopes largely shattered. House
burning had been one thing; killing was another. At Miles' garrison
house they were greeted with lurid tales of what had happened during the previous two days, tales which only served to confirm their
worst fears. Blood had been freely shed at Swansea, and war was
upon the colonies.

Considering that the several garrison houses were some distance
apart, and that the Wampanoags had struck at diverse points in the
town, it is no wonder that the information obtainable at the moment was incomplete or confused. Nor is it surprising that contem-
poraries who wrote of these events gave ambiguous or contradictory
accounts. Consequently our chance of ever knowing exactly what
happened at Swansea on June 23rd and 24th, 1675, is very slight indeed. By careful comparison of all extant contemporary accounts,
however, we can recreate a fairly accurate picture of these vital
developments.

John Easton tells us that a young English lad shot and mortally
wounded an Indian looter on the 23rd, the Wampanoags having resumed large-scale plundering operations at that time. If this account
is true, then it would seem that it was the English who first shed
blood in King Philip's War. Tradition has it that Philip, having been

informed by his *powaws* that the Indians could win only if the English fired the first shot, caused his men to antagonize the settlers in the hope of bringing this favorable omen to pass. The story may or may not be true, but at least it is not contrary to the facts as we know them. Easton implies that the shooting of the Indian looter on the 23rd served as the immediate provocation for what happened on the following day.[16]

June 24th had been designated by the government of Plymouth as a colony-wide day of solemn humiliation before the Lord because of the trouble with the Indians. The appointed day proved to be memorable mostly for additional disasters, including the first shedding of English blood. Major Bradford and the colony treasurer, Constant Southworth, were both at Swansea on the fateful day. Cudworth was on his way with an additional contingent of eighty men. The troops already at Swansea were posted at the Bourne, Miles, and Browne garrison houses to defend the villagers who were congregated in those places. Thus the Indians could rove almost at will so long as they did not attack the garrisons themselves.

Apparently the Wampanoags were free of their last restraints and inhibitions. In groups they had sortied from their peninsula and slipped into the concealing bushes along the roads and paths of Swansea. There they waited their opportunities. At Mattapoiset they fell upon a small party engaged in retrieving corn from a deserted farm some distance from the garrison house, and killed six, including, it is said, the boy who had shot the Indian on the previous day. Elsewhere toward the end of the day the savages ambushed a group of Swansea people returning from public worship. One man was killed, and others in the party were wounded before they could reach safety. That night at Miles' garrison, which was now supposedly a well-guarded military stronghold, the enemy added insult to injury by creeping near and shooting one of the sentries dead. Two others were mortally wounded. Because it was now imperative to obtain medical help for the injured, two men were dispatched toward Rehoboth that very evening to fetch a doctor.[17] Their mutilated bodies were the ones found by the Massachusetts mediators the next day. Altogether, then, nine men had been killed and at least two mortally wounded at Swansea on the fateful 24th of June.

On the afternoon of the 26th the Massachusetts emissaries

mounted their horses for the return journey to Boston. The purpose for which they had been sent was now impossible of attainment, and they would recommend to their government strong military support for Plymouth Colony in order that the Wampanoags might be speedily crushed. Possibly Oliver was sent on ahead to hasten the coming of reinforcements from Boston, since there were growing fears that Philip had already made his escape from the peninsula, and would carry the war into other regions.[18] Savage was escorted as far as Rehoboth by a small mounted patrol of Plymouth men. There he encountered Hutchinson and his party who were just returning from their conference with the Narragansett sachems. Exchanging information, both parties knew that there was little room for optimism now. The Wampanoags had chosen war, and war it would be.

* * *

While the ominous events of mid-June, 1675, were unfolding themselves in the vicinity of Mount Hope and Swansea, English settlements for miles around were shocked and frightened by the wild rumors which were spreading in all directions. The town of Warwick, Rhode Island, held a town meeting on June 20th to decide upon necessary precautions. Here, of course, it was the nearby Narragansetts who were principally to be feared. Within a week Warwick experienced a real scare when a large band of armed Narragansetts appeared at the town, but fortunately they went away again without making an attack. Just what the purpose of this armed demonstration may have been is not clear, but it served as an additional warning to Roger Williams, who was still sojourning at Wickford, that the recent promises of the Narragansett sachems were not to be trusted too far. Pessacus himself had warned the English to take some precautions because he could not guarantee his ability to control the young warriors.[19]

On June 28th the government of Massachusetts directed an official letter to Governor Winthrop of Connecticut, informing him of the outbreak of trouble with the Wampanoags, and giving an account of conditions at Swansea.[20] The letter reached New London on the following day, and was there opened and read by Major Fitz-John Winthrop, the governor's son, who then sent it on to his father at Hartford. It was believed in New London that Philip was counting on assistance from the Mohegans, who recently had been acting in a suspicious manner. One citizen of the town expressed the current general apprehension when he wrote to the governor, "Wee have Great Reason to beleeve that there is an universall Combination of the Indians and fear you canot Ayde us timely." [21] These people, frightened by the wave of bad news, had a real sense of imminent disaster.

Winthrop received this communication from New London on the 1st of July, along with a fearful letter from Stonington telling of Wampanoags discovered on the eastern side of the Pawcatuck River. This latter report was almost undoubtedly erroneous.[22] The whole tone of the Stonington letter reflected mounting panic among a people who felt themselves weak and isolated in the face of deadly danger. As a result of all this bad news, the government of Connecticut ordered troops to the eastern frontier of the colony, and called the General Court into special session. Even remote New Haven was caught up in the spreading wave of fear. At a special meeting of the inhabitants on July 2nd, the townsmen decided to take special precautions for defense and watchfulness lest they be surprised by the sudden spreading of Philip's uprising.[23] Without doubt a wide area of New England was awake to a danger which to some may have seemed exaggerated, but which to many others seemed very real and immediate.

*   *   *

Even before the unsuccessful mediation mission returned to Boston, the government of the Bay Colony had begun to prepare for the mobilization of Massachusetts militiamen. At first it was planned to send two companies of soldiers to the trouble zone if the Wampanoags continued hostilities. Captain Daniel Henchman of Boston was selected to command a company of one hundred men drawn from the militia companies of Boston, Charlestown, Cambridge, Watertown, Roxbury, Dorchester, Dedham, Braintree, Weymouth, Hingham, and Malden. The other company was to be a mounted troop under the command of Captain Thomas Prentice. The Council notified Governor Winslow of these plans, and assured him that supplies of weapons and munitions would be sent to Plymouth

Colony upon request. In fact, that very day a boat for Plymouth was loaded with muskets and ammunition from Massachusetts.[24]

On the 25th the government at Boston created a special committee for the war, and designated John Hull to be the colony's war treasurer.[25] Orders for the mustering of the two companies in the market place at six o'clock that evening were issued. The men being assembled were then quartered for the night, and the actual march began on the afternoon of June 26th, a Saturday.[26] It may have been at the very hour when these troops crossed Boston neck and set their feet on the road to Dedham that the unsuccessful party of mediators led by Captain Savage left Swansea and headed for Boston with the doleful news of Philip's latest activity. The two groups would inevitably meet in the way.

Although the movement of the Massachusetts troops to Swansea cannot be called eventful, it was not without its interesting incidents. On the first night out, while in the vicinity of Dedham, the little army halted as the earth's shadow began to obliterate the face of the moon. The men sat there in darkness, munching food from their knapsacks, talking in low voices, and allowing their superstitious imaginations free rein. Was this darkening of the moon at the very start of their expedition an evil omen? As the soldiers studied the partly obscured moon they could make out a strange shape on its surface, a shape which to some took on the appearance of a scalplock. Quickly the word spread down the line, and the men pointed and watched. For an hour or more the darkness lasted, and then there was moonlight again, and the companies resumed their march.

In the meantime the authorities at Boston made a quick decision to send additional troops at once. Possibly Captain Oliver had arrived sometime after the army's departure, and his account of the critical situation at Swansea and the possibility of Philip's having escaped from the peninsula may have been the cause of this new decision. At any rate, on the night of the 26th at Boston the drums beat for volunteers, and within a matter of hours Captain Samuel Moseley stood at the head of about one hundred brave men and boys, all armed and ready for a fight. This third company included a strange assortment of individuals—apprentices, servants, rough seamen, and even some convicted pirates probably released for the occasion. They had some dogs, too, for hunting out the Indians in the woods. Moseley himself was a hard-bitten adventurer who just a few weeks previously had sailed into Boston harbor with these pirates as his prisoners. A contemporary admirer described him as "an excellent Souldier, and an undaunted Spirit." [27]

The advance force, having received word that more troops were being sent, halted at Woodcock's garrison house near the present Attleboro, Massachusetts, to await the reinforcements. The men had marched some thirty miles since the preceding afternoon, and were glad of the opportunity to rest for a few hours. Probably most of them tried to catch some sleep, as soldiers in the field soon learn to do at every opportunity. But it was not long before Captain Moseley and his volunteers came striding down the trail to join the little army, and in the afternoon the entire force moved forward again.

To the south, Captain Cudworth welcomed the news that help was on its way from Boston, and sent word to the approaching army to hurry. Cudworth now had good reason to suspect that Weetamoo of Pocasset was ready to throw in her lot with Philip despite the attempts of Benjamin Church and some Rhode Island men to keep her out of the struggle. It was feared that the Wampanoags, with the aid of Weetamoo's canoes, might leave their peninsula and carry the war northeastward into the center of the colony. Cudworth had sent additional strength for the protection of Mattapoiset, and now hoped to consolidate his scattered forces into two garrisons. As soon as feasible he intended to send out small patrols to ambush enemy groups wherever they could be found, and of course his chances of success against the Wampanoags would be greatly enhanced by the arrival of the Massachusetts force.[28]

Although officially the governments of the neighboring colonies were in sympathy with Plymouth at this time of crisis, public opinion in both Rhode Island and Massachusetts was far from unanimous in agreeing with the justice of Plymouth's argument against Philip. In view of Rhode Island's earlier history, it is not at all surprising that the greatest amount of criticism originated among the settlers of that colony. But in Massachusetts, too, a number of people were ready to believe that the Bay Colony was being dragged into an unnecessary and unjust war because of Plymouth's stern and unyielding policy toward the Wampanoags. Without doubt, much of the criticism of Plymouth's actions really stemmed from the old issues which had been dividing the English colonies for years: land claims, boundary disputes, and the question of Indian policy.[29] Fortunately for Plymouth, the general fear of Indians and the ties of consanguinity were sufficiently strong so that most of the settlers in Massachusetts were willing to support their government in its policy of helping subdue the Wampanoags. Rhode Island, although it gave some assistance from time to time, remained technically neutral in the struggle.

Exactly what was in Philip's mind in June of 1675 remains something of a mystery. Most New Englanders who were alive at that time seem to have been convinced that the Wampanoag sachem had spent the preceding years organizing a widespread plot against the colonies, and that King Philip's War was the outcome of this conspiratorial activity. Many contemporary observers speak of suspicious intercourse between the Wampanoags and other Indian tribes in the months preceding the war. We read of messengers and presents being sent from Mount Hope to such important groups as the Narragansetts, the Mohegans, the Pocassets, and the Sakonnets. One writer tells how the Indians had prepared secret caches of food, an unusual precaution except in time of war. From various sources in the early months of 1675 the English received distinct warnings of impending trouble. Sassamon spoke plainly, and died on the ice of Assawompsett Pond. On two separate occasions the native ruler of the Christian Indians at Natick told the English of Philip's intentions, a warning which was seconded by others of his own race. Ordinarily these Indians would be considered an excellent source of information, although the possibility of bias against Philip cannot be ignored. At any rate, once the war had started, it was easy for the English to assume that all the earlier warnings were valid, and that the apparently treacherous uprising had been planned well in advance.[30]

If King Philip's War was the result of a prearranged plan among the various New England tribes, why then did it break out and unfold itself in such a strangely haphazard way? Surely an extensive and well-planned conspiracy would have produced an initial attack which was sudden, widespread, and devastating. Instead, there was a long period of petty provocation and quibbling in a relatively small local area before any human blood was shed, and even then the other tribes did not rush to Philip's assistance. Furthermore, Philip himself at the outset apparently sought to avoid hostilities with all other colonies but Plymouth. When citizens of Massachusetts fell into the hands of his men prior to the actual outbreak of full-scale warfare, Philip was careful to treat them with courtesy, and ordered their release.[31] Clearly, he was hoping that the Bay Colony would remain neutral in the developing crisis with Plymouth.

The overwhelming weight of circumstantial evidence does indicate that some sort of plot was being discussed among the Indians in 1674 and 1675. In view of the haphazard way in which the conflict began, and the subsequent lack of unity among the various tribes, it is equally certain that the planned conspiracy was far from complete. Apparently the war came before Philip really wanted it, as the circumstances of the Sassamon Case and the ardor of his hot-blooded young braves forced his hand. Once involved in hostilities, however, there was no drawing back, and so Philip tried to complete in time of war the conspiracy which he had failed to forge in time of peace, while at the same time fighting for his life against the converging forces of colonial military power.

CHAPTER IV

The July Campaign of 1675

CAPTAIN CUDWORTH and his small force of Plymouth Colony men had accomplished very little since their arrival at Swansea, and Governor Winslow clearly was disappointed at their lack of aggressiveness. They had managed to establish themselves in several garrisons for the better protection of the assembled inhabitants, and had sent exploratory patrols to various parts of the town, but that was all. Actually Cudworth himself was far from satisfied with these defensive measures, but he thought it best to await the arrival of the Massachusetts forces before taking more positive action. His impatience was increased by a report that Philip's Indians might soon try to escape from their peninsula by crossing to the Pocasset shore in canoes. In fact, such an escape was the only feasible course left to them, since the Plymouth troops now were in a position to block the one exit by land. Philip probably had a considerable number of canoes available on the peninsula, and Weetamoo was believed to have others hidden along the Pocasset shore to aid in the evacuation. Although the Rhode Islanders could be counted upon to help prevent Philip's escape, their boat patrol was limited, and might prove ineffective against a mass crossing by large numbers of canoes at night. Obviously, Philip on the loose in the open country east of the Taunton River would be much more dangerous than Philip cooped up in his own peninsula; therefore speedy action by the colonial forces was imperative.[1]

The first units from Massachusetts reached Swansea on the 28th of June, and were ordered to join the Plymouth troops already encamped at the Miles garrison house, which then became the army's

main advance base. The building itself served as a general headquarters for the officers, while the troops camped roundabout within
the shelter of a sort of barricade which they erected. Only a short
distance down the road stood the bridge and causeway which led
across a little stream and on into the enemy's country.

Cudworth viewed the arrival of the Massachusetts forces with a
deep sense of relief, for now he had the strength needed for offensive
operations against the Wampanoags. On the evening of June 28th
the English forces stationed at Swansea and vicinity consisted of the
following units: Captain Cudworth's force of well over one hundred
Plymouth Colony men and friendly Indians, Captain Thomas Prentice's troop of about fifty cavalrymen plus a few Indians, Captain
Daniel Henchman's company of about one hundred mounted dra-
goons, and Captain Samuel Moseley's company of about one hundred
volunteers. Opposing them were an unknown number of enemy
warriors, probably several hundred, equipped with modern firearms.

The arrival of a Massachusetts army at the scene of action naturally
raised the question of military cooperation and supreme command.
Cudworth, of course, took his orders from the governor and military
council of his own colony, and exercised direct authority only over
the Plymouth Colony men. The expedition from Massachusetts was
under the command of Major Thomas Savage, who had not yet
arrived on the scene.[2] Governor Winslow, recognizing the dominant
role which the Bay Colony was inevitably coming to assume in the
crisis, suggested that the government at Boston should name the
supreme commander for the combined forces. It is now very difficult
to tell just how the problem was solved at that time. There seems to
have been some working arrangement, for decisions were made, and
operations were conducted jointly by the two forces.

The Massachusetts troops had scarcely arrived at the Miles garrison house and taken note of their surroundings before some of
them began to wonder where the hostile redskins were. About a
dozen of Captain Prentice's men, guided more by enthusiasm than
by sense, wanted to demonstrate their military prowess without further delay, and gained permission from their superiors to make a
foray into enemy territory beyond the bridge. Benjamin Church, who
was probably already chafing at Cudworth's cautious leadership,
readily agreed to accompany them. The whole army watched with

interest as the little party of hot-bloods on horseback trotted out
of the camp and headed toward the bridge. Apparently they intended
to go some distance into the peninsula, for they took with them as
guide a Rehoboth man, William Hammond.

The troopers found their Indians soon enough. No sooner had they
crossed the bridge than a small group of Philip's warriors, hidden in
ambush, sent a volley of bullets whistling through their ranks. The
guide, Hammond, was hit in a vital spot, and slumped helpless in his
saddle. Quartermaster Joseph Belcher was shot in the leg, while his
horse was killed under him. Corporal John Gill felt a bullet smack
into his body, but was relieved to find that his tough outer jacket
plus a thick layer of paper which he wore beneath it had saved him
from anything worse than a bruise. The rest of the startled and
confused troopers, their martial ardor somewhat cooled by this unexpected turn of events, galloped back to safer ground, while the
hundreds of soldiers around the garrison house stood open-mouthed
at the sight.

The fullest account of what happened next is found in Church's
own memoirs of the war, an account which makes Church himself
the hero of the occasion.[3] As he recalled the episode many years later,
only he and Gill remained undaunted by the sudden volley from
ambush and, seeing the plight of the badly wounded Hammond, they
urged the troopers to return to the rescue. Most of the troopers,
however, now seemed hesitant about moving even one yard nearer
the enemy. Finally Corporal Gill and one other, together with
Church, managed to reach their wounded companion, sling him
across the back of Gill's horse, and carry him back to the English
lines. Hammond's wound, unfortunately, was a fatal one. Still not
satisfied, Church, who had remained in the danger zone alone,
stormed and shouted for the army to come over and pursue the
enemy; but the troops were not ready to move into combat on such
short notice, and they continued to stand and stare. The disdainful
Church thereupon rode back into the camp, convinced that he was
in the company of fools and cowards. Perhaps the Indians thought
so too.

The next day a much larger force advanced across the bridge for a
deeper penetration of the enemy's territory. Beyond the bridge, the
units spread themselves out in a broad scouting line, with flanking

parties on both wings to guard them as they advanced. The separated units proceeded ahead in a manner which clearly showed the army's inexperience in such maneuvers. At one point during the advance a brisk exchange of shots rang out as two groups of soldiers mistook each other for the enemy. Fortunately, only one minor casualty occurred as a result of this error, but the victim was Major Savage's own son, then an ensign in Henchman's company. After scouting some distance down the peninsula, the army turned about and returned to its base. This foray was the total accomplishment recorded for another precious day.

About six o'clock that evening Major Savage, attended by two small mounted companies, arrived from Boston to take command of the Massachusetts forces. Almost equally welcome was the small train of loaded supply carts which accompanied this troop movement, and furthermore, Savage was able to report that his government was dispatching two small ships with additional supplies including foodstuffs and powder. These vessels, of course, would have to make the passage around Cape Cod in order to deliver their precious cargo at Swansea. Cudworth now had reason to feel even more confident. In addition to his own force, he could confront the enemy with a strong Massachusetts contingent totaling now well over three hundred men, enough to give Philip real trouble if properly employed.[4]

June 30th was the day appointed for the long-awaited sweep of the Mount Hope peninsula. The men awoke to find the weather very unpromising, and the march was delayed until shortly before noon. Then at last the various companies formed themselves into marching order, the men shouldered their heavy muskets, and the advance began. Across the bridge they went, and on into the green depths of Philip's homeland. As in the previous day's probing maneuver, parties of horsemen protected the flanks of the advancing army. No doubt the men were nervous at first, expecting at any moment to hear the crash of an Indian volley; but the minutes passed, and there was no sound of hostile fire.

Not long after leaving the bridge, the troops passed by the blackened ruins of English homes, the remains of that little group of Swansea houses which had been built there in the neck so close to Philip's country. Continuing on for two or three more miles, they reached Kickamuit, at the narrowest part of the neck. Here they came upon a sight which caused their scalps to prickle in horror—a group of upright poles upon which hung the severed heads and hands of Englishmen. These were bloody souvenirs of the Swansea men who had been killed at Mattapoiset on the 24th; and, as Church later recalled, these "gash'd and ghostly objects struck a damp on all beholders." [5] After taking down the remains, the grim-faced troops resumed their southward advance. They soon entered the area of Indian habitation, where they saw ample evidence that the savages had made a hasty withdrawal from the vicinity. Wigwams stood empty and abandoned. The cornfields were deserted. Most significant of all, the army found no Indian canoes along the shore. The land seemed empty.[6]

Finally the troops reached the southern shore of the long peninsula and saw before them across the narrow straits the gentle green slopes of Aquidneck Island. Night was drawing on, the army was in the open, and the weather promised to be "very tempestuous, and rainy." [7] Fortunately, some boats from the island were available for transport. Although the records are not entirely in agreement on the episode, the evidence does seem to indicate that some of the Massachusetts troops actually spurned the opportunity to accept Rhode Island hospitality at this time. Apparently they could not forget the old animosities, which boded ill for future intercolonial cooperation in the continuing struggle against the Indians. Cudworth and the Plymouth men seem to have had no such scruples, however, and were glad to accept whatever comforts the Rhode Islanders could offer them.[8]

After spending a wet and miserable night in the open at the southern end of the peninsula, the Massachusetts units returned to Swansea, while the Plymouth men lingered on Aquidneck. It was obvious that Philip and his people had fled, probably on the night of June 29th, and the entire Mount Hope peninsula was now in English hands. Soon the land-hungry English would be estimating its real-estate value in pounds sterling, as though it were ready to be parceled out and occupied. Some in the army acted as though they had just effected a great conquest, but others, including Church, knew better. As Church later said, "The Enemy were not really beaten out of *Mount-hope* Neck, tho' 'twas true they fled from thence; yet it was before any pursu'd them. 'Twas but to strengthen themselves, and to gain a more advantagious Post." [9]

The commanding officers, meanwhile, were trying to decide what to do next. Church argued for a vigorous pursuit of the Wampanoags in the Pocasset country, but instead, the army adopted defensive tactics for the time being. For one thing, there was still a lingering belief in a secret stone fort somewhere on the peninsula. No such fort had been discovered during the recent sweep, but so long as there remained any possibility of its existence the peninsula would have to be watched. Moreover, even if all the Wampanoags really had fled, they might return; therefore the English decided to build a fort of their own on the eastern side of the peninsula near the mouth of the Kickamuit River. Captains Moseley and Page with their companies were designated to keep the peninsula under surveillance, while Captains Henchman and Prentice conducted patrol operations above Swansea.[10] At least one successful patrol action did occur between Swansea and Rehoboth soon after the army's return. A group of enemy Indians were discovered and pursued, with the result that several of them, including a minor sachem, were killed. But such little victories could now have no real effect in putting a stop to the dangerous uprising which Philip had begun.

It now seems apparent that the defensive policy adopted at the beginning of July was a regrettable blunder. It is true that the proposed fort would serve the purpose of denying the peninsula to the Wampanoags if they should decide to return there, but the time and effort expended in building it could have been spent more profitably in a vigorous offensive east of the Taunton River. Both colonies would have been better defended if strong contingents had been sent to the vicinity of Taunton to prevent the Indians from making a westward crossing, while the remainder of the army entered the Pocasset country to track the enemy down. In this way Philip could have been squeezed between the two forces, and the uprising very likely would have come to an end at that point. Instead, the army dallied at Swansea for almost a week after sweeping the peninsula, while Philip sojourned with Weetamoo's people and bound them to his cause. So far, the Wampanoags had completely outmaneuvered their opponents, and had finally placed themselves in a location from which they could strike in a number of directions. Philip was now far more dangerous than when he had been penned up like an animal at bay on the Mount Hope peninsula. Well might the settlers wonder which town would be the next to feel his fury.

*   *   *

Meanwhile, the colonies remained extremely apprehensive over the role which the Narragansetts might come to play in the war. The assurances which the Narragansett sachems had given to Edward Hutchinson and Roger Williams in the latter part of June had done little to allay English suspicions. There was far too much evidence of Narragansett hostility to be outweighed by mere promises. It was known that Philip had been communicating with the Narragansetts for some time, in hopes of securing their support, and there was even reason to believe that a few Narragansett warriors were with the Wampanoags during the early days of the war. Moreover, the English suspected that Wampanoag women and children were being sheltered in the Narragansett country.[11] So threatening was the outlook there, that many of the settlers had left the area and taken refuge on Aquidneck Island. Yet for the moment, at least, the Narragansetts remained officially at peace with the English.

One interesting side light of the situation concerned the old rivalry between the Narragansetts on the one hand, and the Mohegans and Pequots of eastern Connecticut on the other. The Narragansett sachems looked upon Uncas as a perpetual enemy whom they must continue to oppose in every possible way. Thus, the attitude of Uncas toward the war might well determine the role of the Narragansetts in the struggle, for their natural inclination was always to line up on the side opposite the Mohegans. In Connecticut many people considered Uncas an old villain who was ready to throw in his lot with Philip whenever he thought the proper moment had arrived, but others believed that a wise policy on the part of the authorities at Hartford would bind the Mohegans securely to the English cause. One very hopeful indication of Uncas' intentions came early in July when he sent six envoys to Boston to offer his aid in the war. The English thereupon requested hostages as an assurance of Uncas' sincerity, a demand which was met when Uncas arranged to have his son Oneco's wife and child sent to Hartford.[12] The Narragansetts,

in the meantime, lost no opportunity to inform the English that
Uncas was secretly becoming involved with Philip, while the Mohegans
accused the Narragansetts of the same thing. Which side was telling
the truth? It was a very great question which no-one could answer
at the moment, although as the Reverend James Fitch of Norwich
told Uncas, it would soon "come to the triall who are freinds and who
are foes." [13] The English could not afford to wait too long to find the
answer. If the Narragansetts should enter the war on Philip's side, it
would be a terrible blow to the English, for the Narragansetts were
able to place hundreds of warriors in the field, perhaps as many as
a thousand. Eastern Connecticut as well as central Massachusetts
would be in dire peril from such a force, and the resulting diversion
of English military strength would enable the Wampanoags to increase their destructive activities still further. Clearly, then, the future
status of the Narragansetts was of the utmost importance in the
present emergency.

The uncertainty might have lingered on for weeks if Massachusetts
had not decided to force the issue. This time the authorities at
Boston were determined to negotiate from strength rather than from
weakness. They sent Captain Edward Hutchinson with a small retinue
to demand positive guarantees from the Narragansett sachems, and if
such guarantees were not forthcoming the colony's military forces
would take drastic action. Hutchinson was to have the support of the
Massachusetts units then in the field, and his arrival at Swansea on
the night of July 4th with these orders changed the whole aspect of
the campaign against Philip. All or nearly all of the Massachusetts
troops were diverted to the new project, and this at the very time
when the Wampanoags, having eluded the army, were now at large
somewhere in the southwestern part of Plymouth Colony. Only the
Plymouth forces remained to keep watch, and there could be no real
hope of crushing the uprising until the Massachusetts troops had
returned from their new mission.

On July 5th the Massachusetts army began moving toward the
Narragansett country. Hutchinson, accompanied by Moseley and his
volunteers, traveled by water; the other units proceeded by land
around the head of Narragansett Bay. Apparently this part of the
army was held in reserve somewhere below Providence, for only
Moseley's company was actually present at Wickford, the site of the

negotiations. Once again Roger Williams had consented to lend his good offices in the interests of peace. If the negotiations should end in failure, however, the commanders had every intention of striking a decisive blow without further delay. As Hubbard put it, they were resolved to "go to make a Peace with a Sword in their Hands." [14]

From the time when the Massachusetts officers first arrived at Wickford with Roger Williams, the Narragansett sachems were noticeably cool toward the mission. On July 7th Hutchinson was still vainly trying to arrange a meeting with the sachems, and Williams himself was more than a little pessimistic about the outcome of such a parley even if it should take place. More than anything else, Williams feared a sudden outbreak of violence during the negotiations, which would surely cause a disastrous extension of the war. Yet he saw the importance of bringing the Narragansetts into a well-defined relationship with the English by peaceful means if possible, and was eager to do all in his power to effect such an arrangement.

On the 8th of July the two sides got together for the first time, but under conditions which were anything but promising. The sachems brought with them to Wickford a large following of armed warriors who proceeded to act in a manner which the English considered insolent. However, since the English themselves had come with a strong military force, it was reasonable to expect that the Indians would do likewise. What the Massachusetts officials really wanted, of course, was an abject surrender by the Narragansetts, and the proud sachems were clearly in no mood for this. With the conference at an apparent impasse, the military officers were about ready to send for the rest of the army when Captain Wait Winthrop arrived from Connecticut on July 9th, and persuaded them to postpone such drastic action for the time being. [15]

Young Winthrop had been designated by his government to represent Connecticut in the current negotiations with the Narragansetts. He had departed from Stonington with a small force of English troopers and friendly Pequots, following the well-worn Pequot Path toward Pettaquamscut and Wickford. En route he had paused for an interview with the sachem Ninigret, who was really the biggest question mark in the present crisis. On this occasion Ninigret had proclaimed his friendship for the English, even promising to deliver up any of Philip's men who should fall into his hands. After this rather satisfactory interview, Winthrop had continued on to Wickford in order to participate in the major negotiations there.[16]

It was immediately apparent that Connecticut and Massachusetts differed radically in their attitude toward the Narragansetts. Whereas Massachusetts was ready to use force if the sachems would not give the desired guarantees, Connecticut favored a policy of caution and even appeasement. The Connecticut view was briefly summed up in the words of the governor himself, who wrote, "Its best to keepe and promote peace with them, though with bearing some of their ill manners and conniving at some irregularities." [17] This attitude of appeasement was dictated by practical considerations. Connecticut's eastern frontier was adjacent to the Narragansett country, and the towns there were weak and poorly defended. If the Massachusetts army should goad the Narragansetts into open hostility, Connecticut towns might bear the brunt of Indian fury. Stonington could be another Swansea. Knowing this only too well, the frontier settlements of eastern Connecticut were tense with apprehension during the period of the negotiations at Wickford. One of Wait Winthrop's Stonington friends frankly suggested that the negotiators should "winke at small faultes" for the present, rather than resort to force. Perhaps later in the year would be a better time to attack the Narragansetts, "when the Leaves in the wilderness are dried and burnt and the swampes frozen hard and wee may track them out in the snow." [18]

Why had Connecticut not sent a strong force of troops to defend her eastern frontier? The answer lies in a new outbreak of an old quarrel between Connecticut and the royal province of New York. During the years when New York was Dutch territory, the vast area between the Hudson River and the Connecticut River had been claimed by both colonies. When the Duke of York took over the former Dutch colony in 1664, he inherited this old quarrel with Connecticut, but the dispute remained quiescent until Edmund Andros became governor of the duke's territory late in 1674. Soon after assuming the post, Andros demanded that Connecticut surrender its control of the disputed territory, which included such towns as New Haven, Wethersfield, Windsor, and even Hartford itself. Connecticut of course rejected this demand, while asserting its own prior right by royal grant. Here the matter hung until the outbreak of Indian warfare in New England gave to Andros an excuse for action.[19]

On the morning of July 8th two New York sloops bearing Governor Andros and a party of soldiers appeared at the mouth of the Connecticut River and anchored off the town of Saybrook in order to enforce New York's claim. Fortunately for Connecticut, however, Saybrook was ready for this invasion. The local trainband had been reinforced by a body of troops originally destined for the eastern frontier, and these men now manned the fort at Saybrook with a determination which gave pause to the New York governor. There can be little doubt that Andros had expected to seize this area by a sudden show of force, but Saybrook's alertness upset his plan. Andros, however, was not yet ready to give up, so he and his troops calmly remained at anchor near the town, like cats watching a mouse.

Connecticut was now in simultaneous peril on two fronts, and scarcely knew which was the more dangerous. The frontier settlements in eastern Connecticut were crying for troops to defend them in case the Narragansetts should become involved in the war, but the expected contingents from the western counties failed to arrive. They were being held back for the defense of western Connecticut. No wonder the authorities at Hartford felt obliged to appease the Narragansetts at this critical juncture! In a resolution of July 10th the General Court of the colony condemned Andros' action not only because it was illegal, but because it was thought to be a positive encouragement to the Indians. Two days later the government issued orders for the return of Wait Winthrop and his military retinue from the Narragansett country.[20] Massachusetts would have to go it alone in her attempt to force guarantees from the Narragansett sachems.

Luckily for the English, affairs took a sudden and remarkable turn for the better just at this time. After four or five days of waiting at Saybrook, Andros realized that he had failed, at least for the present, and made up his mind to depart. On the other front, the Narragansetts finally weakened in their attitude toward the English demands, and the negotiations reached a successful conclusion. It was also extremely fortunate that Winthrop's orders to return to Connecticut did not arrive soon enough to disrupt the arrangements. On July 15th the terms of a treaty were formally accepted by both sides, greatly diminishing the immediate threat of war. In essence the agreement obligated the Narragansett sachems to remain loyal to the English, and to treat the Wampanoags as enemies. This required among other things giving up of any Wampanoags now held or later taken on Narragansett territory. The English, in turn, promised payment for all Wampanoag captives or heads surrendered to them. As part of the agreement the sachems confirmed all previous grants of land to the English. Finally, the Narragansetts were required to yield up four of their own people as hostages to guarantee that the terms of the treaty would be faithfully observed.[21] Presumably these hostages would be held in custody until the Narragansetts had performed such acts of violence against the Wampanoags as would ensure the future enmity of the two peoples. It is perhaps significant that the treaty itself had not been signed by the really important sachems, but by four Indians styled as "councellors" to the sachems. Quite possibly the real leaders of the Narragansetts, or some of them, had not been able to swallow the terms proposed by the English, and so the Massachusetts officers had gone through the motions of signing the treaty with a group of minor leaders whom they could coerce. Of one thing we can be certain—the treaty was accepted by the Narragansetts only under extreme duress, and the terms of the treaty in no sense represent the real will or intentions of the Narragansett sachems.

In view of what later occurred, it now appears clear that these negotiations were a waste of time. The whole plan of forcing compliance upon the Narragansetts—in fact, of issuing an ultimatum backed by the threat of troops there present—was ill conceived and poorly timed. Up to that moment the Narragansetts had actually done little to aid Philip, although there was real danger that they might do more later. But with Philip loose in the Pocasset country, it was little short of folly to dispatch an important segment of the army on a purely diplomatic mission. The inevitable result was more delay in the offensive against the immediate enemy. Actually, the whole campaign to suppress the Wampanoags was thrown out of gear for about ten days while the Massachusetts officers were browbeating the Narragansetts into signing a treaty which they could ignore later whenever they wished.

As if this were not enough, the expedition to the Narragansett country also had the effect of irritating Rhode Island at a time when wholehearted cooperation by that colony was badly needed in the war against Philip. The Narragansett country itself, as we have seen, had long been claimed by both Connecticut and Rhode Island, while Massachusetts considered the Narragansett Indians to be under her special supervision. Hence every move made by either Connecticut or Massachusetts with respect to this area was viewed with extreme suspicion by the Rhode Islanders. Is it any wonder, then, that the converging of sizable armed forces from both Connecticut and Massachusetts on the Narragansett country caused deep concern to the government of Rhode Island? Governor Coddington expressed the opinion that the real purpose of the expedition was to seize control of the disputed area, and tempers were not sweetened when the Massachusetts officers at Wickford placed a Rhode Island official under arrest for questioning the army's right to be there.[22] Although Coddington's assertion was largely disproved by the subsequent withdrawal of the troops after the completion of their mission, the harm had been done, and Rhode Islanders remained suspicious of their neighbors' intentions. All in all, then, there is much reason to question the wisdom of what was attempted by the Massachusetts forces during the period from July 5th to July 15th. Vigorous action against Philip would have paid bigger dividends.

*   *   *

While the Massachusetts army was preoccupied with the negotiations in the Narragansett country, the Plymouth forces were able to accomplish little of military value, for they were too weak to undertake a major offensive in the Pocasset country. Consequently, their efforts were largely defensive in nature, including the construction of the fort on the Mount Hope peninsula. Strangest of all, Cudworth actually led a considerable part of his little army all the way back to Plymouth, thus leaving the frontier protected only by a very small defensive force. Historians of the war have tended to overlook this significant retreat to Plymouth which occurred either in conjunction with, or soon after, the march of the Massachusetts units toward Wickford. Apparently Cudworth's withdrawal was caused by an acute shortage of supplies resulting from the fact that the colonial governments had not yet been able to organize an efficient service of supply. Not only were the colonies inexperienced in dealing with such a problem, but the very nature of the war itself had produced general confusion, in addition to the ordinary difficulty of transporting bulky goods over long distances through the forest. Cudworth's stay in Plymouth was a short one, for he and his troops were allowed to remain there only one night, after which they headed back for the frontier once again.[23] What Cudworth had hoped to accomplish by his march to Plymouth is a subject open to speculation.

In the meantime, there had been some talk of a military mission to influence the Pocasset Indians in the same way that the Narragansetts were being led to conform with English wishes. Such an attempt was actually made by a detachment of Plymouth soldiers during the time when the Massachusetts units were absent in the Narragansett country, but it met with no success. Nevertheless, the episode is not without its interest, for it resulted in one of the most amazing little battles of the entire war.

Captain Matthew Fuller had only about three dozen men with him when he left Aquidneck Island and headed for Weetamoo's territory on the eastern side of the Sakonnet River. It was now several days since the Massachusetts troops had left Swansea, and fighting men were scarce. Fuller's assistant in this venture was Benjamin Church, whose memoirs must again be relied upon as our major source of information. Church was delighted at the opportunity for two reasons: first, he was anxious to have another meeting with Awashonks in order to confirm her as a friend of the English; second, he had only contempt for the current project of building a fort on the Mount Hope peninsula, and was glad to be able to turn his back on the whole affair.

Having landed on the Pocasset shore, Fuller's stout little party began its operation with all the efficiency of an army from Gilbert and Sullivan. They spent the first night in two separate groups, bivouacked in darkness, hoping that some Indians would inadvertently walk into their grasp. The plan was foiled because some of the men in Fuller's group "being troubled with the Epidemical plague of lust after Tobacco, must needs strike fire to Smoke it," thereby revealing their presence to a group of approaching Indians, who at once took to their heels.[24] Church's disgust at this folly can be better imagined than described, but there was no use in crying over spilled milk, and so the next thing to do was to eat breakfast to strengthen themselves for the day's march. Imagine Church's face now as the soldier in charge of their provisions shuffled forward and confessed that he had left their entire food supply on the island. The rest of the day's work had to be done on the energy furnished by a few small cakes which Church himself had providentially stowed in his pocket before leaving Aquidneck.

After finishing their "slender breakfast," the men divided themselves into two groups of about twenty men each, which went their separate ways, supposedly being attended by a number of boats operating along the shore. This division of forces was surely a tactical blunder in view of their numerical weakness. Fuller's party soon had a brush with the Indians, and took refuge in an abandoned house near the waterside, from which they were fortunately rescued by boat and carried back to Aquidneck. Church's experiences were somewhat more remarkable. Moving southward toward Sakonnet, Church and his party came upon a fresh track which they decided to follow inland. They soon found themselves in country infested by rattlesnakes "which the little Company seem'd more to be afraid of than the black Serpents they were in quest of. . . ." [25] Church felt sure that the track would lead them to Indians; but, fearing the snakes, the group abandoned the track, and continued on in a southward direction.

On Punkatees Neck in an abandoned pease field they discovered a pair of Indians, who quickly ran into the woods, despite Church's attempt to speak with them. Soon a murderous volley came blasting from the woods, and it was only by the greatest good fortune that none of the men were hit. Church knew now that he was in for an exciting time, and those of his companions who recently had been chaffing him because he had as yet shown them no Indians were now silent. There were Indians enough and to spare. Church later recalled that the hillside above them "seem'd to move, being covered over with *Indians*, with their bright Guns glittering in the Sun, and running in a circumference with a design to surround them." [26] Fortunately, the pease field was close to the shore, and Church immediately saw that their best hope was to form a tight little defense perimeter on the beach, where they might be able to hold out until rescued by the boats from Rhode Island. Even as these thoughts flashed through his mind, Church could see a gathering of men and boats over on the Rhode Island shore. He ordered his men to strip off their coats so that the Rhode Islanders would see their white shirts, and know that they were Englishmen.

The shore offered little shelter from the enemy's fire, but by piling up the rocks one on top of the other they were able to give themselves some slight protection. The Indians had every advantage of numbers, terrain, and natural shelter, yet the little band of soldiers stood fast. They had no choice, of course, and they had seen the severed heads which the Wampanoags had left behind them on the Mount Hope peninsula. Worst of all, time was against them, for their powder supply was dangerously low.

One boat from the island ventured near, but withdrew again after getting a taste of the enemy's fire. This only served to encourage the Indians, who were now yelling with excitement as they peppered the beach with their bullets. So desperate was the position of the English that some of the men even talked of trying to make a running escape through the woods, but Church knew the complete futility of such an attempt, and persuaded his party to stick together where they were. Yet night was approaching, and darkness would mean death.

Suddenly they sighted a sloop moving down from the direction of Gould Island. Nearer and nearer it came, while the hard-pressed Plymouth men fought to hold off the surrounding mass of Indians. Finally the sloop anchored well within the range of the enemy's guns, and let her tiny canoe drift in to the shore. Two of Church's sweating men clambered aboard and paddled desperately for safety. Again and again the little canoe drifted to shore, and each time it returned to the sloop, carrying a pair of trembling, tired men. All during this gradual evacuation the musketry of the crew helped hold off the yelling Indians. Church, of course, was the last to leave, and he fired one more defiant shot at the enemy before quitting the shore.

Church knew the skipper of the sloop, Captain Roger Goulding, and was never more glad to see an old acquaintance in his life. The fight had lasted from midafternoon until about dusk, and by the time the evacuation was completed the weary defenders had used up practically all of their powder. Probably another few minutes on that beach would have been fatal. As it was, all of the men who had originally gone out with Fuller and Church returned safely, although one or two of Fuller's party had been wounded. This adventure certainly had an ending more happy than anyone would have had a right to expect, although the hope for a successful parley with the Pocassets had proved futile.

Meanwhile, Philip had been doing all he could to strike hard at the English settlements on the frontier. His stealthy raiding parties brought terror and destruction to a widespread area, and no-one knew where the Indians would strike next. Confusion and panic swept through the exposed towns, and the normal work of raising crops had to be neglected as the people abandoned their homes and crowded into the local garrison houses. From these they could sometimes see the smoke rising from their own burning homes and barns. Nearby, the rotting carcasses of horses and cattle littered the ground.[27]

Since the original outbreak at Swansea, both Rehoboth and Taunton had been attacked, and on July 9th the tiny settlement of Middleborough felt the heavy hand of the enemy, with the result that most of the houses there were burned down, and the town was soon abandoned. At about the same time hostile Indians fell upon the town of Dartmouth in the extreme southern part of the colony, killing a number of the townspeople, as well as destroying many houses.[28] Worse still, other Indians besides the Wampanoags were now trying their hand at this kind of activity. Providence had already suffered some depredations, probably by hot-blooded young Narragansetts.[29] Now, on the 14th of July, a group of Nipmucks launched a sudden attack against the small frontier town of Mendon in the southern part of Massachusetts, killing several of the surprised inhabitants.[30] The epidemic of Indian hostility was showing dangerous signs of spreading.

The Indians were so skillful at slinking through the forest and awaiting their chance to attack unsuspecting settlements that there seemed no practical way to prevent such depredations short of cutting out the very heart of the uprising, Philip himself. Because this fact was becoming increasingly clear to the military commanders, they continued their operations in the Pocasset country. The peasefield fight was only the first of several lively skirmishes in that area. Unfortunately, the terrain was extremely disadvantageous for the English because it included a number of trackless swamps into which

Philip and his followers could quickly disappear whenever they were pressed too closely. Thus the sweating English troops were forced to work hard at their task without achieving any notable success. But at least the skirmishes proved that the enemy was present in the vicinity, and so the English would know where to strike hard when the chance came.[31]

*   *   *

One thing that the English commanders soon learned by experience was that friendly Indians could be very useful in the fight against the enemy. There could be no doubt that the natives had a skill in tracking and forest maneuver which the English sorely needed, but did not themselves possess. It was a common complaint in these early days of the war that "the English wanted not courage or resolution, but could not discern or find an enemy to fight with, yet were galled by the enemy." [32] Friendly Indians were present with the Plymouth forces at Swansea soon after the outbreak of the war, and Massachusetts sent a group of more than fifty Christian Indians to the army on July 6th. Although some of the English soldiers were not a little suspicious of these native warriors, the friendly Indians remained loyal to the English cause, and performed good service against the enemy.

Although Philip was still at large, he was now thought to be isolated from other major Indian groups such as the Narragansetts and the Nipmucks. Meanwhile, large numbers of troops remained in the field, which meant that the summer's work on the farms was being neglected, and the colony governments were being put to heavy expense. Would it not be possible to demobilize some of the troops at a great saving to the taxpayers? Governor Winslow thought so, and suggested to Governor Leverett that all but about a hundred of the Massachusetts soldiers might now be withdrawn from duty in Plymouth Colony. At the same time, he advised Cudworth to retain only about a hundred of his own best men to continue the pursuit of the enemy.[33] This would mean that the task of crushing the Wampanoags would be left in the hands of only about two hundred English soldiers plus some friendly Indians, an amazing proposal in view of the uncertainty of the situation.

While these plans were being considered, the last units of the

Massachusetts army had returned from the Narragansett country, and were rejoining the Plymouth forces for a new blow against the Wampanoags. The combined army moved forward toward the Pocasset swamp country on July 19th, and was met by a band of hostile Indians who attacked their *forlorn*, or advanced guard, killing two men.[34] Undaunted by this sharp attack, the English forces pushed on to the great cedar swamp where the bulk of the enemy lay concealed. There was no question about the nearness of the enemy; the great difficulty was to get at them. The swamp was extensive and thickly covered with a tangle of wild growth which made it extremely difficult to penetrate, especially under fire. Nevertheless, the Massachusetts forces moved courageously into the swamp, with the Plymouth troops close behind them. The retreating savages made good use of the natural cover afforded by trees and bushes, and inflicted a number of casualties on the advancing soldiers. Despite this galling fire from ambush, the English pressed on, capturing a large number of abandoned shelters, but were never able to get their hands on the elusive Indian warriors. The best they could do was to capture one old man who informed them that both Philip and Weetamoo had recently departed.

The English now found themselves deep in the swamp, and obviously at a great disadvantage. Because of the terrain and the tangle of brush, they were seriously handicapped by their cumbersome muskets and other equipment. Confusion had invaded the ranks, and the advancing troops were endangering each other as they nervously fired at every moving bush. Moreover, night was approaching, and a swamp like this was no place for the army after dark. The commanders therefore called a halt to the attack, and the weary soldiers straggled back through the thickets and out to the nearby shore. It had been another frustrating day.[35]

Contemporary accounts of the number of casualties suffered by the English forces during this encounter vary somewhat, but it is probably safe to say that at least seven or eight soldiers were killed or mortally wounded, while a number of others received lesser injuries. Some Indians later said that if the English had pressed their attack for a little while longer, Philip would have been ready to surrender. If so, the war would have ended then and there. But of course even if this were true, the English had no way of knowing the desperate condition of the enemy; they knew only that they themselves had had their fill of such terrain. As Hubbard put it, the commanders now realized "how dangerous it is to fight in such dismal Woods, when their Eyes were muffled with the Leaves, and their Arms pinioned with the thick Boughs of the Trees, as their Feet were continually shackled with the Roots spreading every Way in those boggy Woods. It is ill fighting with a wild Beast in his own Den." [36] The Reverend John Eliot, the famous apostle to the Indians, expressed the current feeling even more succinctly when he remarked, "We were too ready to think that we could easyly suppresse that flea; but now we find that all the craft is in catching of them, and that in the meane while they give us many a soare nip." [37] Mr. Eliot apparently knew fleas as well as he knew the Indians.

The swamp fight of July 19th convinced the English commanders that aggressive action of that kind was not worth the difficulty and danger involved. Therefore Cudworth and his colleagues decided upon a new approach to the problem of ending the uprising. Since Philip and his followers were now definitely located, the English reasoned that the wisest course was to keep them penned up in their swamp until hunger forced them to surrender. No longer would the English forces rush precipitately after the Indians wherever they could be found. Instead, the commanders decided to reduce the size of the army as Winslow had suggested, maintain a small garrison in the fort on the Mount Hope peninsula, build another fort on the southwestern side of the Pocasset swamp to keep the Wampanoags from reaching open water, and organize a small but efficient mobile force to harass the enemy by cutting off their supply of food. Whenever necessary, this flying army could hurry to any threatened point on the frontier. Of one thing the English were now reasonably certain—the uprising had been successfully localized, and it was only a question of time before the beaten Indians would come crawling out of their swamp to seek mercy.

In accordance with this plan, a series of significant troop movements took place almost immediately. Four out of the five companies of Massachusetts men withdrew from Plymouth Colony altogether, the units led by Savage, Moseley, and Page returning to Boston, while Prentice's troop proceeded to the vicinity of Mendon. Apparently Cudworth with all or most of the Plymouth troops crossed back to the Mount Hope peninsula, intending to utilize that area as a base of operations. Henchman's company of about 125 soldiers and seventeen friendly Indians remained at Pocasset to construct the new fort there while keeping a close watch on the enemy in the nearby swamp.

The decision to send a large proportion of the army home after the skirmish of July 19th was unquestionably the greatest blunder of the entire campaign. There were reasons for doing so, of course. A large army was expensive to maintain. Even more important, the shortage of supplies remained acute, constituting a real handicap to any large-scale offensive operations. The English believed that the Wampanoags now hidden in the cedar swamp would be most anxious to reach the shore of Mount Hope Bay, and perhaps return to their own peninsula to secure their corn. Such a movement, they thought, could be effectively blocked by Henchman's small force at Pocasset, since the fort was being constructed between the swamp and the waterside. Basically, the strategic disposition of the troops after July 19th was not without some merit. Presumably a force based on the Mount Hope peninsula and Swansea could move quickly upriver toward Taunton if the enemy should emerge from the northern end of his swamp. But the forces available never should have been reduced as they were, especially at a time when a few more days of vigorous action might have settled the issue then and there. The necessary supplies could have been scraped up somehow. As one close student of the July campaign has stated, "At no time during the whole Indian war were King Philip and his warriors cornered and confronted by such an overwhelming number of armed soldiers. . . . The military tactical error of the English in withdrawing their superior forces at the very time when victory was in their grasp . . . is something new in the history of wars. . . ." [38]

Indeed, the whole July campaign must go down in history as a failure of the first magnitude, a failure which resulted in the further spread of the war, with untold suffering for the settlers of New England and the Indians as well. It would be an understatement to say that the military leadership in the field left much to be desired. We can only assume that the apparent inadequacies of the English forces were due to their inexperience in strategy and tactics, and their failure to understand the real nature of the situation which confronted them. Those who analyze military campaigns ought to be lenient in their judgments, for it is one thing to study a battle while seated in a comfortable library chair, and quite another to be making life-and-death decisions during the confusion and pressure of actual war. Military commanders in battle never know all of the facts which later will be at the disposal of the historian. They must make their decisions on the basis of whatever information they happen to have at the time, and this factor of uncertainty should always be taken into account by later critics. Nevertheless, we learn by studying past errors, and therefore history insists upon judgment.

It is clear that the military organization and tactics of the English were not well suited to the kind of war in which they now found themselves. This seems strange, in view of the fact that the colonists had been close observers of the Indians for years, and should have known their methods. Unfortunately, the colonial governments had continued to place too much faith in the old European drill manuals, which had not been written with American conditions in mind. Fast-moving, forest-wise Indian war parties repeatedly were able to baffle the ponderous English units, retreating successfully when necessary. The colonial troops were learning everything the hard way.

After the departure of Savage and the bulk of the Massachusetts troops, Cudworth made one more serious mistake. Governor Winslow was anxious to have part of the army pay a call on the devastated settlement at Dartmouth, some thirteen miles southeast of Pocasset. The badly frightened people there were in need of encouragement and support. Accordingly, Cudworth decided to lead a strong force to the Dartmouth area to do what he could for the inhabitants. On July 29th, leaving twenty-one men to guard the fort on the Mount Hope peninsula, Cudworth and his company of about 112 soldiers embarked for Pocasset, where they found Henchman and his men still busy constructing the new fort. From here they continued on their way to Dartmouth, leaving Henchman to keep Philip bottled up in the swamp.[39]

In the meantime, Henchman's men continued their labor at the site of the new fort, all the while probably congratulating themselves on the approaching end of the Indian uprising. Sometime after nine o'clock on the evening of July 30th, two officers arrived at Pocasset by boat, and hastened to Henchman's camp. One of the men was Lieutenant Nathaniel Thomas, who had just come from Rehoboth.

The other was Lieutenant James Brown, a Plymouth Colony Assistant. Henchman must have known from their faces that something
was up, and they wasted no time in making their report. Philip and
his followers had escaped from the Pocasset swamp, crossed the
Taunton River, and were heading northward toward Massachusetts
and the Nipmuck country. Cudworth's march to Dartmouth and
Henchman's preoccupation with the fort had enabled the Wampanoags to make a sudden dash toward freedom and opportunity. Thus
ended the futile July campaign of 1675.

CHAPTER V

The War Spreads

IN July of 1675, at about the same time as the Narragansetts were being forced to sign a treaty of fidelity, and while the war was still confined largely to the western reaches of Plymouth Colony, the English were also investigating the attitude of the Nipmucks. Like the Narragansetts, the Nipmucks were a loosely organized people residing in scattered villages, each separate group having its own sachem. Although these various rulers might confer on important matters from time to time, there seems to have been no single, clearly defined, over-all structure of government for the entire tribe. The Nipmucks had formerly been closely bound to the Wampanoags, and still might be under their influence. Hence it was extremely important to determine their attitude toward the uprising which Philip had begun. The government of Massachusetts wanted to obtain from the Nipmuck sachems, if possible, firm guarantees of fidelity, to prevent any spreading of the war in that direction. However, instead of sending an army, as in the case of the Narragansetts, the authorities placed the matter in the hands of Ephraim Curtis, a young trader who owned a trading post or storehouse deep in the Nipmuck country, and who knew these Indians from firsthand experience.[1]

Despite warnings that the Nipmucks were in a very dangerous frame of mind and might even try to kill him if he penetrated their country, Curtis set out from Marlborough during the second week of July, accompanied only by two other white men and a few friendly Indians. They proceeded southward and westward along the narrow trails which led through the native villages of Hassanemesit, Manchage, and Chabanakongkomun to Senecksig. Here they found

73

numerous signs of Indian habitation, but no Indians. Apparently the natives had abandoned their usual haunts for some new and unknown locality. This fact alone was ominous, but to turn back now would mean failure. Curtis was determined to find the Nipmuck sachems and speak with them despite all peril, and so the little party pressed deeper into the wilderness. They eventually came across a track which led them in a generally northward direction past several abandoned campsites to the vicinity of the "leadmine" near the present town of Holland. Riding beyond this point, and following fresh tracks, the scouting party soon captured a terrified Indian who stammered out the news that the Nipmucks were located nearby.

Curtis now sent one of his own Indians on ahead to announce his approach and to indicate his desire for a conference in the interests of peace, but the messenger returned without a satisfactory answer. In spite of this discouraging reception, however, the young trader and his companions continued on to the place where the Indians were gathered. Summoning up all his reserves of courage, Ephraim Curtis forced his way into the very midst of the hostile, menacing assemblage, and delivered his message of peace from the Massachusetts government. Then he took his departure, apparently satisfied that he had made some progress toward cooling the Indians' dangerous anger against the English. What Curtis did not yet know was that even while he was engaged on this mission, a party of Nipmuck warriors, led by Matoonas, had fallen upon the village of Mendon, Massachusetts, murdering several people there.[2] Boston was shocked by the outrage, for it was the first time that open violence of this kind had broken out within the borders of the Bay Colony.

Between the 16th and the 24th of July Curtis made another official visit to the Nipmuck sachems, and this time he was received with somewhat more courtesy than on the previous occasion. He read to the sachems a message from Governor Leverett, receiving in turn a promise that two of their leading men would visit the governor in the near future, but the march of events decreed that this promise would never be kept.

The two dangerous missions of Ephraim Curtis not only had enabled the English authorities to reach the ears of the Nipmucks with their message of peace, but had also produced some valuable information about the Indians themselves. Apparently in the midst of the current tension and excitement raised by Philip's revolt, the Nipmucks had gradually become divided into a pro-war party and an anti-war party, with the former faction now in the ascendancy. The bellicose sachem Muttaump had achieved a position of leadership, or perhaps dominance, over the other Nipmuck rulers, and was supported in his policy by the majority of the Indians, especially the hotheaded young braves. Without question, the Nipmucks were in a belligerent mood at this particular time.

When Philip escaped from the Pocasset country at the end of July, New England was shocked into alertness. Now, unless Philip were stopped at once, the storm of war might lash across the whole countryside, with tribe after tribe joining the orgy of destruction. No longer hemmed in by natural geographical barriers, the savages would be able to range through the forest almost at will, attacking wherever they found a weak point. New England's last chance of escaping such fury rested in the hands of those who now sought to overtake Philip and cut him down before he could reach the council fires of the Narragansetts or the Nipmucks.

The Wampanoags, after making their escape from the unguarded northern end of the Pocasset swamp on the night of July 29th, had moved cautiously up the eastern bank of the Taunton River until they were able to make a crossing. From this place there was only one feasible way to reach the relative safety of the Narragansett country or the Nipmuck country, and that was to pass across Rehoboth plain, and so beyond the Pawtucket River. A more northerly route would bring the Wampanoags far out of their way and dangerously close to the outlying settlements of Massachusetts. But passing close to Rehoboth involved a danger too, for in that vicinity there was much flat, open country to cross, and the risk of detection would be great.

Not daring to remain east of the Pawtucket River even for a single day, Philip and his men, together with Weetamoo and her people, tried to continue their journey by daylight on July 30th, but their presence was discovered by some Taunton men who quickly sent the alarm on to Rehoboth. Stung into action by this frightening news, the English quickly set in motion a hue and cry, lest their adversary escape to do his mischief. As we have seen, Lieutenant Nathaniel Thomas hastened to Pocasset to notify Captain Henchman of Philip's escape. The news was also dispatched to the Narragansetts, in the hope that they might honor their recent treaty with the English by helping to intercept Philip as he rounded the upper end of Narragansett Bay. In the meantime, local forces from both Providence and Rehoboth had begun the active pursuit. Among those who marched from Rehoboth was a well-armed party of Mohegan warriors led by Oneco, the eldest son of Uncas.[3] These Indians had recently come to Boston from Connecticut, offering their services to the English as a proof of Mohegan fidelity. The English had accepted their offer, and so it was that the Mohegan warriors happened to be at Rehoboth at the very time when Philip was attempting his escape. Oneco and his men readily joined in the attempt to overtake and destroy the fleeing Wampanoags.

Before either the Providence group or the Rehoboth group could take effective action, however, Philip was across the Pawtucket River and on his way toward the Nipmuck country. Nevertheless, the pursuing English and Mohegans, realizing now how weak the fugitives actually were, continued the chase until they came to a place called Nipsachuck, some twelve miles northwest of Providence. Here the weary Philip and Weetamoo had halted temporarily to make camp. On the evening of July 31st, as darkness closed over the scene, the men from Providence and Rehoboth studied the situation, and laid their plans for smashing the Wampanoags on the morrow.

Henchman, meanwhile, after learning of Philip's escape, had delayed his departure from Pocasset until daybreak of the 31st. Then he had embarked a large part of his force on boats, taking them ultimately to Providence, where they found quarters for the night. Thus it was that Henchman's troops were not present at Nipsachuck during the early morning hours of August 1st, when the English and Mohegan pursuers were making ready for their attack.[4] Although the men at Nipsachuck knew that Henchman was coming, they dared not postpone the assault lest the enemy slip through their fingers while they were waiting. Therefore they fell upon the weary Wampanoags early that morning, and apparently took the Indians by surprise. Philip's men lost no time in abandoning their positions, leaving behind much equipment and other plunder which later fell into the hands of the Mohegans. Sensing the kill, the excited English and their Indian allies pressed their advantage, and engaged the reluctant Wampanoags in a sharp skirmish. This action came to an end about 9:00 A.M. when the defeated enemy took refuge in a swamp. Here they lay hidden for the rest of the day, expecting all the time to be assaulted again. There is some reason to believe that if the attack had been renewed at this time, many if not all of the Wampanoags would have given themselves up, and the war might have come to an end much sooner than it did. This possibility was made all the more likely by the arrival of Henchman and his company about an hour after the end of the first skirmish. Surely now, with Henchman in command of the combined forces, the attack would be resumed with vigor, and pressed to a victorious conclusion. But such was not the case. Despite his overwhelming strength and the apparent weakness of the enemy, Henchman dallied until the next day, by which time the Wampanoags had made good their escape.

Henchman's lack of speed and aggressiveness on this occasion has justly been criticized both then and since. If Henchman really understood the importance of his opportunity at Nipsachuck, he failed to take advantage of it, and so the moment and the chance passed forever. Weetamoo and her people branched off to the southward, seeking refuge with the Narragansetts, while Philip and his warriors proceeded on to join the Nipmucks. Thus by the failure of the English on August 1st, the flames of war were allowed to burst out of western Plymouth Colony into the ready tinder of the Nipmuck country.

*　　*　　*

Late in July the government of Massachusetts had initiated one more attempt to secure the allegiance of the Nipmuck Indians. At this time the mood of the authorities at Boston was not entirely one of appeasement. They were ready to demand that Matoonas and the other Indians who had taken part in the murders at Mendon on July 14th be delivered up to justice, and they wanted a firm and definite treaty of peace with the Nipmuck sachems, guaranteed, if possible, by the surrender of hostages. Captain Edward Hutchinson, having just returned from his successful treaty-making mission to the Narragansetts, was given the responsibility of trying to obtain these desired commitments.[5]

On the 28th of July Hutchinson took his departure from Cambridge, and proceeded by way of Sudbury into the great forested reaches of the Nipmuck country. With him went Ephraim Curtis and three friendly Indians as guides and interpreters, plus some twenty or more troopers under the command of Captain Thomas Wheeler. En route to their destination they passed through a number of Indian villages in which the huts stood empty, the fireplaces cold. It was like passing through a land of the dead. All of this simply confirmed the earlier observations of Curtis, and indicated very clearly that the Nipmucks were assembled at some central rendezvous, instead of living dispersed as in times of peace.[6]

In the very heart of the Nipmuck country, on a hilltop overlooking the forest for miles around, lay the tiny frontier village of Brookfield, otherwise known as Quabaug. A comparatively new settlement, this village in 1675 contained perhaps twenty families all told. In addition to being a farming community, Brookfield was important as a stopping point on the long Bay Path which ran from the vicinity of Boston across Massachusetts to Springfield on the Connecticut River. Springfield was the nearest English town, and that lay almost thirty miles to the west by trail through the woods—a good day's journey. Indeed, scarcely a town in all of Massachusetts could claim the dubious distinction of being more isolated than Brookfield. Into this remote little village rode Hutchinson and Wheeler with their party of mounted men, and enlisted the help of the local authorities for their important mission. They found these people firmly confident that their Indian neighbors, with whom they had had such close relations in the past, would remain on good terms with the English despite all evidence to the contrary.

Upon learning that the main body of the Indians were assembled at a place about ten miles northwest of Brookfield, probably Menameset on the Ware River, Hutchinson on August 1st sent Curtis and several other men to arrange a parley.[7] The messengers found the atmosphere at the Indian camp anything but friendly. Nevertheless, the sachems finally agreed to meet Hutchinson at eight o'clock the next morning at a designated spot within three miles of Brookfield. At the very moment when Curtis was making these arrangements, forty miles to the southeast Philip and the Wampa-

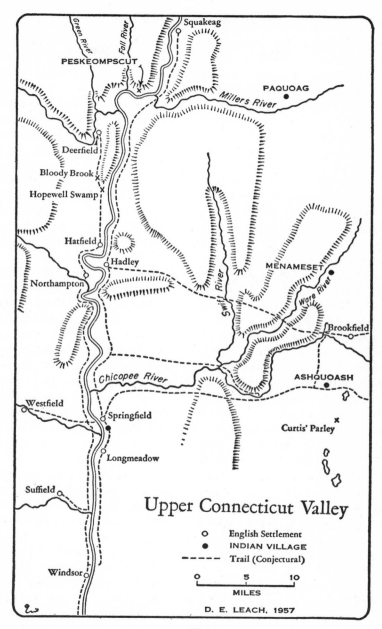

Green River · Fall River · Squakeag

PESKEOMPSCUT

PAQUOAG

Millers River

Deerfield

Bloody Brook

Hopewell Swamp

Hatfield

Hadley

MENAMESET

Northampton

Swift River

Ware River

Brookfield

ASHQUOASH

Chicopee River

Westfield

Springfield

Curtis' Parley

Longmeadow

Suffield

Upper Connecticut Valley

○　English Settlement
●　INDIAN VILLAGE
- - -　Trail (Conjectural)

0　　　　5　　　　10
MILES

Windsor

D. E. LEACH, 1957

noags were cowering in the swamp at Nipsachuck, not yet aware that they were about to make good their escape.

On August 2nd, after an early breakfast, Hutchinson's entire party started for the rendezvous, accompanied by three of Brookfield's leading citizens, men so convinced of the fidelity of the Indians that they reportedly did not even carry arms on this occasion. But when Hutchinson arrived at the designated place no Indians were to be seen, and it soon became evident that the sachems were not going to keep their appointment. Accordingly, the leaders of the expedition held a quick conference to decide what to do next. Against the fervent advice of the three Indian scouts, Hutchinson was finally persuaded by the Brookfield men to proceed to the place where the Indians supposedly were, in the expectation that the sachems would consent to a parley on the spot if confronted with the chief English negotiators.[8]

Hutchinson's better judgment might well have risen up within him again as his little force resumed its northward march through the wilderness. Who knew what hidden eyes were watching as the troopers and the three complacent citizens approached a place where the narrow way threaded into a defile marked by a thick swamp on the left hand and a steep, rocky, brush-covered hill on the right? Here the trail was so narrow that the horses were forced to proceed in single file, the most vulnerable of all military formations in such a place. They must have made a brave show, horses and men, as they jogged on, the buff-coated troopers sitting in their saddles like veterans, peering from under their visors to left and right. When the entire party was well into the defile, the steep hillside and the brushy swamp suddenly blazed with musket fire, and Hutchinson realized in one dreadful second that he had ridden into a well-laid ambush.[9] Unable to move forward because of the unsure ground, the bewildered troopers instinctively thought of turning and dashing out the way they had come, but this too became impossible as the enemy skillfully closed in behind them. The swamp at the left offered no choice but to charge up the steep hill on the right in the face of galling enemy fire.

It must have been a scene of wild confusion, with each man seeking to save his life by desperate riding. Here and there men tumbled from their mounts as the Indian bullets found their marks, while the screams of wounded and frightened horses added to the din. Up the hillside the survivors scrambled, and through the enemy lines, leaving behind them on the ground eight men dead or wounded, including the three complacent citizens of Brookfield. Even after the lucky survivors had fought their way clear of the scene of action their plight remained desperate, for they were many miles from Brookfield, and the savages would soon be on their trail. Moreover, the party now included several wounded men, among them Hutchinson and Wheeler, who could not in honor be left behind. Fortunately, the two remaining Indian scouts knew how to reach Brookfield without following the main trail, and so the shattered little group, hearts pounding with exertion and terror, not daring to stop even to stanch the bleeding of the wounded, raced the long miles back to Brookfield knowing that life or death depended on whether the enemy reached there first. Their salvation lay in the fact that the triumphant Nipmucks lacked horses.

Having won their desperate race against death, the exhausted English hastened to make themselves as secure as possible in one of the principal houses of the village. The frightened inhabitants of Brookfield likewise rushed to this shelter, abandoning their own homes to save their lives. Altogether about eighty people, the majority of them women and children, cooped themselves up in this one house on the hill, and prepared to defend themselves against the expected attack. Thus began one of the classic sieges of New England's history.

It was imperative that help be obtained speedily, for the defenders of the garrison could not hope to hold out long against such overwhelming odds. Therefore two brave men, Ephraim Curtis and Henry Young, mounted horses again and headed eastward down the hill, hoping that perhaps one of them might slip by the enemy and reach Marlborough. They had not gone far, however, when they encountered Indians, and were forced to return. Not long after Curtis and Young had regained the shelter of the garrison, the enemy closed in upon the house, and commenced the attack. Apparently well supplied with ammunition, the Indians poured their shot through the walls, all the while "shouting as if they would have swallowed us up alive." [10] Inside, the terrified women and children crouched behind any available shelter, while the men tried to fire back at the Indians

to keep them from coming any closer. The din and confusion must
have been terrific. There were wounded men there too—the ones
who had been injured at the time of the ambush. They needed care,
and probably it was the women who ministered to their wants in
the midst of the awful siege.

As the long hours crept slowly by, there was no sign that the
savage enemy was tiring of his sport. On the contrary, the attacking
force seemed to grow in strength, and the hideous yelling of the
Indians told of the fierce exultation which spurred them on. Henry
Young lingered too long at a window, and fell mortally wounded.
Another poor fellow tried to make his way to a nearby dwelling to
fetch some goods, but fell into the hands of the Nipmucks. They cut
off his head and used it as a football. Then they further mocked the
garrison by mounting the bloody trophy on a pole in full view. This
at least warned the English what surrender could mean.

The indomitable Curtis made another attempt to get through to
obtain help, this time on foot, but again was forced to turn back.
Later he tried once more, crawling through the darkness on his
hands and knees, fearing at every second that he would be discovered and killed. This time, however, his experience as a woodsman
and scout paid off, for he finally found himself clear of the Indians,
and was able to make his way on foot to Marlborough, some thirty
or more miles away, where he arrived exhausted. As it happened,
news of Indian trouble at Brookfield had already been brought to
Marlborough by some people who, in traveling along the Bay Path
toward Brookfield, had been forced to turn back because of the signs
of danger. It was Curtis, however, who brought the first word of the
exact situation in Brookfield.[11]

In the meantime the Nipmuck warriors were maintaining their
tight siege of the Brookfield garrison. They further strengthened their
position by fortifying themselves in the adjacent barn, where they
could lie in relative safety and pour shot into the house. When bullets
alone failed to overcome the garrison, the Indians resorted to fire.
They shot flaming arrows into the roof of the house, but the people
inside cut holes in the roof, and extinguished the flames before they
could spread. The Indians piled combustible material such as hay
against one corner of the building, and set it on fire, but some of the

English dashed from their shelter and put out the blaze. Once again the Nipmucks tried, this time by lighting their fire against the wall of the building, and then concentrating their strength in the vicinity of the door to prevent another sortie, but the desperate defenders broke down part of the wall in order to extinguish the fire. Next, the warriors built an ingenious mobile torch. This consisted of a barrel to which were attached a pair of extremely long shafts constructed by splicing many long poles end to end. The shafts rested upon a series of paired wheels which had been taken from captured farm vehicles. By pushing on the extreme ends of the two shafts the Indians could move the barrel up against the wall of the garrison house, without themselves coming too near the guns of the English. However, a sudden rainstorm soaked the combustibles, and temporarily saved the garrison from the flames. No wonder the people inside the house believed that Providence had intervened to preserve them at least for another hour.

By now it was the 4th of August, and the siege had been under way for almost forty-eight hours. Unknown to the people at Brookfield, help was at last approaching. At the first news of Brookfield's danger, the people of Marlborough had sent a messenger to inform Major Simon Willard, who was known to be at Lancaster with a strong force of troopers. By the time the messenger arrived there, Willard and his men had already left the town on a special mission to the westward. A rider raced to overtake them, however, and when Willard heard the message he at once abandoned his immediate assignment in order to lead his men to the scene of action.[12] It was a long ride to Brookfield, but the troopers covered the distance as rapidly as they could. Upon nearing the center of the village they were guided to their destination by the hideous sounds of an Indian siege, sounds which apparently helped to drown out the signal shots fired by Nipmuck sentries who had noticed their approach. Probably for a number of reasons which Cotton Mather summed up as an *"unaccountable besotment"* of the enemy, Willard and his troopers were able to make their way almost to the very door of the garrison house before being discovered by the main body of the besiegers.[13] After a brief skirmish, Willard's men entered the bullet-riddled house to receive the most fervent welcome they had ever experienced in

their lives. Also there to greet them, if one contemporary account
is to be credited, were several babies born during the course of the
siege.[14]

With the timely arrival of Major Willard's force, the Indians
decided that victory would now be too costly, and so, after burning
the remaining buildings in the vicinity, they disappeared into the
forest. Brookfield was left to reckon its losses. In three short days
a peaceful farming community had been transformed into a tragic,
blackened shell. The dazed inhabitants, still scarcely able to believe
that they were alive and safe, wondered what to do next, for to them
the future seemed like an ominous mystery. The wounded Hutchinson was moved to Marlborough on August 14th, and died there five
days later. Captain Wheeler recovered. The man who had rescued
them all, Major Simon Willard, remained at Brookfield for a number
of weeks, directing military movements in that area. Soon, however,
it became apparent that under the circumstances the difficulty of
maintaining an adequate garrison in Brookfield was too great, and the
town was completely abandoned.

*   *   *

Meanwhile, the clouds of war were spreading to other areas.
Enemy Indians were reported south of the Merrimack River, and the
frontier villages in that vicinity earnestly pleaded for help, whereupon Captains Samuel Moseley and Samuel Appleton with their
companies were dispatched to reinforce this northern frontier.[15] On
the 22nd of August violence broke out at Lancaster when a group of
unidentified Indians slew seven inhabitants of that town. At first,
suspicion fell upon the local Indians then residing at Marlborough,
but the truth of the matter seems to be that the Nipmucks, encouraged by the presence of Philip and the Wampanoags in their
country, were now beginning to extend the range of their operations.[16]

The authorities at Boston were also concerned about the attitude
of Wannalancet, sachem of the Pennacook Indians, who dwelt in
the upper Merrimack Valley. Wannalancet's father, the old sachem
Passaconaway, had consistently maintained a policy of peace with
the English, and had bequeathed this policy to his son. Since Wannalancet now had no desire to be dragged into the interracial war

which had broken out, he and his people withdrew northward up the river, but this only served to arouse the suspicions of the English. Hence the rough-handed Moseley led his men deep into Pennacook territory in September, and burned an Indian village there. Still Wannalancet refused to strike back. One cannot help feeling that Moseley's actions at this time were directly comparable to the wanton destructiveness which was supposed to be characteristic of the savages themselves. The authorities at Boston, at least, did not approve what Moseley had done, for they were most anxious to restore close relations with the Pennacooks. Accordingly, various attempts were now made to get in touch with Wannalancet and persuade him to take up residence at Wamesit, near Lowell, or at least to renew articles of friendship with the English. But all such attempts failed. Wannalancet had disappeared into the northern woodlands to assure for his people the peace which they desired.[17]

The exact whereabouts of Philip and the Wampanoags during the month of August is something of a mystery, and will probably always so remain. As a much-wanted fugitive, Philip naturally was not eager to advertise his location, at least until he had been able to forge all of the disaffected tribes into a powerful force of resistance against the English. Meanwhile, conflicting rumors and reports were flying about the countryside. On August 6th Philip and his men were reported to be within eighteen miles of Stonington, Connecticut, starving and sick. Actually, this must have been Weetamoo's people on their way to take shelter with the Narragansetts. At about the same time, Philip was said to be at Quabaug Old Fort, or Ashquoash, a favorite Indian gathering place about four miles southwest of Brookfield. Probably this report was near the truth. It seems likely that from Ashquoash Philip would then move on up to Menameset, the main camp of the warring Nipmucks.[18]

In the English villages of the upper Connecticut Valley the atmosphere grew increasingly tense as the August days crept by. Strung out for miles along the southward-flowing Connecticut River, these towns formed a thin ribbon of civilization separated from the rest of Massachusetts by miles of wilderness. If disaster struck, it might be days before any considerable help could reach them from the east. Since the great river valley was their principal route of communication and transportation, these settlements in some respects felt more closely related to Connecticut than to Massachusetts, although they were actually a part of the Bay Colony.

The enemy was believed to be hovering somewhere east of the river, between Hadley and Squakeag (Northfield), perhaps in the vicinity of Paquoag, an Indian locality some twenty miles northwest of Mount Wachusett.[19] Chief responsibility for military affairs in the upper valley rested upon the shoulders of John Pynchon of Springfield, prominent merchant, Indian trader, and civic leader. Upon first learning of the trouble at Brookfield, Pynchon had procured troops from Connecticut, subsequently reinforced by additional men under the command of Major John Talcott of Hartford. In this way Connecticut acquired almost overnight a real and immediate interest in the military situation in the upper valley. The government at Hartford wrote to Pynchon that "we stand a tiptoe for Inteligence, and earnestly desire as any comes to your hand it may be posted away to us." [20] Massachusetts companies were also hastening into the area, army headquarters were established at Hadley, and soon units from both Massachusetts and Connecticut, together with a considerable number of Mohegan Indians, were seeking the enemy. Despite all danger, the inhabitants of remote Deerfield and even Squakeag continued to cling to their little areas of settlement, reluctant to abandon their hard-won homes to the fury of the savages.

Like many towns in New England, the settlements along the upper Connecticut River had their nearby groups of Indians who, although hitherto peaceful, were now viewed with increasing distrust by many of the English. Other men, Pynchon among them, scoffed at the scare talk, and urged a cautious and moderate policy toward these Indian neighbors, a policy which also was being advocated by the government of Connecticut.[21] Among the local Indians now coming increasingly under suspicion was a group which lived in a sort of enclosed camp not far from the village of Hatfield on the western side of the Connecticut River. Members of this group were known to be blood relatives of the Quabaug Indians, who had already proved so treacherous. Then too, the Mohegan Indians with the English forces declared that the warriors of this village, who also had gone out with the army, had behaved in a very suspicious manner when near the enemy. Because of a great popular demand, therefore, the local authorities on August 24th ordered these Indians to surrender

their weapons as a precaution against treachery. The natives pro-
crastinated, and under cover of darkness that night they slipped out
of their camp and headed northward up the river, after having
killed one of their chief men who opposed their design.

The neighboring English, of course, soon learned of this escape,
and very early the next morning a force of about a hundred soldiers
led by Captain Thomas Lathrop of Beverly and Captain Richard
Beers of Watertown went in hot pursuit. They came up with the
fugitives at Hopewell Swamp just to the south of Sugarloaf Hill,
about halfway between Hatfield and Deerfield. The Indians, unwilling to be seized by the English troops, put up a stout fight in
the swamp, and killed or mortally wounded nine of the soldiers.
After this lively skirmish the English force withdrew, and the Indians
continued on their way.[22] Now the river Indians had been blooded,
and all hope of keeping them loyal, or at least neutral, went glim-
mering. Connecticut arranged to send additional reinforcements,
and the river towns braced themselves for more trouble.

The first two days of September brought additional tragedy to
the upper Connecticut Valley. At Deerfield one man was killed and
some dwellings were burned, probably by the very Indians who had
fled from Hatfield. Soon after this, eight Squakeag men were surprised and killed in the woods. By this time it was clear that the
northernmost of these frontier settlements would have to be abandoned, and on the 3rd of September Captain Beers with a company
of about thirty-six men and a couple of carts was sent up the river
to effect the evacuation of Squakeag. When just about two miles
from their destination, on the morning of the 4th, Beers and his
men marched into an Indian ambush, and suffered a disastrous defeat. Beers himself was slain, as were more than half of his men.
Most of the exhausted survivors straggled into Hadley that night
and the next day.[23] Two days after this debacle Major Robert Treat,
the commander of all the Connecticut troops in the upper valley,
successfully evacuated the garrison at Squakeag. While engaged in
this mission Treat and his men came across a gory display reminiscent
of the Mount Hope peninsula and Brookfield—a group of poles on
which were mounted the severed heads of some of Beers' soldiers.

During the next two weeks more troops arrived in the upper valley
to strengthen the army, among them Captain Moseley's veteran

company. The Indians attacked Deerfield again on the 12th of September, making off with one unfortunate prisoner. Now it was decided to evacuate Deerfield also, and Captain Lathrop was ordered to bring the inhabitants and their goods to safety. On the 18th of the month Lathrop's company, while returning toward Northampton with loaded carts, was successfully ambushed at a spot since known as Bloody Brook, about five or six miles due south of Deerfield, and only a short distance from Sugarloaf Hill. The men were taken completely by surprise, and the bewildered company, fighting for life, was soon pitifully reduced. Fortunately, Moseley's company was in the vicinity. Being notified of the situation by Lathrop's bugler, who had managed to escape, these hardy troops hurried to the scene, and tore into the yelling Indians with a fury which helped to lessen their earlier advantage. Meanwhile, Major Treat at Hadley had also learned of the emergency, and was now hastening up with additional forces to save the day. With the arrival of these reinforcements, the enemy fled northward, making a successful escape.[24]

Moseley retired to Deerfield that night, and there he and his grim-faced men were taunted from a distance by a group of enemy warriors who gleefully displayed articles of clothing taken from the English dead. The next day Moseley's company returned to the scene of action, and buried sixty-four English bodies. Lathrop himself had paid with his life for the surprisal of his company. The contemporary historian Hubbard called this day of defeat "the Saddest that ever befel *New-England*," and lamented "the Ruine of a choice Company of young Men, the very Flower of the County of *Essex*, all called out of the Towns belonging to that County, none of which were ashamed to speak with the Enemy in the Gate." [25]

In the meantime the Commissioners of the United Colonies had been meeting at Boston to consider the weighty problems raised by the Indian war and its rapid spread. Despite differences of opinion on certain matters, they were able to reach some important decisions. They now officially declared the war to be the joint concern of the three United Colonies, and decided to raise a combined force of a thousand men, of whom Plymouth would contribute 158, Connecticut 315, and Massachusetts 527. The chief command of all units operating in western Massachusetts was assigned to Major Pynchon, despite his earnest desire to be relieved of such heavy military responsibility. Connecticut's Major Treat would thus be subject to Pynchon's orders as long as the army was in that area. On September 22nd the Commissioners decided that the army in the west should immediately be brought to a total strength of five hundred men, of whom Connecticut would contribute two hundred, and Massachusetts the remainder.[26]

The abandonment of Squakeag, Deerfield, and Brookfield left only five inhabited towns in all of western Massachusetts. Of these the most prosperous and important was Springfield, which in 1675 had a population of five hundred or more. For years Springfield had enjoyed excellent relations with its neighboring Indians, partly as a result of the good influence of Pynchon. At this time the local natives were living in a sort of fort about a mile below the town, where they could be closely supervised by local officials, and there were still a number of men in Springfield who refused to believe that the local sachem, Wequogan, and his people could be anything but loyal to the English. Even after some unidentified Indians burned Pynchon's mill and other buildings at Stony Brook on September 26th, men argued that the local Indians were not to blame.[27] Complacency was lingering even yet.

On October 4th all of the troops in Springfield marched out of the town to join the main body of Pynchon's army at Hadley for a new expedition against the lurking enemy, leaving Springfield defenseless except for the weapons of the inhabitants themselves. That night there arrived from Connecticut a post rider bearing an ominous report. An Indian of Windsor had revealed the existence of a plot contrived by the Springfield Indians in conjunction with Philip's men. It was said that several hundred of the enemy Indians had actually been admitted secretly into the nearby Indian fort. The startled authorities at Springfield sent this news on to Hadley, and impatiently waited for morning to come.

When it was light, Lieutenant Thomas Cooper and Constable Thomas Miller, with perhaps a few other Springfield men, set out on horseback for the Indian fort to investigate the situation. Cooper, apparently, was one who believed firmly in the faithfulness of the local Indians, but his trust proved to be ill-founded. The little party never reached the fort, for on the way they encountered Indians who fired upon them with deadly effect, killing the constable and mortally wounding Cooper. By a great effort the dying Cooper managed to cling to his horse while urging him back toward the nearest garrison house. There he gave the warning to the gaping inhabitants, and expired.

The townspeople had little time to digest this latest development before the hordes of Indians were upon them, Wequogan himself being "ringleader in word and deede," as it was later reported.[28] Fortunately, the warning of the previous evening had been sufficient to place the inhabitants on their guard, so that nearly all were in or near some place of refuge when the Indian fury struck. Not willing to risk an attack upon fortified garrisons, the enemy contented himself with putting the torch to the dozens of undefended houses which had been abandoned for safer shelter. The sky was filled with columns of seething smoke and glowing sparks, while all the time the exulting Indians yelled their defiance at the English. It was a wild scene of destruction, a Brookfield on a much larger scale.

While this was going on, two military groups were advancing toward Springfield. Major Treat was leading one force in from Westfield where it had been on garrison duty, and Pynchon himself was hastening down from Hadley with Captain Samuel Appleton and a force of about two hundred soldiers. The march from Hadley was maintained at a pace which put the men into "a most violent sweate," for Pynchon had recognized the potential danger to his own town as soon as he heard the report from Connecticut. [29] We should not infer that Pynchon's magnificent haste on this occasion was prompted primarily by his own extensive holdings in Springfield, but at least this personal interest was an added incentive to cover ground with the least possible delay.

Treat and his men arrived first, but were prevented from reaching the burning town by their lack of boats. Although a small group of daring Springfield men did manage to get a boat across to the western shore, a return crossing with a load of troops was foiled by heavy enemy fire from the eastern shore. Treat and his men were able to do nothing but watch the destruction of Springfield from the opposite bank, an infuriating and frustrating experience.

Pynchon and his breathless column burst upon the scene about two or three o'clock that afternoon, whereupon the savages immediately disappeared into the forest. The newcomers were treated to a sad scene of desolation. More than thirty homes and many barns lay in smoking ruins. The air was heavy with the smell of burning wood and hay. Altogether some forty families, probably about a third of all those in the town, were left "utterly destitute of subsistence" because of the heavy loss of property.[30] In fact, within the village proper only a few more than a dozen houses were left standing, although many homes in the outskirts and across the river remained untouched. Thanks to the advance warning which the town had received, the total casualties, in addition to Cooper and Miller, consisted of only one woman killed and three or four people wounded.

* * *

It must be obvious by now that the war effort of the New England colonies was both inadequate and inept. One might even venture to say that the colonists were rapidly losing the war, even though as yet there was no immediate danger of annihilation. Blunder had followed blunder in almost incredible succession, and one must pause to ask why the English were not able to resist the Indians more effectively.

The rapid spread of the uprising had really taken the colonists by surprise, finding them without adequate preparations or plans. Moreover, the very nature of the enemy's tactics had produced a serious disruption of normal economic activity even in areas far removed from the immediate zones of combat. As one officer noted, the people were "very much discouraged in their spirits and thereby dissuaded from their callings." [31] It was not that the people were cowardly; they simply did not know how to care for their crops and provide for the security of their families under the constant threat of an enemy who lurked everywhere and struck without warning. One of the serious effects of the spreading of the war was the growing shortage of food for men and cattle, caused by the fact that ordinary work in the fields had become dangerous for small isolated groups.

The experience of Brookfield taught the grim lesson that any remote town which was attacked by the savages must expect to defend itself without any outside help for at least the first few hours of the ordeal. Throughout New England local communities were hastening preparations for their own defense, and this took many precious hours which normally would have been devoted to farming.

For example, Wallingford decided to fortify two of its houses, and ordered the whole town to help complete the project. Topsfield planned to build a stone wall around its meetinghouse, with a watchhouse at one corner. Beverly decided to construct four defensive works, including one about the meetinghouse. Marshfield, where Plymouth's Governor Winslow had his residence, voted to maintain three watch stations within the town. New London planned to establish six fortifications for the protection of its inhabitants. Bridgewater decided to build a fortification around its meetinghouse, and specified that the structure "be made with halfe trees seven foot hie above the ground 6 rood long and 4 rood wide beside the flankers. . . ." [32] The fact that the meetinghouse was so often selected to be a center of defense is further evidence of the central position which this building of many uses occupied in the life of the typical New England town.

On a higher administrative level, the colony governments were also issuing elaborate and sometimes confusing precautionary orders. In Massachusetts local committees of militia were granted wide powers in providing for the defense of their communities, and citizens were required to help build fortifications if so directed by local authorities. To some extent the people of the colony were being brought under a form of martial law.[33] The government of Connecticut established requirements for guard duty in the various towns of the colony, specifying that on any given day one-quarter of the local militia were to be on guard. This program was supplemented with a plan for regular patrolling of the paths leading from town to town.[34] The Province of New York also took certain precautions in this time of danger. Governor Andros sent an armed sloop into Long Island Sound to prevent any crossing by Indians from the mainland, and ordered the towns in his jurisdiction to provide places of refuge for women and children.[35] Over a wide area people were deeply concerned about the situation, for no-one knew where the Indians might rise up next.

From a purely military point of view, New England's greatest weakness in these opening months of the war stemmed from the inexperience of the military forces and their leaders. The laxness of discipline in the ranks caused increasing concern to the authorities until finally, on the 26th of October, the General Court of Massachusetts adopted a strict code for the government of the colony's troops. Early in January Connecticut followed suit.[36] Even more dangerous than loose discipline, however, was the army's ineptitude in strategy and tactics. The long list of military failures from Pocasset to Springfield clearly reflects poor leadership at all levels. Commanding officers seemed painfully slow in learning the lessons of forest warfare. All during the July campaign the Indians had demonstrated their skill at scouting, swamp fighting, and laying ambushes; but many of the colonial officers still believed that such cowardly brutes as the Indians would never be able to prevail against English soldiers properly drilled and led. The formations and tactics which had served Cromwell on the battlefields of England yielded but slowly to the hard lessons of defeat and death in the American forest. Because there was a lingering feeling that civilized gentlemen must not fight like savages, the lives of many civilized gentlemen were lost. Hubbard, who was no tactician, actually blamed Lathrop's defeat on his attempt to imitate Indian tactics by having his men fight as individuals from behind trees rather than in a compact body.[37] But Governor Leverett, who had served as a cavalry captain under Cromwell, urged that the soldiers "bee comanded to attend the Enemies method, which though it may seeme a rout to ours, is the best way of fighting the Enemy in this brushy wilderness." [38] This was good advice. If only the colonial governments had adapted their military tactics to American conditions during the long period prior to King Philip's War, many lives could have been saved in 1675.

As always in wartime, a number of people suggested new methods of combating the enemy. Someone even proposed that troops move through the woods in enclosed horse-drawn chariots built with loopholes so that the men inside could fire out upon the enemy. What would prevent the Indians from immobilizing the chariots by shooting the horses was not stated.[39] The real answer to the problem of how to deal with the skulking tactics of the enemy, as time was to show, lay in the intelligent adaptation of standard English tactics to forest conditions, and especially the systematic use of friendly Indians as scouts with every English force that moved through the woods. These natives were experts in the art of detecting the presence of other Indians, and whenever they were used ambushes became much less of a danger.

The New England colonies were also hampered in their common struggle against Philip by certain other distracting problems. Massachusetts, for example, had to deal with an outbreak of Indian trouble along the Maine coast in September. For the remainder of the war, the Bay Colony was forced to devote a considerable portion of its strength to that area, while still engaged in the desperate struggle against Philip. Connecticut, likewise, still felt obliged to keep one wary eye fixed on Governor Andros, in case he should repeat his attempt to seize the land west of the Connecticut River. Such distractions, of course, meant that fewer men could be spared for operations in the upper Connecticut Valley.

As the warfare spread, moreover, the various towns which believed themselves to be in danger called for more local protection, and sometimes objected very strongly when troops were called out for distant operations. Connecticut towns were showing increasing reluctance to strip themselves of their own defensive forces in order to send reinforcements to western Massachusetts. Many Connecticut people were coming to feel that Massachusetts was not sending her fair share of men to the combat zone. "Why may they not send 500 men as well as we one hundred?" asked a New Haven man, with some heat.[40] Governor Leverett, in answer to these charges, pointed out that up to this time Massachusetts troops had borne the brunt of the fighting, and had sustained the heaviest losses. In addition, the Bay Colony was forced to protect a great number of widely scattered towns, not only on her southern and western frontiers, but also along the coast of Maine.[41] The problem was further aggravated by the fact that Massachusetts was now having some difficulty raising additional troops, as many individuals sought to evade conscription.[42]

Relations between the two Puritan colonies were not made any smoother by Connecticut's almost constant criticism of the way the situation in the upper valley was being handled by Massachusetts authorities. The government at Hartford clearly felt that the outbreak of hostilities in the valley might have been avoided if the Massachusetts people had not been so rigorous in their dealings with the local Indians. Especially was it charged that the authorities had made "Imprudent demands" upon the Indians at Hatfield, thereby precipitating the action of August 25th.[43] Connecticut also objected strenuously when her troops in western Massachusetts were held on garrison duty rather than employed in vigorous offensive operations. These men had been sent north to help defeat the Indians in the field, not just serve as guards for Massachusetts villages. If the latter was to be the extent of their usefulness, then Connecticut would prefer to have them guarding towns in their own colony. On the other hand, the Massachusetts military commanders were torn between their inclination to provide adequate forces for each exposed town and their desire to end the war by engaging the main body of the enemy in the field. With the forces then available, one or the other of these two courses had to be neglected. Actually, neither course seemed to be really satisfactory. The Indians possessed every advantage of mobility and surprise. Their effectiveness as scouts enabled them to determine when and where to strike with the greatest advantage, and when they did attack a village the defenders were almost invariably outnumbered. Yet whenever the English forces left their garrisons and took to the field, the Indians either evaded them or skillfully caught them in ambush, as the ghosts of Hutchinson, Beers, and Lathrop could testify.

The attack on Springfield added still more fuel to this dispute over military policy. Prior to the attack, the Commissioners of the United Colonies had given firm backing to Connecticut's contention that the army should be kept on the offensive. However, many people in the upper valley, including Pynchon himself, had deplored this decision, for it seemed to give the military commanders no choice but to withdraw all of the soldiers from the towns, thus leaving these settlements with none but their own inhabitants to protect them against a sudden attack.[44] The people of Springfield had not been happy to see the troops march out of their town on the 4th of October, and the very next evening these people, as they rummaged through the ruins of their homes, were bitterly exclaiming, "We told you so!" The truth of the matter is that the job at hand was simply too big and too difficult for such a small and inexperienced army as was then available.

*   *   *

After October 5th the morale of the people in the upper Connecticut Valley, especially Springfield, reached a new low. In that fire-scarred town the inhabitants and the soldiers were now living crowded together in the houses which were still left standing. Having lost much of their own corn and hay as well as their homes, and having now no mill for the grinding of grain, the discouraged settlers talked of abandoning their town and leaving it to the Indians. Pynchon himself was terribly disheartened, but he realized that if Springfield were abandoned the three river towns to the north would also become untenable. Thus all of the upper valley would be lost to the enemy, who would then be free to descend upon Connecticut or eastern Massachusetts or both. Fearing this prospect, the river towns from Windsor on down were bustling with activity as the settlers hastened to lay in supplies of corn from the outlying farms, and threw up emergency defensive works about their towns. The people of southern New England were especially shocked at the perfidy of the Springfield Indians, who had long been considered among the most peaceable and dependable. Now their defection to the enemy caused the English to be increasingly suspicious of neutral or friendly Indians everywhere, and made the lot of such Indians even more difficult than before.

Soon after the burning of Springfield, Samuel Appleton of Ipswich succeeded Pynchon as commander in chief in the western theater of operations. The decision to change commanders had been made by the government of Massachusetts prior to the attack on Springfield, and at Pynchon's own request. It was fortunate that the change was made no later than it was, for after the Springfield tragedy Pynchon, by his own admission, was "more and more unfit and almost Confounded in my understanding." [45] He seemed bewildered by the blows which Fate continued to rain upon him.

The army of which Appleton now assumed command consisted of various companies from Connecticut and Massachusetts with a total authorized strength of five hundred men. Its actual strength at any specified time is virtually impossible to determine because of the lack of exact records and the shifting of various units. Connecticut's troops and their Indian auxiliaries were commanded by Major Robert Treat, who also served as second-in-command of the army. Among the Massachusetts forces the most famous unit was the veteran company of Captain Samuel Moseley, a company which had distinguished itself in every major operation since the outbreak of the war. Plymouth Colony had no troops in the western army.

Appleton inherited not only the difficult military situation, but also the quarrel with Connecticut, which at this time was becoming even more intense. The Commissioners, at the time of their decision against regular garrison duty for the troops, had also stipulated that none of the troops were to be withdrawn from the area except "by spetiall order of the comitioners, or by the joynt advice and consent of their own councill of officers when they shall see it nessessary upon the remoovall of the enemy else where." [46] Shortly after the attack on Springfield, hostile Indians were reported to be in the vicinity of Hartford and Wethersfield, which caused the government of Connecticut to recall Major Treat and sixty of his men from the upper valley, contrary to the order of the Commissioners. Appleton was greatly upset by this situation, and reported to his superiors that the army was "at present in a broken posture uncapable of any great action." [47]

Trouble continued to mount. When Appleton ordered one of the Connecticut companies to report at his headquarters for a mission, only its commanding officer, Lieutenant Seeley, appeared, and coolly informed Appleton that he doubted if his commission from the government of Connecticut permitted him to employ his company as ordered. After considerable debate, Seeley finally agreed to obey orders, but was later instructed by Treat not to take his company into the field. Presumably Treat's order was prompted by the desire to have Seeley's men available for quick recall to Connecticut in case of need. There can be no doubt that Connecticut really feared an outbreak of hostilities within her own borders at any moment, but her actions at this time also were prompted to no little extent by anger at the retention of troops on garrison duty and the apparent slowness of Massachusetts in sending additional soldiers to the western theater.[48] Massachusetts, in turn, was highly indignant at the arbitrary conduct of her sister colony, and charged that Treat's recall was a violation of the agreements entered into by the United Colonies. The authorities at Boston told Appleton that if Treat should return he was to be clearly informed that he would not be allowed to depart again without proper authorization.[49]

In the midst of these difficulties, of course, Appleton had to continue his prosecution of the war. By October 13th the army was again concentrated in the Hadley-Northampton-Hatfield area, with Appleton's headquarters at Hadley. Scouts were sent out toward Squakeag on the 13th and 14th, but they accomplished little. On the following day Appleton led the army northward from Hadley with the intention of marching up the eastern side of the river, but scarcely had they left the vicinity of their base when a message from Hatfield caused them to change their plan and cross to the opposite bank. Scouts from Hatfield had discovered tracks indicating that a large body of the enemy was on the western side of the river. With darkness already closing in, the army headed northward toward Deerfield. They trudged along for some miles in the darkness with a storm brewing, until finally Moseley and the other officers, fearing that the Indians might fall upon the river towns in their absence, conferred with Appleton and persuaded him to turn back.[50] The troops marched back into the towns after an evening of wasted effort.

Further reports of Indian activity in the vicinity convinced both Appleton and Moseley that an assault upon one or more of the three towns was imminent.[51] No-one could tell which of the settlements would be the enemy's prime target, or whether all three would be attacked simultaneously. Each of the towns contained a civilian population clamoring for more protection. Appleton hardly knew what to do next. At this time the general location of units was as follows: Lieutenant Seeley's company was at Northampton, Captains Moseley and Poole were at Hatfield, and Appleton himself was at Hadley.

The 17th and the 18th of October passed without bringing the expected attack. In the meantime Major Treat had returned from Connecticut, bringing much-needed additional strength to the defenders. On Tuesday, the 19th, Moseley's men at Hatfield saw smoke rising from a point in the woods several miles away, and a scouting party of ten men was sent to investigate. Actually the fires had been set by the Indians for the express purpose of attracting an English force, and the ten scouts fell neatly into the trap which the enemy had laid. Only one or two survivors escaped to give the alarm.[52]

Moseley quickly summoned additional forces from Hadley and Northampton, with the result that when the hordes of the enemy did launch their assault upon Hatfield that day, they found the town well defended by a large number of troops. A hot fight ensued, with both sides suffering casualties, but for once the Indians had met more than their match, and they finally retreated in much confusion.

Early the next morning the defeated Indians were seen withdrawing from the vicinity in a somber procession, their dead and wounded on the backs of horses. The fight at Hatfield on October 19th helped to compensate for the Springfield disaster, for it restored to the English some of their lost confidence, and taught the Indians that they were up against a foe who could fight very effectively under favorable circumstances.

Hatfield was the last major effort by the enemy in the Connecticut Valley that year. Nevertheless, groups of marauders did continue to lurk about the river towns for some time afterward, occasionally striking harassing blows at isolated groups of settlers. On October 25th some Northampton people on their way to work in the fields were surprised by Indians, but all managed to get back into the village safely. Four days later the raiders struck at Northampton again, this time killing several people at work in a meadow. On the 26th some Indians fell upon a group of Springfield men who were at Westfield for the purpose of grinding their grain, Springfield's mill having been destroyed. After killing three of these men, the Indians turned their attention upon Westfield itself, and burned down several houses. These attacks were additional warning to the settlers in the valley that anyone who ventured into the fields or woods without the protection of armed soldiers was in danger of sudden death.

Meanwhile, the quarrel between Connecticut and Massachusetts over the question of military operations was approaching a new crisis. Massachusetts had lost faith in her sister colony, and expected little cooperation. The authorities at Boston finally referred the matter to the Commissioners of the United Colonies, charging that Connecticut's attitude was hindering the conduct of the war; but still no solution was forthcoming. Hartford continued to send orders directly to Major Treat, thus by-passing Appleton.[53]

Treat himself suspected that the enemy was moving southward toward his own colony, and he longed to lead his men in active pursuit. Finally, with the backing of his subordinate officers he presented his case to Appleton, but was told that the army must remain together under a single command. The commander in chief expressed doubt that the enemy had actually departed from the area, and stated that the army's present job was to discover the enemy's whereabouts. After some further argument, Treat returned to his troops dissatisfied. The seriousness of the split is indicated by the fact that Treat had even begun to challenge the legality of Appleton's appointment as commander in chief, on the grounds that the appointment had never been officially confirmed by the Commissioners of the United Colonies.[54] Actually, Massachusetts did have the right to name the commander in chief, since the intercolonial army was operating within her borders. On November 15th the government at Hartford informed Appleton that if he continued to hold Connecticut soldiers on garrison duty, the Connecticut forces under his command would begin to conduct their own operations.[55] Under such harassing conditions as these, it is no wonder that Appleton felt unequal to his responsibilities.

While these developments were taking place, the mystery of the enemy's whereabouts was beginning to unravel itself. About the beginning of November in the area east of Brookfield a large group of Christian Indians belonging to Magunkaquog, Hassanemesit, and Chabanakongkomun was suddenly beset by a strong force of enemy warriors. Resistance was useless, and the enemy soon persuaded or forced the Christian Indians to accompany them into the wilderness. Presumably some of the "captured" Indians were easily persuaded to join the enemy, but others, less willing, escaped from their captors and brought news of the incident to the colonial authorities. Troops under Captains Henchman and Sill were dispatched to the area, and during the next few days they had several minor encounters with enemy groups.[56] All of this seemed to confirm a growing suspicion that the hostile Indians were leaving the war-ravaged upper Connecticut Valley, and moving to other parts. Whether this transfer of activities was the prelude to mass attacks against English communities elsewhere, or was merely part of a movement into winter quarters, no-one could yet tell.

*　　*　　*

There can be no doubt that during the fifteen weeks since Philip had escaped from Pocasset the New England colonies had received a severe setback. On the frontier the loss of life and property had been extremely heavy, while the normal activity of the people in general, even in areas remote from the actual fighting, had been painfully upset. For the colonists, these tragic weeks were a time of testing and suffering, a time when they were absorbing grievous defeats while learning the hard lessons of war. That the colonial governments were quarreling so bitterly among themselves in the midst of their troubles only added to the difficulty of the situation.

During this period Philip remained something of a ghost leader. His Wampanoags gave added strength to the Nipmucks, but Philip himself can not be identified in any of the important actions of the time, although he may have directed them to some extent. Probably he was devoting much of his attention to the problem of coordinating the efforts of various Indian groups, while trying to cement them together in the great confederacy which was his only hope of victory. To all of the hostile Indians Philip was the great living symbol of resistance to encroaching English civilization, for he was the first of his generation who had dared to raise the tomahawk against the white men.

The greatest chance of suppressing the uprising before it became general had been lost through the failure of the military forces to bottle up the Wampanoags on their own territory. Although there had been widespread disaffection among the other tribes of New England, they had hesitated to commit themselves against the English until Philip proved that he was not going to be easily trapped by his enemies. The speed with which the war had enlarged itself after Philip's escape shows how widespread was this disaffection. Whether or not they had previously been bound to a prearranged conspiracy, one group after another had now seized the opportunity of Philip's uprising to vent their own wrath against the English. For large numbers of the Indians, the prospect of revenge and booty was too alluring to be long resisted. Some of the settlers, as we have seen, believed that the friendly or neutral Indians should be treated with leniency and gentleness to prevent the growth of dissatisfaction among them. Others insisted that the only safe way to deal with such Indians was to pull their fangs—that is, to disarm them and keep them under rigid surveillance. Probably neither of these courses alone could have prevented the spreading of the war. Certainly the vacillating policy which was actually followed was a failure, and the conflict had to run its tragic course.

As early as the 23rd of October the authorities at Boston had told Appleton that he might expect to receive orders recalling his army from the Connecticut Valley. When subsequent developments indicated that large numbers of the enemy were actually moving away from the valley in a southeasterly direction, the necessary orders were issued on November 16th. On the following day Appleton, probably even before he had received these orders, finally released the Connecticut forces under his command. Once he had learned the decision of his government, the commander in chief made all necessary arrangements for the maintenance of small garrison forces in the river towns, and then withdrew the bulk of his army from the valley.[57] For these men the long weeks of hard campaigning were over. They who had experienced the fatigue of marching and countermarching, the boredom of garrison duty, the prickling terror that comes with Indian warwhoops, and the nauseating smell of war's destruction, were now on their way toward Boston, and perhaps their own homes.

CHAPTER VI

Men, Matériel, and Money

WE have watched the most dangerous Indian war in New England's history get under way and spread. Now it is time to pause briefly in our narrative to see how the colonial governments handled the three administrative problems common to every war effort—recruiting, supply, and finance.

Armed forces ready to fight were of course the first essential. Generally speaking, the colonies preferred volunteers to conscripts, with impressment being resorted to only if prescribed quotas remained unfilled. Increasingly, however, as the months went by, the supply of volunteers dwindled, and the long arm of the press officer became more active in New England towns. To anyone who has dealt with the intricacies of modern selective service, the press mechanism of 1675 seems unbelievably simple. For purposes of illustration let's assume that the government of Massachusetts is faced with the problem of raising a force of five hundred men to march against the Indians. Immediately the authorities at Boston will assign to each town in the colony a quota based upon the relative size and strength of the town. Shortly thereafter an official courier will ride into the town of, say, Reading, and will hand over to the constable there a warrant from the governor and Council, ordering him to impress sixteen men from the town, and to have them properly equipped and ready to march by a specific date.

From this point on, the matter rests completely in the hands of the local authorities. How the sixteen men are chosen out of the town's population is no concern of the central government at Boston. If Reading is lucky, sixteen men will come forward and volunteer, but more likely than not some portion of the quota will have to be met by impressment. Perhaps the selectmen of the town will hold a meeting at someone's house to decide who can best be spared by their families. Indentured servants as well as freemen are subject to call, and their departure for the army will mean real financial loss to the families claiming their service, for the time spent by such servants in the army will be included in their term of indenture.[1] Possibly the town authorities have a grudge against some ne'er-do-well or a certain family that has proved uncooperative in civic affairs. Such persons may find their names at the top of the list. A man of means, however, can usually hire a substitute to go in his place.[2] Although the method of selection may be haphazard, it at least has the virtue of being flexible, and the local authorities are able to decide each case on the basis of firsthand knowledge. Once the list has been drawn up, it is the constable who has the duty of riding around to the various homes in order to notify the men of their selection. Then on the appointed day Reading's sixteen new soldiers will assemble on the green and march off to a central point of rendezvous, probably Boston, where they will be assigned to a company in the new expedition.

The forces being sent out to combat the Indians required a constant flow of supplies in support of their operations, which meant that means had to be devised for purchasing, assembling, storing, transporting, and distributing large quantities of products ranging from bread and rum to shoes and bullets. And all of this had to be done in a sparsely populated wilderness, large areas of which were open to devastating enemy raids. In a way it was fortunate that the colonists hadn't yet heard of vitamins, calories, and balanced diets, for such knowledge would have shown the inadequacy of army food under forest conditions, and might have discouraged the hard-marching, bread-and-beef eating kind of expedition that eventually won the war for the English. Bread was the army's staple food. Whenever a new expedition was being planned, care was taken to see that a quantity of grain was collected and brought to the mills, where it was ground into flour, and then carried to local kitchens to be baked into loaves. Sometimes biscuit was also used, being, as one colonist noted, "most conservable and transportable provision for a woods march, and may serve alone in case of need." [3] Other kinds of food were also used in the field whenever possible. Captain Henchman, an experienced field officer, recommended cheese or raisins as a supplement to the usual "biscake." [4] Meat also was favored. This was usually beef or pork, preserved and packed in barrels. The monotonous diet was occasionally varied by the addition of such foods as peas and dried fish. For liquid refreshment the soldiers relied on rum, wine, brandy, and the good clear water of New England's brooks and springs.

Clothing was largely an individual affair, with little attempt at uniformity. Usually the soldier provided his own clothing. In summer he would be dressed as though for an extended hunting trip, with homemade leather shoes, woolen stockings, trousers of leather or wool, open-necked shirt, jacket or waistcoat, and cap. Wintertime would require the addition of warm mittens, an overcoat, and perhaps a scarf. Officers generally showed their rank by finer and more elaborate clothing, although this made them a more likely target for enemy marksmen. The rough life in the woods caused the men's clothing to wear out rapidly, so that replacements were an almost constant necessity. The commander of the garrison at Marlborough reported that his men needed "shoes, and stockins and shurts very much," but he dared not let them go home to obtain these articles for fear they would not return.[5] Sometimes when the troops had leisure they themselves could do much to replace or renew their worn clothing, for in those days farmers knew how to mend shoes and make serviceable garments of cloth and leather. Without this patchwork skill, many a colonial soldier would have gone barefoot and cold for lack of supplies from the rear areas.

The problem of providing shelter for the troops was handled with equal simplicity. Whenever they were located in established communities, the men usually found quarters in various houses, sheds, and barns, but in the field they were less fortunate. Tents apparently were seldom if ever used by New England troops at this time. The men were expected to make whatever shelters they could out of material available on the spot, or else sleep in the open. Often the soldiers could take advantage of old abandoned buildings or even Indian wigwams. Frequently they enjoyed no other shelter than the lee side of a stone wall, or a hastily built lean-to, or a pile of brush. Many times they merely huddled around open campfires, and hoped for dry weather.

Fortunately, in comparison with the apparatus of modern war the equipment carried by the soldiers in King Philip's War was simplicity itself. This fact alone kept the supply problem within manageable bounds. The typical foot soldier carried a knapsack, a sword or hatchet, probably a hunting knife (for eating as well as fighting), a bandoleer or cartridge belt, a bullet pouch, and a flintlock musket. Troopers usually preferred pistols or carbines to the unwieldy muskets. Ammunition was rapidly used up in battle, requiring constant replenishment. Powder, lead, and all kinds of bullets were transported in barrels or rundlets, and doled out to the men as needed. Troops had to be reminded not to waste the precious powder which had been so laboriously brought to the combat area.[6]

Besides food, clothing, and military equipment, other types of supplies were sometimes needed for special purposes. When a fort or a magazine was to be constructed at some advanced point, tools and nails had to be sent up to the site. Medical supplies, including instruments, linen for dressings, and liquor, were a constant necessity wherever the army was located. Ordinarily, the surgeons had their own personal tool kits with them, but the expendable items needed by the sick and wounded had to be sent out from base towns such as Boston and New London.

In order to keep their forces supplied with all the essentials of war, the colonial governments reached out to a number of sources both here and overseas. The food, of course, was available locally. New England farms provided most of the wheat, corn, beef, pork, and mutton used by the troops, and the nearby sea afforded whatever fish was added to the diet. The liquors as well as the sugar came in by ship from distant ports. Home, shop, and mill played an essential part in providing such items as flour, clothing, shoes, leather goods, and containers of various sorts. Bullets could be molded locally, but most powder and practically all firearms had to be brought from overseas. Guns, of course, were in great demand, which caused the colonial governments to resort to such measures as confiscation in order to assure an adequate supply for the army. Persons of means might even gain exemption from military service by furnishing three guns for public use.[7]

Even the forest itself might be considered a source of supply. Men accustomed to the woods, as were many of the soldiers, knew of ways to obtain food and shelter there. Deer and other game animals were plentiful, and many a good feast of venison must have been enjoyed by soldiers weary of salt pork and moldy biscuit. Fish, too, were obtainable in the ponds and streams. One party of English soldiers and friendly Indians, starting out on extended scouting operations along the Merrimack River, was instructed to carry a supply of twine from which the Indians could make nets. Thus the Merrimack would provide all the fish they needed.[8]

Only waterways and cartpaths were available as routes for carrying the supplies needed to enable the widely scattered military forces to continue their fight against a fast-moving foe. Boston was the great supply center for all of New England. From there ships carried cargoes of food, guns, and ammunition to other important bases such as Plymouth, New London, and Hartford. Narragansett Bay afforded access to Indian country in three directions, and Rhode Island supply vessels were able to move freely between Newport, Swansea, Providence, Wickford, and Jireh Bull's trading post at Pettaquamscut. Local supplies from Connecticut towns on Long Island Sound were picked up by coastal craft and carried to bases at Hartford, New London, or Norwich. Of course, the rapids above Hartford prevented seagoing vessels from passing that point, but on the upper reaches of the river small boats proved useful as a means of transportation from town to town.

Where boats were unable to go, carts and horses were used. Supplies of all kinds in boxes and barrels, hogsheads and rundlets, were loaded into the sturdy carts, and covered with a canvas for protection against the weather. The carts usually moved along the forest roads in groups, under convoy of foot soldiers or troopers. When supplies had to be moved along trails where even the carts could not go, packhorses were pressed into service.[9]

The post of commissary in the army was a thankless one, involving great responsibility, hard work, and not a little ingenuity. Apparently the turnover in these positions was rapid, and new appointments appear again and again in the records. Commissaries often accompanied the armies to their advance bases, where they undertook to set up supply headquarters of a sort, utilizing whatever buildings were available for storage purposes. They were expected to see that the provisions and ammunition were carefully doled out, and were usu-

ally required to keep some sort of record of the supplies that passed
through their hands. Commissary-generals exercised over-all supervision of the flow of supplies, reporting directly to their own colony
government or to the Commissioners of the United Colonies.

In King Philip's War the problem of supply had a direct impact
upon civilians as well as upon soldiers. The difficulty of gathering
adequate supplies of food for the army was tremendously increased
by the fact that food was scarce for the whole population. In fact,
famine was always an imminent prospect. At the time when the war
broke out, crops were just at that stage where they needed much
attention, but the farmers were now forced to spend a considerable
proportion of their time fighting the Indians or building fortifications. Many a good farm, with all its growing crops, was abandoned
when the inhabitants fled to the shelter of fortified garrison houses.
What the roaming cattle then failed to destroy, the Indians tried to
steal or ruin.[10] The demands of the war tended to hamper all phases
of agriculture, and as more and more territory was abandoned, less
and less land was available for crops. In places where the people
were crowded into garrison houses for weeks at a time, efforts were
made to grow food on every available bit of soil within easy running
distance of the house.[11] The colonies were of course anxious to
preserve and protect, insofar as possible, all existing crops and stores
of food. Frequently, when a town such as Deerfield had to be abandoned, troops were dispatched to the scene to harvest the crops and
cart them back to safety. It was on just such a mission that Captain
Lathrop met his disastrous defeat. Attempts were also made to afford
added protection to farmers at work in the fields, especially at the
times of planting and harvesting, by assigning guards to watch over
the workers. Community plans were developed, whereby the people
worked in groups for greater safety. Sometimes these plans went so
far as to establish a temporary form of communism in which all
farm work was assigned by a committee, the land was worked in
common, and the harvest was shared by all participants.[12]

One of the weakest links in the chain of supply from farmland to
table was the town mill, for all the townspeople depended upon the
local mill to grind their grain into bakable meal or flour. The Indians
knew this, and often directed their attacks at the mills, with the result that a large number of these important establishments were

destroyed or rendered useless. Pynchon's letters from Springfield after the great attack on that town tell of the hardship caused by the fact that not one mill was left standing in the vicinity. Some towns made special efforts to assure the safety of their mills by placing them under military guard.[13]

The general shortage of foodstuffs caused individual colonies to place restrictions upon exports, sometimes to the detriment of neighboring colonies who might be even more hard-pressed. For example, on October 19, 1675, the General Court of Connecticut forbade the export of corn, grain, meal, bread, and similar products, without special license. At about the same time Massachusetts placed a similar embargo upon all sorts of provisions except fish. When the Bay Colony made an official application for supplies from Connecticut, she was given assurance that the needs of her army would be recognized, but "as to the opening the doore wider, at present, we dare not adventure; corne being very scarse with us, and the seate of the War being in our borders, and danger of being thereby prevented of sowing and planting. . . ." [14] Massachusetts did not accept the Connecticut restrictions with good grace, especially when some of her merchants were prevented from removing grain which they had previously bought in Connecticut and stored in warehouses there. The Commissioners of the United Colonies sided with Massachusetts in this controversy, and pointed out to the authorities at Hartford that Massachusetts merchants had been forced to import thousands of bushels of wheat from Bermuda for the maintenance of the armed forces. The Bay Colony even threatened to clamp a retaliatory embargo on ammunition and other commodities needed by Connecticut. Fortunately, the situation was eased by a conditional repeal of Connecticut's embargo on May 13, 1676, thus ending a dangerous controversy which had seriously threatened the war effort of the United Colonies.[15]

The people of New England soon found that a major Indian uprising could be not only dangerous but expensive. In those days the colonial treasuries were chiefly dependent upon personal property taxes for their replenishment. Each town would assess the estates of its own inhabitants, and these values formed the basis for tax levies by the colony government. In normal times a tax of one "rate" was required annually, the "rate" being simply a designated proportion of the taxpayer's holdings, expressed as a certain part of each sterling pound of value. A standard rate, for example, might be set at sixpence on the pound. With the tremendously increased expenses brought on by the war, the old system of a single annual rate quickly gave way to frequent multiple assessments. On July 9, 1675, the General Court at Boston ordered that a single rate be levied, with the understanding that a total of three such rates would be levied within twelve months. Obviously, the authorities still had no conception of the staggering expenses which would soon confront the colony. By mid-October the true financial picture was seen more clearly, and the government decided that seven single rates must be levied. In Connecticut the usual levy of sixpence on the pound was doubled, so that the single rate now took 5 per cent of a man's estate. This percentage could be applied again and again as often as the government saw fit.[16]

The towns also had expenses of their own, adding local taxation to that imposed from above. Special town rates were sometimes assessed for the purpose of providing clothing and other equipment for local inhabitants called into military service. Such funds were also used to maintain local supplies of powder and bullets.[17] Town records sometimes provide a good picture of the tremendous increases in taxation during King Philip's War. Dorchester, for example, paid taxes in three separate years as shown in the following table: [18]

	COLONY TAXES	TOWN TAXES
1671	£ 28–04–04	£50–03–08
1675	408–16–10	15–06–10
1678	111–10–07	23–12–10

Recognizing that the burden of taxation was rapidly approaching its practical limit, the government of Massachusetts in February of 1676 began to solicit loans, offering as security "all publicque and common lands within this jurisdiction, and all the interest that this colony hath . . . in any conquered lands in any other jurisdiction. . . ." [19] The idea of basing war loans on the spoils of a victory still to be achieved indicates that certain practical-minded men in Boston had their eyes fixed on valuable Indian land, probably including that at Mount Hope and in the Narragansett country.

Soldiers were usually paid their wages under a system of pay chits or debentures. Upon release from service a man was supposed to obtain from his commanding officer a debenture showing the actual number of days served. The soldier would then present this evidence to the government in order to receive his pay minus deductions for equipment and supplies. The financial condition of the colonies being what it was, payment was not prompt, and the soldiers often went months and even years without receiving all the wages owed them.[20]

The officials who controlled the government purse strings during the war carried a heavy load of responsibility. In all cases they were carefully chosen for the work because of their ability and experience in financial matters. Massachusetts was ably served by Richard Russell, the colony treasurer, and John Hull, the war treasurer, who stepped into the former position after Russell's death in May of 1676. Similar services were performed by Constant Southworth in Plymouth Colony, Major John Talcott and William Pitkin in Connecticut, and Peter Easton in Rhode Island. These men, and a large number of others who served the cause at all points along the lines of supply, deserve some recognition along with that which is usually reserved for heroes and generals. They too helped make final victory possible.

CHAPTER VII

The Campaign Against the Narragansetts

WHILE the Indian uprising was rapidly spreading through Massachusetts, the colonial authorities were having continued difficulties with the Narragansett tribe. It will be recalled that on the 15th of July, under coercion, the Narragansetts had solemnly promised to remain loyal to the English, and to surrender any of Philip's subjects who might fall into their hands. Firm as these commitments seemed to be, they quickly became a ground of contention between the Narragansett sachems and the United Colonies, and for the next three or four months, while the upper Connecticut Valley glowed with the flames of burning houses, relations between the English and the Narragansetts were characterized by mounting suspicion and friction.

The Narragansetts were a powerful tribe, potentially the most dangerous Indian group in southern New England. Furthermore, their strategic location made it possible for them to strike either northward into Massachusetts or westward into Connecticut. With Philip's uprising already well out of control, it is no wonder that the United Colonies feared what the Narragansetts might do. The one element in the situation working in favor of the English was the fact that the tribe was apparently divided on the question of the Wampanoag war. Ninigret, the sachem of the southern Narragansetts, or Niantics, seems to have thought that Philip was doomed to failure, for he was doing everything he could to convince the English of his continued good will and fidelity. Perhaps he was already counting the benefits to be reaped by those Indians who supported the United Colonies against Philip. But the other powerful sachems, including Ninigret's sister Quaiapen (sometimes known as the Old Queen or the saunk squaw), Pomham, Pessacus, and the two nephews of Pessacus, Canonchet and Quinnapin, were biding their time. In retrospect it would seem that the main body of the Narragansetts was, for the moment, trying to glean every possible advantage from a neutral position, while waiting to see which side appeared to be gaining the upper hand. Yet their policy reflects not so much cold calculation as hesitant confusion, emphasized by the fact of their own internal division.

From time to time Narragansett warriors seized enemy Indians by force, as though eager to abide by the treaty of July 15th. Only about ten days after the signing of the treaty Ninigret sent the severed head of a Wampanoag to New London, demanding a coat in payment as the English had promised. The town officers were somewhat taken aback by this unusual business transaction, and asked the government at Hartford whether they were expected to go on paying a good English coat for every such grisly trophy. In reply the Council advised them to pay if necessary, but to urge the Indians to deliver their trophies elsewhere in the future. On two subsequent occasions the Narragansetts brought in the heads of Indians said to be followers of Philip, which would seem to indicate that for the time being they were perfectly willing to shed Wampanoag blood for the coats it would bring.[1]

Gradually, however, the pattern of Narragansett behavior began to take a new form. As we have already observed, soon after the fight between Philip and the English at Nipsachuck, the Wampanoag sachem and his men continued on into the Nipmuck country, while Weetamoo and her people headed southward to seek refuge with the Narragansetts. There, in the Narragansett country, the fugitives were treated more like guests than like prisoners. Of course such a large influx of strange Indians did not go unnoticed by the English, and during the next few weeks the status of Weetamoo and her people became a focal point of the growing dispute between the colonial authorities and the Narragansett sachems. In this instance the Narragansetts seemed to be playing the enemy's game while violating the terms of their treaty agreement with the English. Those who were closest to the situation saw the danger of it most clearly. Richard Smith, the famous Indian trader of Wickford, expressed the opinion that the sachem Pessacus was actually inclined toward peace, but that the unruly young fighting men of the tribe were eager for action. Already the English settlers along the western shore of Narragansett Bay were feeling a mixture of apprehension and anger because of Indian vandalism in the area. Smith counseled a policy of moderation for the present, lest the aroused Indians make the Narragansett country untenable for the English.[2] Wickford had no desire to be another Swansea.

Unlike the other sachems, Ninigret was most active in trying to ingratiate himself with the English. His trusted aide in this project was a prominent Indian leader by the name of Cornman. The two kept in close touch with both Richard Smith at Wickford and Thomas Stanton at Stonington. When Ninigret conferred with Pessacus and learned that the Narragansetts were now sheltering upward of four hundred refugee Indians, he passed this information on to Stanton, promising that the fugitives would be surrendered to the English upon demand. But the scheming Ninigret put forward his own suggestion as to how the matter could best be handled. He proposed to bring a few Wampanoags to Stanton, whereupon Stanton would give them back to him, urging that they be well treated. The news of this remarkable leniency would soon reach the ears of all the other Indians held by the Narragansetts, and would encourage them to surrender themselves also, especially if Ninigret should intimate that they would undoubtedly be allowed to settle once more in their own country. In this way the Wampanoag captives would be persuaded to go to Aquidneck Island where they could be quickly taken into custody by the English, and disposed of as the authorities thought best. Stanton was intrigued by this perfidious scheme, but it was never put into effect.[3]

Ninigret even envisioned himself in the grandiose role of peacemaker for the entire war. Perhaps he had enough of a sense of history to feel that this was the moment for a master stroke of diplomacy, a great gesture which would place him high above all other sachems in the favor of the English, and would open for him the door of prestige and power. He now let it be known that he could and would end the war between the two races, using even his own wampum if necessary. Ninigret proposed that he be sent in company with Captain Wait Winthrop on a mission to the Mohawks and other western tribes to prevent their joining Philip's uprising.[4] Presumably all such

Museum of Art, Rhode Island School of Design

A 17th-century New England Indian, supposedly Ninigret, sachem of the Niantics (southern Narragansetts). If authentic, this is probably the only such portrait of a New England Indian prior to King Philip's War. There is no authentic portrait of Philip.

Governor John Leverett of Massachusetts, who was quick
to send aid to the stricken Plymouth Colony

Governor Josiah Winslow of Plymouth Colony, who
commanded the army in the Great Swamp Fight

Governor John Winthrop, Jr., of Connecticut, who died at Boston in April, 1676, while serving as a Commissioner of the United Colonies

Indians would then remain faithful to the English, and Philip's revolt would fizzle out from lack of support. This part of Ninigret's diplomacy likewise was not put to the test.

About the 22nd of September an important conference between the Narragansetts and the English was held at Wickford. The assembled Indians were given a message from the Commissioners of the United Colonies, then in session at Boston, urging compliance with the rightful demands of the English, including the surrender of all fugitives. But there seemed to be a strange reserve in the attitude of most of the sachems, which betrayed their unwillingness to deliver the Wampanoag refugees into the hands of their enemies. Ninigret alone continued steadfast in his resolve to comply with the agreement of July 15th.[5] It was clear to those who attended this conference that the split between the Niantics and the rest of the Narragansetts was growing ever wider.

One concrete result followed the meeting at Wickford. Cornman, escorted by Richard Smith, undertook a mission to Boston for the purpose of conferring with the authorities there. The leaders of the Bay Colony knew, of course, that this Indian and the sachem for whom he spoke might well hold the key to life or death for hundreds of settlers, and they were anxious to retain their good will. Imagine their shock, then, when a rough bystander in Boston suddenly hurled himself upon the Narragansett emissary, throwing him to the ground. The authorities quickly placed the fellow under arrest, and he was fined for his offense the following day, Cornman being consoled with a part of the fine.[6] Fortunately, there were no serious repercussions from this episode.

Cornman was probably instrumental in laying the groundwork for a formal reaffirmation of the July treaty. This new document was signed at Boston on October 18th by Cornman, on behalf of Ninigret; and the young sachem Canonchet, on behalf of himself, Pessacus, Quaiapen, Pomham, and Quinnapin. By the terms of this agreement the Narragansetts pledged themselves to remain at peace with the English, and promised to deliver at Boston no later than October 28th every enemy Indian now in their custody.[7] Actually, this treaty of October 18th contained nothing to which the Narragansetts were not already bound by the previous treaty except the definite date for delivery of the refugees. This fact may explain why

Canonchet was willing to sign such a document at a time when he and his warriors were giving every indication of following a completely independent and pugnacious course. It is also possible that Canonchet may have felt himself under duress in Boston, although his later record leaves no doubt as to his personal courage. Cornman, of course, signed willingly, for the terms of the treaty were completely in accord with Ninigret's basic policy, or at least his professions. At once the Narragansetts began to find new excuses for not yielding up their Wampanoag guests, so that the authorities at Boston can hardly have been surprised when October 28th came and went without the arrival of any prisoners.[8]

In the meantime the English had been accumulating a body of evidence which gave room for a growing suspicion that the Narragansetts were actually much more deeply implicated in Philip's uprising than would appear by their statements and promises. Greatest importance was attached to the fact that the sachems were not abiding by their promises to surrender enemy Indians, but the English were also alarmed by reports that the Narragansetts seemed to receive extremely prompt intelligence of enemy successes in the upper Connecticut Valley, and appeared very pleased at such news. It was even suspected that Narragansett warriors were secretly participating in combat, which seemed to be confirmed by reports that wounded Indians had been seen moving toward the Narragansett country. In fact, it was reckoned that the Wampanoags, Nipmucks, and Pocomtucks alone could not possibly have put in the field as many warriors as were then thought to be active against the English in the western theater of operations.[9]

Toward the end of October the English authorities received another startling piece of information. An Indian belonging to Plymouth Colony had just returned from a visit with the Narragansetts, claiming that Canonchet was definitely planning to fall upon the English the following year. The informant also confirmed the suspicions of the English that the Narragansetts were already giving aid and support to Philip. In the eyes of the Commissioners of the United Colonies, the evidence against Canonchet and his people was becoming irrefutable. As the General Court of Massachusetts expressed it, "wee Judge they doe but jugle with us." [10] Only Ninigret and the Niantics gave continued promise of fidelity to the English.

To the relatively few settlers who lived at Warwick, Wickford, and Pettaquamscut these events seemed increasingly ominous, and the danger to them was very near and personal. For weeks they had been living under a cloud of fear, weighing every development according to its possible effect upon their security. Now they could sense that affairs were approaching a crisis. As early as the third week of October there were rumors that a military expedition would be sent into the area to overawe the Narragansetts, and that might mean bloodshed. Some of the settlers were even leaving their homes and moving out of the Narragansett country to escape the impending trouble.[11] As often happens, rumors were the forerunners of actual fact.

*   *   *

The Commissioners of the United Colonies, at the conclusion of their sessions in October, had adjourned until the 2nd of November. Now with that date upon them, and knowing that the Narragansetts had already failed to observe the agreement of October 18th, they faced what was probably the most difficult decision of the war. They were generally agreed that the Narragansett sachems had violated their solemn engagements with the English and were deliberately playing the enemy's game. The question with which the Commissioners had to contend was whether the United Colonies should now coerce the Narragansetts by military force, thereby running the extreme risk of enlarging the war. Already the colonies were fighting desperately against a cruel and destructive foe. Could they afford to give Philip a thousand more warriors by driving the Narragansetts to open resistance? The Commissioners reversed the question and asked whether the English could afford not to strike a decisive blow at once, rather than permit their enemies to gather their strength, accumulate munitions, and choose their own time for making war upon the settlers. If the Narragansetts were allowed to wait until summer, they would then have the additional advantage of the concealment afforded by the leafy foliage of the forest.

Even as the Commissioners deliberated, they could look out of the windows and see the bareness of the trees in Boston. Winter was coming early this year. To all New Englanders, the great difficulties and dangers of a winter campaign in the wilderness were obvious.

An army in the field at that bitter season would be in constant peril from the weather and lack of supplies. Men forced to camp in the open woods and fields might be as effectively crippled by the cold and dampness as by enemy bullets. Snow drifting over the long forest paths, and ice locking up rivers and harbors, could block the usual lines of supply. Yet despite these somber possibilities, many responsible men were coming to believe that the best course of action was to smash the power of the Narragansetts immediately, without waiting for them to complete their own preparations for war. Probably by this time both Plymouth and Massachusetts were convinced that positive military action was the correct answer. Connecticut still clung to the hope that peace might be secured through milder measures. Unfortunately, the Connecticut delegation was for the moment incomplete, for Governor Winthrop's colleague, James Richards, was still detained at Hartford. The Massachusetts men were eager to reach a decision for action, all the more so since the recent episode in which a large group of Christian Indians near Hassanemesit had been taken off by enemy warriors, among whom were thought to be some Narragansetts.[12] Winthrop, however, insisted that the Commissioners could not legally act until the Connecticut delegation was complete. So the matter hung fire.[13]

By November 5th the patience of the Plymouth and Massachusetts delegates had about reached its limit. They tried to persuade Winthrop that the matter was urgent and could not wait for the arrival of another Commissioner from Connecticut, but the governor refused to budge from his original position, all the while probably hoping that time was on the side of a peaceful resolution of the problem. When it became clear that Winthrop could not be moved, the four other Commissioners angrily affixed their signatures to a statement declaring that the defection of Connecticut was "an absolute violation of the maine ends of the Articles of Confederation." [14]

In all probability several more days passed before any major decision could be reached. By the 12th, however, the Commissioners were once again functioning smoothly as a joint planning committee. This was made possible by the fact that Hartford had authorized the governor's son, Captain Wait Winthrop, to serve as the colony's second Commissioner, thus completing the Connecticut delegation.[15] Now the crucial decision had been made—the United Colonies would send an army of a thousand men to force the stubborn Narragansetts to observe their treaty obligations, including the surrender of all enemy fugitives. If the Narragansetts still refused to cooperate, they should be dealt with as open enemies. This decision was embodied in a document which has often been called a declaration of war against the Narragansett tribe. Actually, it was not intended as such, for the army was to strike only if it could not otherwise force the sachems to comply with the demands of the United Colonies.[16] Most men, however, probably felt that military action was now virtually inevitable. In view of the past history of intercolonial rivalry for control of the Narragansett country, we can hardly doubt, too, that a number of prominent gentlemen in Connecticut and Massachusetts were greatly comforted by the prospect of military conquest in the area. Conversely, the colony of Rhode Island might well feel that the impending expedition was a potential threat to its own claims.

A great amount of preparation would be necessary before the expedition could take the field. The Commissioners decided that one of their own number, Governor Winslow of Plymouth Colony, should command the army, and reserved to Connecticut the privilege of designating a second-in-command. A contemporary observer, commenting on Winslow's new assignment, spoke of his physical frailty, but concluded, "I know noe man fitter for this great servis. . . ."[17] Probably it was hoped that the selection of a Plymouth rather than a Massachusetts man as commander in chief would smooth the intercolonial tensions which had developed over Appleton's leadership in the upper Connecticut Valley.

Each of the participating colonies was expected to raise a certain proportion of the men needed for the expedition, and the Commissioners expressed the hope that only "men of strength corrage and activity" would be sent on this arduous mission.[18] With the soldiers would go a number of surgeons and chaplains to provide for their special needs. It was decided that the army should be assembled and ready to commence its mission no later than December 10th, and certain towns were specified as points of rendezvous for the various units.

Very prudently, the Commissioners also decided to seek the full cooperation of Rhode Island in the venture, and accordingly told Governor Coddington of their plans in a letter dated at Boston on

November 12th. They invited Rhode Island to send a contingent of
men if she so desired, and also requested that sloops and other vessels
be made available for the transport of men and supplies. Although
the letter did not actually ask Coddington's permission to enter
Rhode Island territory, it was not offensive in tone, and seemed to
be a sincere bid for cooperation. Naturally, the governor was urged
to keep the plan under a veil of secrecy. Coddington assured the
Commissioners that his colony would provide the necessary vessels
for the expedition. Newport, in turn, sent word to Providence and
Warwick concerning the impending operation, in order that these
exposed settlements might be on their guard against retaliation by
the Indians.[19] It was most fortunate that Rhode Island was willing
to cooperate, for without such assistance the problem of transporting
supplies across Narragansett Bay or down through Providence and
Warwick would have been greatly magnified.

On the same day that the Commissioners drafted their letter to
Rhode Island, Governor Winthrop wrote to his own government at
Hartford notifying them of the decision which had been reached,
and explaining in some detail the reasons behind it. Hartford officially acquiesced in the plan, and named Major Treat to command
the Connecticut contingent and serve as second-in-command of the
entire army. As in Rhode Island, the more exposed plantations were
notified to be ready for possible trouble.[20]

The Commissioners and the governments which they represented
wasted little time in attacking the complex problem of how to keep
the troops properly supplied during the course of their operation.
Winter was approaching rapidly, which served to emphasize the
absolute necessity of establishing and maintaining adequate lines of
supply into the Narragansett country. The success or failure of the
whole venture, and the lives of hundreds of men, hung upon this
difficult problem. The elaborate planning which was now undertaken
gave every reason to believe that the lessons of the summer and early
fall had been well learned, and that henceforth the military forces
would be kept properly furnished with all the necessary items of food
and equipment. In fact, this was the first campaign in New England
history that was really supposed to be carefully planned before it
was set in motion.

The small village of Wickford, on the western shore of Nar-

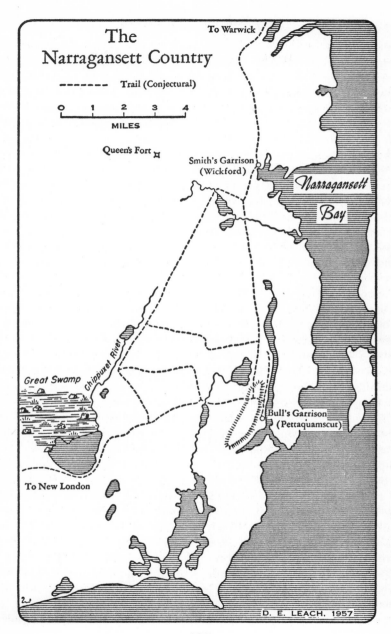

The Narragansett Country

Trail (Conjectural)

0   1   2   3   4
MILES

Queen's Fort

Smith's Garrison
(Wickford)

Narragansett
Bay

To Warwick

Great Swamp

Chipuxet River

Bull's Garrison
(Pettaquamscut)

To New London

D. E. LEACH. 1957

ragansett Bay about nine miles below Warwick, was selected as the
army's advance base. Here Richard Smith had his trading post where
he had carried on business with the Narragansetts for years. Smith
knew the country and the Indians there from long experience. In
addition, he was recognized as a man who would cooperate with
the United Colonies. Upon learning that his plantation was needed
as a base for the army, Smith changed his own plans for a voyage
abroad in order to be on the scene in person.[21] Near Smith's garrison
and trading post were other houses which might furnish additional
shelter for troops and supplies. Wickford was located on a small
harbor only eleven miles by water from Newport, thirteen miles
from Portsmouth, and twenty-three miles from Rehoboth. Even New
London was only a day's sail away if the wind stood fair. Barring
unforeseen circumstances, then, the vessels of Newport, New London,
and Boston could keep the base at Wickford well provided with
supplies.

Contemplating a field army of a thousand men or more, the
Commissioners spent busy days at Boston planning for the accumulation and transportation of an adequate backlog of supplies. They
decided to provide initially enough food and ammunition for a two-
month operation,[22] with each colony undertaking to furnish these
supplies for its own troops. The Commissioners also issued a special
warning that the men must be adequately provided with warm
clothing against the bitter cold of the winter season.

Connecticut chose New London as her main base of supply. From
there her troops could march eastward along the well-known Pequot
Path to Wickford, while more bulky supplies could be carried by
the sea route around Point Judith. In order to assure an adequate
store of foodstuffs for the expedition, the Council at Hartford laid
a two-month prohibition on the export of all sorts of provisions
from New London County. Bakers were kept busy making bread
out of the hundreds of bushels of grain which were collected in
various parts of the colony. Stephen Barrett was appointed commissary for the Connecticut forces, and into his hands fell the responsibility for receiving, storing, and distributing the food and equipment
which now came pouring into New London. The Council ordered
that three barrels of powder, seven hundredweight of lead, and a
stock of flints be added to the supplies of powder and bullets already

stored in the town.²³ Plymouth and Massachusetts, of course, were making their own similar preparations at the same time. On the 16th of November Appleton's army in the Connecticut Valley was ordered home, for it was now apparent that the bulk of the enemy had moved toward winter quarters in the Narragansett country and elsewhere. General Winslow, meanwhile, was in Boston conferring with the other Commissioners and with his subordinate officers.²⁴

In the various towns of the United Colonies men were being enlisted or conscripted to make up the required quotas for the coming expedition. Everywhere the soldiers were checking their weapons, gathering the warmest clothing they could find, and making last-minute preparations before saying goodbye to their families. Massachusetts was forced to deal with a discouraging wave of draft dodging, undoubtedly caused by the already heavy demands of war and the special hardships connected with a winter campaign. A special proclamation was issued, explaining to the people why their colony had become involved in the Indian war, and justifying the coming campaign against the Narragansetts.²⁵

The colonies observed Thursday, the 2nd of December, as a special day of prayer. Before the hushed congregations the solemn-faced clergy invoked God's blessing for the coming venture, and urged the soldiers to remain steadfast in faith and prayer. Soon after this date the men began to move along the roads from town to town, converging on the designated points of assembly. Plymouth Colony's troops were ordered to be at Taunton on December 8th, and at Rehoboth on the 9th. Massachusetts arranged for her forces to rendezvous at Dedham on the morning of December 8th. Connecticut's contingent gathered at New London.²⁶ It was to be the greatest military force that New England had ever seen, and the hearts of the people went with it.

*   *   *

Dedham was a scene of bustling activity and martial display as the Massachusetts companies prepared for their departure on December 9th. Altogether there were well over five hundred men in this contingent, organized in six companies of infantry and a troop of cavalry, the whole force being commanded by Major Appleton. The troopers, about seventy-five strong, were led by Captain Thomas

Prentice. The companies of foot, averaging about seventy-seven men each, were commanded by Major Appleton and Captains Samuel Moseley, James Oliver, Isaac Johnson, Nathaniel Davenport, and Joseph Gardiner.[27] General Winslow and his special aide, Benjamin Church, were at Dedham with the troops, which gave them their first opportunity to size up the men who had been chosen for this hazardous expedition. They were a mixed lot of farmers and artisans, apprentices and seamen, hard-bitten veterans and men who had never seen combat. Already the country was in the grip of an early winter, and the men shivered in the cold as they listened to instructions from their officers, and checked their equipment.

Before sending the troops on their way, the government of Massachusetts made a pledge which was designed to encourage the men in their endeavor. The assembled troops were told that if they were successful, they could expect to be rewarded with benefits in land as a supplement to their regular pay.[28] With this welcome promise ringing in their ears, the companies swung into line and started their march down the long path toward Rehoboth and the Narragansett country.

Prentice and the troopers went ahead as an advance force, billeting that night at Rehoboth; the foot companies spent the night at Woodcock's, and then moved on to Rehoboth the next day. Here they joined with the contingent from Plymouth Colony, consisting of two companies of infantry commanded by Major William Bradford and Captain John Gorham, with a total strength of about 150 men. Again Prentice moved ahead, crossing the Seekonk River to Providence, and continuing on toward Wickford, but the bulk of the army remained at Rehoboth that night. Captain Johnson and some men were sent over to Providence to surprise an Indian camp near that town. Winslow hoped, of course, that by wiping out any such enemy outposts en route he might prevent word of his approach from reaching the Narragansetts. In this case, however, the Indians made their escape before Johnson's men arrived.[29]

In answer to a previous request, Rhode Island sent several vessels to meet Winslow's army at Rehoboth. Richard Smith was there also, ready to conduct an advance force to his garrison. From Winslow's point of view, it was imperative to establish some military strength at Wickford at the earliest possible moment, lest the enemy destroy the base before the army could arrive. Accordingly, Moseley's company and Benjamin Church embarked on the Rhode Island craft, and proceeded to Smith's garrison to prepare for the arrival of the other companies.[30]

Winslow and the rest of the army were ferried across the Seekonk River by means of a pontoon raft built of canoes and planks. At Providence they picked up the old Pequot Path and followed it southward to Pawtuxet, where they took up quarters. Until now Winslow had received no positive information concerning the movement of Connecticut forces assigned to operate under his command. In fact, the general could not even be sure that Connecticut would dispatch her troops in accordance with the orders of the Commissioners. This state of uncertainty was somewhat eased on December 12th when the army at Pawtuxet intercepted a messenger bearing a letter from Major Treat to the Commissioners at Boston. Eager to gain any news of Connecticut's contingent, Winslow broke open the letter, and was greatly relieved to read that Treat had arrived at New London several days previously with about three hundred men. The general sent the messenger on his way again, and dispatched orders ahead for Treat to continue his advance toward the rendezvous.[31]

Having heard that sachem Pomham was then situated near the upper reaches of the Pawtuxet River, the army resumed its march on the evening of December 12th with the hope that by advancing in the dark they might completely surprise Pomham and his people, and thus prevent them from escaping to the main body of the Narragansetts. In the bitter cold and the darkness, however, the guides missed their mark, and the coming of daylight found the troops still some distance from their objective. Pomham, apparently, had made good his escape. Discomfited by this failure, and fearing that the enemy might already have fallen upon Wickford, the army hastened on to Smith's garrison, where they found all in order, and the advance force waiting to greet them.[32]

The next few days were spent in vigorous scouting activity in the vicinity of Wickford. Before long the army had a sizable collection of enemy prisoners, who were subsequently sold to Captain Davenport and transported to Aquidneck Island for safekeeping. One captive, however, was not sent away, and for a very important reason.

This Indian, known as Peter, had turned traitor to his own people, agreeing to serve as a guide to the English forces. It was probably upon information given by this Indian that Winslow led a large force into the field on the 14th. During the course of this highly successful excursion the English fell upon two Indian villages, one of them belonging to the Old Queen, inflicted a number of casualties, and burned down a large number of wigwams. Some of the prisoners taken were found to be Wampanoags.[33] There is no evidence to show that Winslow had attempted to open further negotiations with the Narragansetts before engaging in such acts of hostility. In this respect, the army's attempts to cut off any outlying groups of Indians during its march from Rehoboth are significant. Indeed, the stated purpose of the expedition seems to have dissolved in the general urge to smash the potential foe as quickly as possible.

By this time, of course, the Narragansetts were perfectly aware of the army's presence at Wickford, and had probably guessed its intention quite accurately. Yet they must have felt reasonably secure, for they had nearly completed construction of a great secret fortified village on a small island in the midst of the Great Swamp north of Worden's Pond. Here the Narragansetts and their friends—men, women, and children—had congregated to pass the winter, safe from intrusion. Past experience had shown the Indians that the English were poor swamp fighters, and the secret island was thought to be virtually inaccessible to any who did not know the proper way of approaching it. But the English now had control of Indian Peter, who knew the location of the Narragansett stronghold.

On December 15th a Narragansett by the name of Stonewall John came to army headquarters and attempted to negotiate for peace. His real mission may have been to obtain information about the strength and plans of the army. At any rate, Stonewall John aggravated the officers by his boastfulness, and was sent back with the admonition that if the Narragansetts wanted to speak with the English they must send sachems.[34] It afterward appeared that Stonewall John had been attended by a body of warriors who lay concealed not far from Smith's garrison, for in a matter of minutes after the emissary had departed the Indians killed or mortally wounded three of the soldiers nearby. A little later they slew two of Captain Oliver's men who were stationed at a house about three miles from head-

quarters. Winslow sent three companies to go and bring back Appleton's company, which at that time was several miles away from
headquarters. En route they were fired upon by the lurking enemy,
and in the brief skirmish which followed, one Indian was killed.

While these events were taking place, Winslow was impatiently
wondering what had become of Treat and the Connecticut forces.
Every passing day increased the difficulty of the situation, for additional supplies expected from Massachusetts had not yet arrived,
and provisions were becoming dangerously scarce. Furthermore,
should there be any severe winter storm it might prevent any large-
scale movement of troops for days. Presumably, the Connecticut
contingent would come by way of Pettaquamscut, a small settlement
about nine miles south of Smith's garrison. Here Jireh Bull maintained a large stone garrison house which would serve quite well
as a jumping-off point for an attack aimed at the heart of the
Narragansett country, the Great Swamp. Winslow sent Prentice's
troop down to Pettaquamscut, probably to look for the Connecticut
forces. The troopers came back on the 16th with grim news—the
enemy had fallen upon Jireh Bull's garrison house, killing most of
the people in it, and destroying the building by fire.[35] Pettaquamscut
was now almost useless as a base for the army. Furthermore, the
Connecticut troops still had not made their appearance.

The gloomy tidings of the 16th were considerably lightened on
the following day when news reached Wickford that Treat and his
Connecticut soldiers were actually at Pettaquamscut, and ready to
join the rest of the army in offensive operations. This represented an
important increase in Winslow's effective strength. Included in
Treat's regiment were five companies commanded by Captains John
Gallop, Samuel Marshall, Nathaniel Seeley, Thomas Watts, and
John Mason, with a total strength of more than three hundred men.
In addition, Treat had with him about 150 Mohegans and Pequots
led by Oneco and Catapazet. Now the army was complete, and
Indian Peter was ready to guide the English to the secret fort in
the Great Swamp. With food running low, Winslow believed that
he must act at once, or perhaps lose the chance forever. This was
the moment to make his great bid for a decisive victory.

*   *   *

Leaving at Wickford a sufficient number of men to protect Smith's garrison, the Plymouth and Massachusetts contingents on December 18th marched down to Pettaquamscut, where they found the Connecticut forces awaiting them. There being no adequate shelter remaining at Pettaquamscut, the men camped that night in the open around the grimly black ruins of the garrison. This experience proved to be a severe test of their hardihood, for the weather was cold and stormy, and the troops had little real protection from the elements. Probably the wet and the bitter cold prevented sleep, so that by morning the men were more than glad to resume their march. Already a number of soldiers were found to be suffering from frozen limbs, and had to be left behind.

By now there was a heavy fall of snow on the ground, and the weather remained unfavorable. With the first gray light of dawn filtering across the frozen landscape, the weary troops resumed their shuffling advance through the deep snow, each man carrying his weapons, ammunition, and a small quantity of food. Like a sluggish gray snake the long procession wound its way inland in a generally westward direction, guided by Indian Peter, who undoubtedly marched with Moseley's company in the van. Next came the other companies of Massachusetts troops followed by General Winslow's party and the two companies of Plymouth men. The five companies from Connecticut brought up the rear of the long, plodding column. The men were miserable during the entire long march, and the officers permitted no rest periods even for eating. As they trudged along, the soldiers blew upon their stiffened fingers, and occasionally gnawed at some of the food from their knapsacks. Every weary mile took them farther from civilization and nearer to danger. Their route lay over Tower Hill and across the Chippuxet River, probably somewhere between Larkin Pond and Thirty Acre Pond. Beyond the Chippuxet lay miles of woodland and swamp virtually unknown to white men. All now depended upon their captive guide who alone could pick out the proper route for the advancing army.

Early in the afternoon the leading troops reached a position on rising land some two miles beyond the present village of West Kingston. Before them to the southward lay the unknown depths of the Great Swamp,

A place which nature coyn'd on very nonce
For tygers not for men to be a sconce.[36]

There was no time for gloomy reflection, however, for at the edge of the swamp the English encountered a picket party of Indians who quickly returned the fire of the army's advance troops, and then withdrew into the wasteland. Without awaiting further orders from Winslow, who had not yet arrived on the scene, the leading companies impetuously dashed into the swamp after the retreating enemy. Fortunately, the remarkable cold of the past few weeks had completely frozen the muck and water of the swamp, so that the English were able to advance across terrain which under normal conditions would have been impassible.

The onrushing troops suddenly saw before them in the gloom of the swamp a small piece of upland, perhaps five or six acres in extent, and upon it the shaggy outlines of what appeared to be a great walled Indian village. The wall itself was constructed of tall stakes set upright in the ground, and around its perimeter was piled a thick mass of tree limbs and brush several yards thick. Moreover, this formidable outwork was further protected by a number of small blockhouses from which the enemy could pour a raking fire upon any body of men attempting to assault the fortification. Enclosed within the main wall was a village consisting of many crowded huts. Probably at this time a thousand or more Indians of all ages and both sexes were sheltered in this unusual fort. The English, in all their experience with native construction, had never seen anything quite like it.

As fate would have it, the first English troops to arrive came upon the one vulnerable spot in the entire structure. At one corner the palisade was not complete, leaving a gap which had been temporarily blocked by the trunk of a tree placed in a horizontal position about four or five feet from the ground. As compared with the rest of the wall, this gap seemed to offer the English their best chance to fight their way into the village, despite the fact that it was protected by a nearby blockhouse. Heroically, the first companies raced toward the gap and clambered over the horizontal trunk in the face of galling enemy fire from the blockhouse. Captain Johnson was killed as he led his men into the breach, and Captain Davenport fell dead just within the fort. Nevertheless, the highly excited troops hurled themselves forward. As more and more soldiers poured through the gap in the wall, the Indians were forced to give ground; but soon they gathered their strength once more, and drove the hard-fighting English back into the swamp. Thus the first phase of the battle came to an end with nothing gained by either side.

With the arrival of other companies at the scene, the English determined upon another attempt to capture the fort, and so once more the troops rushed for the gap in the wall, clambered over the barricade, and poured into the area of wigwams. The Indians again retreated stubbornly before the advancing soldiers, yielding ground only gradually. As the battle developed into a contest of firepower and marksmanship, both sides took advantage of the shelter afforded by the many closely huddled wigwams. The cold, crisp air was alive with the flash of muskets and thick with the smell of powder.

General Winslow and his immediate party remained on the high ground just outside the swamp, listening to the sound of the furious battle, and probably receiving reports by messenger. The general's aide, Benjamin Church, was no man to be long satisfied with such a passive role, however, and upon his request was given permission to lead a body of volunteers in to the scene of combat. By the time Church and his party of about thirty men reached the fort, the English were gaining control of the area within the walls, although many Indians were presumed to be hiding within the wigwams. Recognizing Captain Joseph Gardiner, Church started toward him, when suddenly Gardiner sank to the ground with a bullet through his head. Obviously, the fight was not yet over.

Orders were given to set the wigwams on fire as the safest means of routing the enemy within the walls. Church tried to have the order countermanded, for he was convinced that the army should preserve the fort and wigwams for its own use that night. Moreover, the Indian huts were well-stocked with grain and other food which the army sorely lacked. But he pleaded in vain, for although Winslow at first seemed disposed to take his advice, others interposed and overrode Church's argument. Soon the village was an inferno of flame. How many old men, women, and little children perished inside the wigwams will, of course, never be known. Hubbard's comment on this tragic episode, intended to be grimly humorous, scarcely does credit to the author. He reported that the English troops first launched their attack at a time when the Indians were preparing dinner, "but one sudden and unexpected Assault put them besides that Work, making their Cookrooms too hot for them at that Time, when they and their Mitchin fryed together." [37]

With the mopping-up operations completed, the army was able to take some account of its situation. English casualties amounted to at least twenty dead and some two hundred wounded, or about 20 per cent of the total number engaged. Now the afternoon was waning, and dusk was approaching. The wind and the sky gave clear warning that the wintry storm was still not played out, and might yet wreak havoc on the victorious army. Winslow also feared that the enraged enemy would regroup and launch a massive counterattack upon his tired men. The fort was now impossible as a place of shelter; Pettaquamscut offered little more; and the only practical course seemed to be a night retreat directly to the main base at Wickford. The troops busied themselves bandaging the wounded and collecting the weapons of those who had fallen in the fight. Then, probably about 4:00 P.M., the retreat began.

Twelve of the dead and some of the more seriously wounded were hoisted onto the backs of horses for the long march. The rest of the English dead had to be left behind, and these were later found and buried by Ninigret's men. For the wounded especially, the retreat to Wickford was an agonizing experience. They felt every jolt and stumble caused by the darkness of the route. They winced as the frozen blood and the caked bandages cut into their wounds. They shivered constantly in the penetrating cold, for their clothing was inadequate to shut out the icy winds and the snow, and their condition and mode of transportation made it hard for them to exercise their stiffening limbs. Always there was the terrible fear that the Indians were on their track and circling the flanks for an ambush. A number of the wounded, perhaps twenty or more, never lived to see the welcome light of Richard Smith's hearth fire. Most of the army managed to reach Wickford about two o'clock in the morning, after a march of some fifteen miles or more. One group of about forty men, including the general and the chaplains, became separated from the rest in the darkness, and didn't arrive until seven.[38]

Records of the army's first few hours at Wickford after the retreat are sparse, but imagination can supply the deficiences of fact. The majority of the returning men quickly found what food and shelter they could, and then dropped down to sleep the sleep of exhaustion. Food was desperately scarce. The wounded were gathered into the best available shelters, and thawed out before roaring fires, while surgeons and others set about to do whatever was possible for the sufferers. Doubtless, emergency operations had to be performed in order to save the lives of the most severely wounded. Hands more used to the plow than the bandages and basins of sickrooms aided the doctors in their overwhelming duties.[39]

On the day after the Great Swamp Fight the English troops buried thirty-four of their dead at Wickford, while in the following days still others of the wounded succumbed. A month after the battle the total number of dead was approaching seventy, and both Hubbard and Mather subsequently placed the figure at more than eighty. Of the company commanders, seven out of fourteen were killed or mortally wounded in the battle, and one other, Captain Gorham of Plymouth Colony, contracted a mortal fever. In this battle the officers had demonstrated a bold and spirited leadership which would long be remembered in New England, but the loss of so many of them left the army woefully short of experienced leaders. The inclement weather also took its toll of casualties, in addition to those caused by the battle itself. Although the army escaped the ravages of epidemic disease, many of the men were disabled because of frozen hands and feet.[40] Without question, then, the successful blow against the Narragansetts had cost the colonial army a heavy price, rendering it temporarily unfit for further campaigning.

It is impossible to give any accurate figures for Indian casualties in the Great Swamp Fight. Contemporary reports, based on the impressions of participants and the statements of prisoners, vary widely. The English tended to overestimate the number of Indians who fought against them and the number who fell in battle. Prisoners under questioning were prone to give erroneous figures to confuse the English, or to please them, or simply because they did not know the true facts. The Reverend Joseph Dudley, one of the chaplains with the army, estimated that the enemy had lost at least two hundred men in the battle. Captain James Oliver reported that the English had killed at least three hundred warriors and more than three hundred women and children. Other estimates went much higher.[41] There can be no doubt that the losses of the Indians were grievously heavy, and that many innocent noncombatants perished in the flaming wigwams. Those who managed to escape from the fort found themselves without shelter in cold wintry weather, and many of them undoubtedly died soon after the battle. But perhaps from the long-range point of view the most significant loss to the Indians was the destruction of their winter food which had been so carefully accumulated and stored in the wigwams at the fort. Henceforth the English would have an important ally—hunger—stalking the Indian camps.

The story of the Great Swamp Fight raises a number of interesting questions. Why was the army sent forth on December 18th without any reserve rations sufficient to last more than a day or two? Church testified that by the time the fight was over, the Plymouth soldiers *"had not so much as one Biscake left. . . ."* [42] Under normal circumstances the troops never should have been sent on such a mission without being issued a considerable reserve of food. But these were not normal circumstances. The well-intended plans for supplying Winslow's army had broken down under adverse conditions of weather, with the result that by the 18th of December Wickford was virtually stripped of provisions suitable for a field march. Apparently, then, the troops took with them on their march nearly all of the food still left, hoping that by the time of their return some vessels with fresh supplies would have arrived. Seen in this light, the attack on the Narragansett stronghold appears as nothing less than a desperate gamble.

Furthermore, the expedition seems to have been undertaken without any clear decision as to how the assault would be conducted, and what would be done after the battle had been won or lost. The impetuous way in which the leading companies rushed into the swamp upon the first contact with the enemy reveals a dangerous lack of battle discipline. In the subsequent fighting, many casualties among the leading companies apparently were caused by careless shooting on the part of the troops farther back.[43] This tragic circumstance is not uncommon in the history of warfare, but among well-trained and well-led troops it can usually be kept to a minimum. Historians may argue endlessly as to whether Church was right or wrong in his proposal to remain at the fort rather than retire to Wickford. Possibly many lives would have been saved if the army had utilized the food and shelter which they had captured, rather than consigning it all to the flames. Possibly, too, the army might have been able to strike further damaging blows at the dispossessed Indians, using the fort as a base. But there were also dangers in Church's proposal. The men, bone-weary as they were, might not have been able to withstand a determined counterattack by a reinforced enemy. Our principal criticism, however, must be directed at the fact that the various contingencies apparently had not been thoroughly considered, and alternative courses of action decided upon, before the army undertook its march. For this, Winslow must bear the major portion of blame.

Still another question raised by the Great Swamp Fight is what actually happened to poison relations between the Connecticut troops and their comrades from Massachusetts. Soon after the battle the Connecticut men began to complain that some of their guns had been stolen by Massachusetts soldiers. Apparently what had happened was that during the interval between the end of the battle and the arrival of the army at Wickford a number of guns belonging to Connecticut casualties had disappeared. Connecticut soldiers claimed that they had collected and bundled these guns at the fort just before the retreat, but that later some Massachusetts men had made off with them while the Connecticut soldiers were preoccupied. Possibly these much-needed weapons were taken by mistake during the hasty departure of the army, and then, being heavy, were discarded during the difficult retreat. Or they may have been left behind altogether. At any rate, they were not returned to the Connecticut contingent, and this caused a great deal of bitter feeling. Whether any pilfering of clothing and other personal effects took place after the return to Wickford cannot now be determined with certainty. All question of actual guilt aside, the situation was most unfortunate in that it helped to aggravate relations between the troops of the two sister colonies at a time when intercolonial relations were already under considerable strain.[44]

In one all-important respect luck had been with Winslow. If the march against the Narragansett stronghold had been postponed even a day or two beyond the 19th of December, it could not have been undertaken for a number of weeks because of snow conditions and adverse weather. The general happened to choose the last feasible day for his attack, and that decision was largely dictated by the arrival of the Connecticut troops at Pettaquamscut and the imminent exhaustion of the army's supply of food.

The victory over the Narragansetts brought a much-needed moment of satisfaction to suffering New England, tempered by sadness at the heavy losses suffered by Winslow's army. This had been an adventure never to be forgotten by those who participated and survived. On many a cold New England night for years afterward the howling of the wind would remind the old veterans of flame-lit scenes of horror in the Great Swamp. Then, their faces aglow with the light of blazing hearth fires, they would tell their children and their grandchildren how they marched with Josiah Winslow to drive the savage red men out of their secret lair, and how they staggered back to Wickford that night through the darkness and the snow.

*   *   *

Because Wickford lacked the facilities necessary for the proper care of the seriously wounded, it was decided to send them to Newport where additional surgeons were available. The evacuation began shortly after the army had returned to its base. The wounded men were bundled up in whatever blankets and clothing were available, and carted down to the waterside where the boats were waiting. Once in Newport, the men were distributed in various private houses. Some of the wounded remained there for weeks before they were well enough to be removed to their own homes. Governor Coddington could not deny himself the satisfaction of pointing out to the Massachusetts Puritans the contrast between the hospitality being afforded their wounded soldiers by Rhode Island, and the customary severity of the Massachusetts government toward Baptists and Quakers. As Coddington expressed it, "Our Houses are now open to receive your Wounded and all in Distress, we have prepared an Hospitall for yors, but you a House of Correction for all that repaire to our Meetings, is this soe do as you would be done by?" [45]

Meanwhile, the army continued to be woefully short of supplies. One ship did reach Wickford soon after the Swamp Fight, which helped to ease somewhat the immediate distress, but this was a

notable exception. Hubbard wrote that the supply vessels were unable
to relieve the army because of ice conditions, and suggested that
the shortage of food at Wickford was an important factor in preventing an immediate follow-up strike which might have brought the
Indians to their knees. The river towns of Connecticut were frozen
in, but the Commissioners noted that the seaside towns still had
access to open water, and they recommended that Connecticut send
enough food for the whole intercolonial army. The proposal was still
being discussed as late as January 6th.[46] Despite all the thought and
energy expended in preparing for the expedition against the Narragansetts, obviously something had gone wrong. Hubbard hinted at
the basic cause of the situation when he wrote that "Care was taken
for Supplies, as the Difficulty of such an Affair . . . did require,
though possibly not with so much necessary Care . . . as had been
desired, if what came afterward to pass could have been foreseen,
(which peradventure might be the Reason Things went on so heavily
for Want of well oyling the Wheels;). . . ." [47] What the planners
had failed to foresee were the unexpected factors which often make
their appearance in war—in this case, the unusual rigor of the season,
and the delay in the arrival of the Connecticut contingent. But
beyond this, the evidence indicates that none of the colonies actually
provided its forces with supplies adequate for a month, to say nothing of the two months recommended by the Commissioners.

The troops at Wickford, living in all kinds of makeshift quarters,
did their best to provide for themselves. They became experienced
foragers, and found good supplies of Indian corn, probably concealed
in Narragansett storage pits. This not only helped the army, but also
hurt the Indians. There were other means of obtaining necessities
also. Richard Smith's property disappeared like magic. He later reported that the soldiers had consumed twenty-six head of cattle,
about a hundred goats, and at least thirty fat hogs. His fences provided fuel for many a cheering campfire. In the meantime, military
operations had largely ceased, although late in December the troopers
did raid Pomham's village near Warwick, destroying a large number
of wigwams which they found there.[48]

For about four weeks after the battle at the fort both sides gave
some indication of a desire for a peaceful settlement. On several
occasions messengers from the Narragansett sachems were received

by the officers at Wickford, but these parleys produced no result. Neither side was willing to make any considerable compromise, although the Commissioners instructed Winslow not to be too strict in his demands. Possibly the Narragansetts were stalling for time while they recovered their strength and decided upon their next course of action. Although the English suspected that the Indians were not sincere in their desire for peace, they continued with the negotiations in order to conceal their own inability to strike another major blow. By the 12th of January, however, Winslow had had enough of this fruitless exchange of messages, and the attempts to effect a settlement came to an end.[49]

Ever since the 20th of December, Winslow had been trying to build up the strength and morale of his crippled army to the point where it could once more take the field against the enemy. His experience gave a miniature preview of what Washington would have to undergo at Valley Forge. The heavy casualties suffered by the Connecticut contingent, together with the shortage of supplies and the severity of the weather, led Major Treat to urge that his forces be allowed to return temporarily to their own colony. But from Winslow's point of view, such a withdrawal would greatly weaken the army as a whole, and render it even more incapable of conducting an offensive. Consequently, Treat's request was at first denied by Winslow and his council. Soon after this, a number of Treat's men deserted their units, making their way back to Connecticut on their own initiative. It was obvious that morale among the Connecticut troops was dangerously low, and so before the end of the month Treat was allowed to take his men back to Stonington for recuperation and reinforcement.

Meanwhile, the Commissioners were attempting to strengthen the army with new recruits, so that Winslow would be able to strike while the Narragansetts were still assembled within range. At this time it was considered likely that Philip and his men were with the main body of the Narragansetts, thus presenting an even more tempting target. A plan to raise a thousand additional men was put into effect, and the colonies were asked to cooperate to the fullest extent.[50] Despite all appeals, Connecticut showed a strong reluctance to throw any considerable number of her men into the united army once more. She acted very much like a child whose fingers have been

burned in the fire. Deputy Governor Leete accurately expressed the
viewpoint of his colony when he argued that Connecticut herself
was now endangered by the enemy, and suggested that Massachusetts
was now in a position to contribute a much greater share of men
for the army. Not without truth, he pointed out that almost one-half
of the casualties suffered by the army as a result of the Great Swamp
Fight had occurred among the Connecticut units. Other influential
men at Hartford likewise expressed doubt that the colony could raise
the additional 315 men demanded by the Commissioners.[51]

On January 6th the Commissioners prodded the authorities at
Hartford with a new letter in which they remarked that the Bay
Colony had already dispatched a good part of its quota, and begged
them not to be remiss in providing their full proportion of troops.
With a show of forced optimism, the Commissioners reminded
Connecticut that it was "no small smile of God upon us that the
enemy is now gathered together into such a place where the advantage to the English is doubtless as great as wee can possibly
expect." [52] The government of Connecticut answered this overture
with a carefully worded suggestion that it would be much wiser
to let the Connecticut forces remain in quarters at their own bases
until such time as they were actually needed for an expedition. Thus,
the extreme difficulties of trying to maintain them at Wickford in
a winter season would be avoided, and the troops themselves would
be better fitted to take the field when called upon. Added to this
argument was a pointed reminder that morale in the Connecticut
units was then at a low pitch. In short, the men were in no mood for
further wintertime adventures in the desolate Narragansett country.[53]

Major Treat went to Hartford to report on the current situation,
and then made a trip into the seaside counties to oversee the
raising of additional men and provisions. More wheat was ordered
to be collected and sent to New London, and efforts were made to
build up stocks of shoes and clothing. The Council at Hartford,
however, saw no grounds for encouraging the Commissioners in their
hope that Connecticut could provide all of the food needed by
Winslow's army. They informed Massachusetts that "it's possible
flesh, and som pease, may be had, but little wheat, or at least, little
bread; mills generally failing this winter season." [54] The mills were
frozen, thus effectively preventing the grinding of wheat into flour.

Many families were forced to eat samp, a sort of coarse hominy.

For some time now, the English had been aware that a renegade white man named Joshua Tefft was living with the Narragansetts, and supposedly serving as their adviser in the war. This man's background and the circumstances under which he became associated with the Indians are still very much of a mystery. Tefft seems to have been a former resident of Pettaquamscut, and we know that in his father's will, dated November 30, 1674, he was cut off with only a shilling, while his brother-in-law was bequeathed the father's house. The mystery is deepened by the strange words of Captain Oliver—"A sad wretch, he never heard a sermon but once these 14 years. His father, going to recall him lost his head and lies unburied." [55] These clues merely hint at what must have been a deep family tragedy.

On the 14th of January Tefft was captured near Providence while in the company of some enemy Indians who were stealing cattle. Taken into the town, he was subjected to close questioning, which produced some extremely interesting allegations. Tefft, who admitted having been with the Narragansetts in the fort at the time of the Great Swamp Fight, claimed that a number of Ninigret's men had been present and had fought against the English. Moreover, the Mohegans and Pequots who were with the Connecticut contingent had deliberately aimed high to avoid hitting their opponents. Commenting upon the present condition of the enemy, Tefft asserted that the Narragansetts were now about ten miles northwest of Smith's garrison, having begun to move toward Quabaug where Philip was staying. Although extremely short of powder, they expected to receive new supplies from the Wampanoag sachem. Pessacus was ready to make peace, Tefft said, but Canonchet and others were still in a defiant mood.[56]

Whether Tefft was actually as much of a traitor as he was thought to be may now be open to doubt. His argument that he had joined the Indians under duress may very well have been essentially correct. However, a number of his statements bear the mark of falsehood, and it is difficult to say how much of truth is to be found in his testimony. His allegations concerning the false behavior of the Mohegans and Pequots were quickly taken up by those who distrusted all Indians, but the story is unsupported by other evidence. From Providence Tefft was taken to Wickford under guard, where he was summarily tried by a military court, and convicted of treason. There, on the 18th of January, only four days after his arrest, Joshua Tefft was hanged and quartered.

By this time Winslow had received the first batch of new recruits from Massachusetts. Commanded by Captains Samuel Brocklebank, Joseph Sill, and Samuel Wadsworth, these men had arrived at Wickford from Dedham and Rehoboth about the 10th of January after a difficult march in extremely cold weather. Other Massachusetts troops were to follow. Connecticut, now convinced that her forces must join in the pursuit of the enemy, ordered Treat to make preparations for a speedy departure with his men, including a considerable number of new recruits. These troops, preceded by a vessel carrying supplies of food, reached Wickford probably on the evening of the 27th. With them was a strong force of Indian allies. Now Winslow's intercolonial army was once more united and, strengthened by new recruits, was ready to pursue the withdrawing enemy.[57]

*   *   *

The winter storms of December had piled the woods and trails high with drifted snow, and the bitter cold weather had continued to hold the land in its grip during the first part of January. Then came a remarkable alteration in the weather—a prolonged January thaw which melted the drifted snow. The half-frozen troops at Wickford must have blessed the change, but a minister of Boston remarked that even in the matter of weather God seemed to be working against the English, for now the Indians had an opportunity to move about and escape their pursuers.[58] Winslow was determined to prevent this if he could.

On the 27th of January a band of enemy Indians made an early-morning raid upon Pawtuxet. They nearly surprised the Carpenter garrison house there, but the men inside put up a spirited defense, and managed to save the building from destruction. The Indians, however, destroyed a number of other buildings in the vicinity, including four dwelling houses; and then made their escape, taking with them a large number of horses, oxen, and sheep. Captains Moseley and Sill arrived upon the scene within a few hours, but thought it unwise to attempt a chase.[59]

Soon after this, probably on January 28th, Winslow departed from

Wickford with his army to begin his long-delayed pursuit of the enemy. A small garrison force remained behind to protect Smith's property against Indian depredations. The army marched northward from Wickford, probably stopping en route to raid Pomham's village, and then took up temporary quarters at a ruined farm about five miles outside Providence. Why did Winslow's forces undergo the discomfort of an open bivouac in midwinter instead of enjoying the warmth of Providence houses? Contemporary accounts give us not even a hint for an answer, but one might venture to guess that the reason had some relationship to the old hostility which still existed between the Rhode Islanders and their overbearing Puritan neighbors. At this time, too, it became evident that all was not well with the army's morale, for a number of men from the Plymouth contingent deserted on the night of January 29th, and made their way to Taunton. When questioned later, these men displayed a bitterness which undoubtedly was shared by many other soldiers who had not gone so far as to leave their units. In all likelihood, the trouble centered around such matters as a strong distaste for further wintertime campaigning, shortage of food, and perhaps the fact that the army had not obtained good quarters in Providence. A clergyman who talked with some of the deserters remarked that "Pride and rebellion against authority . . . doth soe [far] rage in our Armye that the Authority of officers will not procure a silent March." [60] Significantly, this pursuit in which the army was now engaged became known in New England folk history as the "hungry march."

On the last day of January, Winslow's army resumed its march toward the Nipmuck country. Contemporary accounts of what happened during the next few days are unusually vague, but from them the careful reader can glean at least a general impression of Winslow's accomplishments. Moving in a generally northwesterly direction, the army conducted a vigorous pursuit, but never was able to catch up with the main body of the Narragansetts. Groups of the enemy were engaged on several occasions, but the overwhelming victory that Winslow desired was beyond the grasp of his forces. Altogether the army chased the Narragansetts some sixty or seventy miles, and killed or captured a considerable number of Indians, but never fought a decisive battle. In the meantime, the provisions which the men had taken with them were rapidly being consumed, until the army was forced to kill and eat some of its own horses. The frustrating elusiveness of the Indians and the army's acute shortage of food soon convinced Winslow that he must abandon his pursuit. Accordingly, he dismissed the Connecticut contingent with its Indian allies, and led the Plymouth and Massachusetts companies toward Boston, where he arrived on February 5th. For the most part, the army was now disbanded. Many people felt that another good opportunity to break the power of the enemy had been lost, but Winslow knew that he had done his best with what he had.[61]

So far as we can now tell, Philip himself was not present at the Great Swamp Fight and the events which immediately followed. Instead, he and a number of his supporters seem to have made their way to a place on the eastern side of the Hudson River some twenty or more miles above Albany. Probably Philip had the intention of persuading the Mohawks to join his uprising, but the plan went awry, and the New England Indians were chased out of the neighborhood by the Mohawks themselves. Increase Mather related a story to the effect that Philip while near Albany had deliberately slain a group of Mohawks, intending to place the blame on the English, and thus win the New York Indians to his cause. Unknown to Philip, however, one of the victims survived the massacre, and lived to bring a true report to his people, whereupon the Mohawks took the warpath against Philip's band. Although the story has not been completely confirmed, it is certainly not impossible.[62]

The disbanding of Winslow's army raised the question of what should be done about Wickford and the Narragansett country. There was some sentiment in Massachusetts for withdrawing all troops from this area, but Connecticut, prompted perhaps by her old claim to jurisdiction over the Narragansett country, favored retention of the garrison at Smith's trading post. She won her case with an agreement to furnish the necessary provisions for the men on duty there. After February, however, the Narragansett country was by-passed by the war for a number of months, and never again achieved the strategical importance which it had enjoyed when the Narragansetts were concentrated there in full strength. Ultimately the small garrison force at Wickford was withdrawn altogether, and soon enemy marauders applied their torches to Richard Smith's house, destroying Winslow's former headquarters.[63]

The aftermath of the Great Swamp Fight aggravated the long-standing hostility between Rhode Island and the other New England colonies. Some Rhode Islanders blamed the United Colonies for unnecessarily provoking the Narragansetts and then leaving the area exposed to their fury. In view of the fact that Coddington's government had signified its approval of the campaign against the Narragansetts by giving valuable aid to Winslow's army, the force of this argument is considerably diminished. Furthermore, although the government of Rhode Island claimed jurisdiction over the Narragansett country, it had made virtually no effort to provide military protection for the inhabitants there. Whether justified or not, the bitterness of the Rhode Islanders was reflected in the fact that Rhode Island cooperation with the United Colonies in the war effort noticeably decreased after January. On February 28th a prominent resident of Newport advised the defenders of Providence not to seek any aid or support from the other colonies, lest by so doing they permit an entering wedge to be driven into their own independence. In June the colony government ordered the commander of the garrison at Providence not to allow any further intrusion of outside military forces upon Rhode Island territory, even uninhabited territory. With a familiar gesture of injured pride, Rhode Island was again withdrawing into its own shell.[64]

In reviewing the events of the campaign against the Narragansetts, one gains the impression that all of the developments following the Great Swamp Fight of December 19th were simply anticlimax. Perhaps the men in the army at that time formed the same opinion. At least they must have been aware of the contrast between the ambitious and determined way in which the campaign was begun, and the weak and ineffective way in which it petered out. The long weeks of suffering which the troops experienced after the retreat from the Great Swamp ate deeply into the foundations of their morale, while the almost constant wrangling between Massachusetts and Connecticut only made matters worse. The "hungry march" was a fitting conclusion to a campaign which had been so adversely affected by failure of the lines of supply.

Despite all the frustration and disillusionment which grew in the wake of the Great Swamp Fight, it can not be denied that the English forces had dealt the enemy a very hard blow. As a result of this audacious venture the great Narragansett tribe had suffered heavy casualties, had been deprived of a great percentage of its food reserves, and had even been forced to evacuate its own territory. The Narragansetts were now much weaker than they would have been had they been left alone until spring, at which time they probably would have joined Philip's uprising anyway. What the English had attempted, in effect, was a preventive war. Some people then, and many people now, would argue that the blow was cruel and unjustified, but a large number of the settlers in those dangerous days believed that the peril and the provocation were sufficient warrant for what was done. One thing, at least, was certain—the Narragansetts, linked with the Wampanoags and the Nipmucks, were now open enemies, and would take the first good opportunity to vent their rage upon the English anywhere. The weeks and months ahead were sure to be loaded with peril.

CHAPTER VIII

The Problem of the "Friendly Indians"

ONE of the most difficult problems confronting the English concerned their relations with those Indian groups which professed to be loyal to their English neighbors, or at least neutral in the struggle. Obviously, it was of the utmost importance to preserve good relations with such Indians if at all possible, yet how far could they really be trusted? Philip would do everything in his power to entice the New England tribes into his uprising, and it seemed quite possible that under his persuasive urging even the most well-disposed Indians could not long resist the call of their savage kinsmen. The mounting score of Indian successes during the early months of the conflict made this prospect even more of a danger. As we have already seen, during the summer of 1675 the Nipmucks of central Massachusetts had thrown in their lot with Philip, while the Narragansetts began that shifting, temporizing policy which was to bring them into a state of full belligerency a few months later.

It was extremely fortunate for the colonies that the Mohegans and Pequots of eastern Connecticut and the Niantics of southern Rhode Island either committed themselves to the English cause, or at least showed definite signs of continuing loyalty. But even though these tribes were supporting the same side in the war, they were unable to forget the old rivalries which had been nurtured between them for so many years, a fact which often proved to be a considerable hindrance to the colonial war effort. Again and again one group or another sulked because of some fancied slight, often at a time when the colonies most needed their services. The jealous sachems let slip no opportunity to impugn the fidelity of their rivals.[1]

Certain men among the English, because of their place of residence and their connections, specialized in dealing with one or another of these tribes. The minister at Norwich, Mr. James Fitch, usually maintained a close liaison with Uncas and the Mohegans. Thomas Stanton and the Reverend James Noyes of Stonington performed a similar function with the Pequots and the Niantics, while Tobias Saunders of Westerly also had some influence with Ninigret.

An interesting bit of diplomacy which took place early in 1676 serves to illustrate the difficulty of smoothing out the old tribal hatreds in the interests of the common cause. Noyes had watched with growing concern the lingering animosity between the three loyal tribes, and finally decided to lend a hand in trying to dissolve these old hatreds which were so detrimental to the war effort. Accordingly, he suggested that Ninigret send a peace offering to the Pequots as a sign of his willingness to forget past wrongs. At first the Niantic sachem was cool to the proposal. Within a few days, however, he decided to follow the suggestion, but only on condition that Noyes and Stanton actually present the gift as though it came from them. Noyes no doubt was overjoyed at this first encouraging breach in the wall of tribal hatred, and soon organized a small party of English to carry Ninigret's gift to the Pequots. But the peacemakers had underestimated the pride of the Indians. The Pequot leader Mamaho completely rejected the offering, and when Noyes and his party took the gift to Robin Cassassinnamon, the other leader of the tribe, this sachem refused to come near them because they had first gone to Mamaho. The English, their spirits dampened by this cold reception, wasted several days in vain waiting, and then went home, still carrying Ninigret's peace offering.[2]

The triangular rivalry among the Pequots, Mohegans, and Niantics grew sharper in the spring of 1676, with the greater opportunities for plunder that were being presented to English and Indian soldiers alike. If the authorities seemed to give greater privileges of plunder to one tribe, the others were sure to resent it. Edward Palmes of New London, who was in the midst of the situation, strongly urged that a common policy be established for all friendly tribes, and remarked pessimistically that "the great Difficulty . . . is how to keepe freindship with all three; which I see noe possibility of. . . ."[3] Ninigret angrily complained that some Mohegans had wrongfully taken wampum from his wife and brother-in-law. Supporting Ninigret's complaint, Thomas Stanton denounced Uncas' "pride and arogansie and covetiousness," adding that "it will bee well if hee prove not as bad as Phillip to the English. . . ." [4] Meanwhile, Robin Cassassinnamon was loudly complaining that Ninigret owed him the sum of £40. On May 18th the Council of Connecticut, not knowing how to settle all these intertribal controversies without losing valuable Indian allies, advised the aggrieved parties to forget their differences for the present, and devote their energies to winning the war.[5]

Plymouth, and especially Massachusetts, faced a somewhat different problem. In those colonies there were various Indian groups living under direct English jurisdiction, including entire villages of Christian Indians who had their own churches and their own Christian leaders. Many of these Indians were located along the outer fringe of English settlement, and numbers of them were related by blood to the more hostile Indians of the interior. How far could these outwardly loyal natives be trusted? Was it safe to let them remain in their usual places of habitation? Was their Christianity stronger than their savage instincts and their kinship with the enemy? These questions were a matter of life and death for the English settlers as the flames of Indian warfare swept along the frontier.

English suspicion of even those Indians who had long been peaceful and friendly was greatly stimulated by the few examples of deliberate treachery which occurred early in the war. The unprovoked attack made by the supposedly neutral Nipmucks on Hutchinson and Wheeler near Brookfield on August 2nd was widely publicized, tending to undermine English confidence in all Indians. A few weeks later when the Springfield Indians, who had long been friendly toward their English neighbors, joined in the devastating assault against Springfield, public faith in converted natives was further jarred. In vain Daniel Gookin, a warm supporter of the Christian Indians, pointed out that the treacherous Indians of Springfield and Hatfield had never been Christians. The popular tide would not be stilled, and praying Indians were lumped together with all other natives as potential enemies. With unconcealed emotion Gookin later wrote that "the animosity and rage of the common people increased against them, that the very name of a praying Indian was spoken against, in so much, that some wise and principal men did advise some that were concerned with them, to forbear giving that epithet of praying." [6]

The question of policy toward the professedly friendly Indians became a matter of hot debate in Massachusetts. Some men held such strong opinions in the matter that two political factions began to be formed around the leaders who represented the opposing viewpoints. Gookin, Captain Daniel Henchman, and the Reverend John Eliot, the famous apostle to the Indians, were the champions of the minority faction which urged a moderate and lenient policy toward peaceful Indians, and even advocated a certain amount of leniency toward enemy captives. On one occasion Eliot sought mercy for an Indian prisoner whom he believed to be innocent of the atrocities charged against him. Governor Leverett firmly refused to save the Indian from death, and tried to convince the impassioned clergyman of the prisoner's guilt. "I told him," said Eliot, "that at the great day he should find that christ was of another mind, or words to that purpose, so I departed." [7] Eliot's cogent arguments against the practice of selling captive Indians into West Indian slavery fell on equally deaf ears.[8] Increasingly, as the war became more intense, moderates like Eliot, Gookin, and Henchman became targets for public abuse.

The anti-moderation party probably represented the opinion of a great majority of the Massachusetts population, but the beliefs of this group were never systematically recorded for posterity. These people seemed to express themselves most effectively in acts of violence, not in polemics. Without doubt the most dramatic and forceful of the Indian haters was Captain Samuel Moseley, a popular and successful officer in the army. When a small group of Indians living within the town of Marlborough came under some local suspicion because of recent atrocities in the neighborhood, Moseley decided to take matters into his own hands. On August 30, 1675, he and his company appeared on the scene, and subjected the Indians to a rough search and questioning. Then he took fifteen of the suspects, had them tied together by a rope around their necks, and marched them down to Boston for trial. Men like Eliot and Gookin, who were interested in protecting such Indians against unjust persecution, helped conduct their defense. The testimony clearly showed that all of the evidence presented against these Indians was unreliable. Nevertheless, public feeling was thoroughly aroused. The authorities, wishing to release some of the accused Indians who were manifestly innocent, did not dare to do so openly, but instead whisked them out of Boston secretly at night. Later a crowd collected, and marched to the house of Captain James Oliver, who was known to be an advocate of stern measures against Indians. Rapidly the leaders poured out their plan to the astonished officer. They wanted him to lead the mob to the prison, where they intended to drag out one or more of the accused Indians and lynch them. To his eternal credit, Oliver bluntly showed these men the door. Lacking a real leader, the lynch mob dispersed without carrying out its plan.[9] It is clear that the Marlborough case served to whip up the spirits of all who distrusted the loyal Indians, and who favored the use of harsh measures to keep them under control.

An even more serious case soon followed. A small group of Indians accompanied by a colonial officer happened to be passing through the town of Woburn just at the time when the local trainband was engaged in a drill. Suddenly one of the militiamen fired his gun and killed one of the Indians. The soldier was brought to trial on a charge of murder, but as Gookin says, the witnesses "were mealy-mouthed in giving evidence," and the defendant's assertion that the whole affair was an accident seemed convincing to the jury. If we may take Gookin's word for it, the judges were much impressed by the evidence against the soldier, and sent the jury out again and again, but were unable to obtain a verdict of guilty.[10] In the meantime the surviving Indians had resumed their residence at Wamesit on the Merrimack River. Soon a barn fire of mysterious origin was locally attributed to the Wamesit Indians, whereupon a gang of Chelmsford men set out to take the law into their own hands. Arriving at the Indian village, they called to the natives to come out from their wigwams. The Indians, not expecting any harm, stepped forth. There was a blast of gunfire, and an Indian boy dropped dead, while four or five others, including the boy's mother, were wounded. Shocked by this latest outbreak of unlawful violence, the authorities ordered the arrest of the two men who had done the actual shooting. Both were quickly brought to trial, and both were acquitted of killing the Indian boy, although the Court of Assistants did order them bound over for later trial on the lesser charge of wounding the other Indians. Afraid to live any longer in proximity to the English, the Indians of Wamesit sought safety in flight. Within a few weeks hunger had forced most of them back to their village, but in February they took to the woods again, and this time they remained away from civilization until the end of the war began to draw near.

Early in 1676 Captain Moseley found another chance to show his arrogant hatred of the loyal Indians. Sometime the previous fall the government had placed a group of Indians under the personal supervision and care of John Hoar at Concord. Hoar constructed a sort of workhouse for the Indians where they could earn their living by industry during the daytime. At night he locked them in for security's sake. Some of the local inhabitants resented the presence of these peaceful Indians in the town, and secretly sent for Moseley, whose reputation as an Indian hater was now well known. The captain and his soldiers arriving at Concord on a Sunday, they went to the meetinghouse, where they found the people at worship. After the meeting Moseley addressed the congregation, and accepted the opinions of a vocal minority as the real sentiments of the town. Accordingly he and his men, with a large mob trotting at their heels, marched to the Indian workhouse, and forced Hoar to let them inspect the frightened natives. Moseley had absolutely no warrant or commission to justify his actions; he was proceeding solely on his own initiative. Hoar, on the other hand, had been authorized by the government to protect the natives under his care. That night Moseley kept a guard at the workhouse, and the next day he dragged the Indians into the open, lined them up under guard, and marched them all down to Boston, where they were interned on Deer Island in the harbor.[11]

John Hoar's Indians were not the first of their race to be forcibly isolated on the bleak and wind-swept islands of Boston Harbor, nor were they the last. By early March, 1676, the population of Deer Island was about four hundred, mostly women and children. Confined to a relatively small and barren terrain, these poor unfortunates suffered greatly from lack of adequate clothing and shelter. Their food supply was at best precarious, and for the most part they lived on clams and other shellfish which they could find in the mud at low tide. Eliot and Gookin paid visits to the islands at intervals to comfort the miserable Indians, a kindly service which perhaps as much as any material aids helped to sustain their spirits.[12]

Cold and hunger were not the only perils feared by these Indians. Sometime in February the authorities learned of a vicious plot against the unarmed natives on Deer Island. Apparently about thirty or forty men from the vicinity of Lynn were planning to invade the island and slaughter the Indians there. The timely discovery and squelching of the plot served to focus the rage of the Indian haters against Gookin, Danforth, and other responsible men who were concerned about the plight of the Christian Indians. On the evening of February 28th Richard Scott, a former soldier, drank himself into a roaring rage, and loudly denounced Major Gookin for his friendliness to the Indians, whereupon Scott was arrested and held for trial.[13] The case caused no little stir in Boston, for just at this time a melodramatic plot against the lives of Gookin and Danforth was being talked of in whispers. Small slips of paper bearing the following message were being surreptitiously planted in strategic places, or handed to chosen men:

Reader thou art desired not to suppresse this paper, but to promote its designe, which is to certify (those traytors to their King and Countrey) Guggins and Danford, that some generous spiritts have vowed their destruction, as Christians we warne them to prepare for death, for though they will deservedly dye; yet we wish the health of their soules.

By the new Society
A. B. C. D.[14]

The very fact that these papers were being circulated seems to indicate that the real design of "the new Society" was more to scare Gookin and Danforth than actually to kill them. In April matters came to an exciting climax when Gookin, Eliot, Danforth, and several others, en route to the islands in a sailboat, were run down by another craft and nearly drowned. The authorities made some attempt to link the collision with the popular prejudice against these men, but the evidence in the case does not lend strong support to this view. The collision may well have been accidental.[15]

When, in the May election, Gookin lost his place as an Assistant, the Indian haters enjoyed a moment of triumph. However, by this time the authorities were coming to realize the folly of keeping the

Indians cooped up on the islands where they had little means of sustaining themselves. Accordingly, about the middle of May, Gookin was able to make arrangements for some of the Indians to be removed to Cambridge. Here they were allowed to set up their wigwams on a neck of land adjacent to the Charles River, where a nearby fortification promised them shelter in case of emergency.[16] Gookin and his wife, together with John Eliot, saw that proper food and medicine were procured for these innocent victims of the war, and tried to offset the hardships of the past year with kindness and understanding.

No discussion of the loyal Indians would be complete without mention of the services actually performed by them as soldiers in the war. The use of native troops, of course, raised certain issues and problems which had to be seriously considered by the colonial authorities. First of all, there was the danger of treachery. Indian troops had to be furnished with guns and ammunition in order to be effective against the enemy, which meant that they could take a favorable opportunity to attack the English if they were so inclined. This possibility had to be weighed against the certain advantages of using the skill and fighting strength of loyal Indian tribes. But aside from this, there was also the very practical question of how to recognize friendly Indians when they were encountered in the field. Tragic consequences might well be expected if these were mistaken for enemy warriors, or vice versa. To prevent such happenings, white men were frequently sent along with the Indian soldiers to guard them against attack by friendly forces.[17] At other times, special signs or signals were prearranged as a means of ready identification at a distance.

Indians, because of their forest training, were able to perform certain valuable functions which Englishmen could not do so well. They were especially useful as scouts, operating in the van or on the flanks of an English force in the woods, because of their knowledge of the terrain, their skill in tracking, and their unusual ability to march rapidly along the forest trails with a minimum of noise. Gookin liked to tell about an incident that occurred on one of the expeditions during the war. An English soldier in a mixed group of English and Indians was wearing a pair of shoes which uttered loud squeaks at every step. Finally a Mohegan chief in the party, afraid that the noise would be heard by enemy scouts, insisted that the soldier exchange his shoes for the chief's own moccasins. The Indian then slung the squeaky shoes on his back, and continued the march in his bare feet.[18]

Indian troops knew how to "live off the land" when necessary, thus requiring a minimum of civilized food which had to be carried along difficult lines of supply. They were used to a simple field ration of parched meal or "nokake" which could easily be carried in a small bag slung on the belt.[19] They were more at home in the forest than were the English soldiers, and knew how to shelter and clothe themselves with the materials available in the woods. In addition, faithful Indians were sometimes able to act as spies, mingling with the enemy Indians, and gaining valuable information about their strength, their weakness, their past losses, and their future plans.

Of all the New England colonies, Connecticut made the most extensive and most efficient use of loyal Indian troops. Contingents of Mohegans, Pequots, and other friendly Indians were almost invariably present with the Connecticut armies in the field. Massachusetts and Plymouth were more hesitant in this respect, especially during the fall and winter of 1675–1676, but later they too came to make increasingly effective use of Indian auxiliaries. Even Captain Moseley realized the value of native troops, and asked permission to obtain fifty or sixty trustworthy Indians to operate with his own men.[20] There seems to have been growing a new current of opinion which was beginning to undercut the strength of the Indian-hating faction in Massachusetts.

Gradually, through bitter experience, New England's military officials learned the lesson that English troops, unless accompanied by Indian scouts, must never be allowed to pursue enemy Indians in heavily wooded country. More than this, the use of native troops in battle was being recognized as a positive advantage. As one colonist frankly admitted, "Had it not pleased god to draw forth some other Indeans (such as were) former enemies to our now enemies: to aid the English to finde their enemies: and overtake them (when the English cannot) we might have bin driven to great straits, And had the Indeans bin all our enemies: and could have gotten powder: they might have forced us to Islands for safety. . . ." [21] It is indeed fortunate that the English colonies learned this lesson before the Indian wars became completely merged in the international struggle for control of the North American continent.

The unfair and cruel persecution of friendly Indians during King Philip's War, even allowing for the excitement and danger of the moment, can only be deplored. It is true that in some instances Indians who were supposed to be peaceful and friendly actually turned on the English and did great damage. Supposedly friendly Indians were also suspected of committing isolated acts of sabotage against persons or property. There is reason to believe, however, that some of this damage was actually done by enemy Indians as part of a deliberate attempt to poison the relations between peaceful Indian communities and their English neighbors.[22]

In view of the suffering imposed on the loyal Indians by the English, the fact that many of these Indians not only remained faithful to the colonial governments, but even retained their Christian faith, seems almost miraculous. Certainly it constitutes a tribute to the men like Eliot, Gookin, and Bourne, who had labored so earnestly to enlighten the Indians. Shallow conversions would not have stood up under the suffering of Deer Island. The evidence indicates that at least some of the seed planted by the missionaries had taken root in fertile ground, and would live to flourish in later, happier years.

CHAPTER IX

A Time of Troubles (February-May, 1676)

DURING the month of January, following the Great Swamp Fight, there seemed to be a lull in the war, for the only major activity which occurred was the futile northward pursuit of the beaten Narragansetts by Winslow's haggard army. Then when the army gave up the chase and disbanded early in February, for a few days virtually nothing happened, and the gods of war seemed to be pausing to catch their breath. During this interval all of New· England, like a great wounded beast, lay trembling in the snow, while the icy winds of winter sobbed over the land as though in mourning. Among the settlers the prevailing mood was one of apprehension. As the people went about their affairs, heavily muffled against the cold, they cast frequent nervous glances toward the surrounding forest, being careful not to get too far away from the fortified garrison houses which would be their refuge in case of attack. New England in those cold gray days of early February might be likened to a man who finds himself trapped in a locked and darkened room, realizing that he has just disturbed and infuriated a nest of hornets.

The Indians, meanwhile, were passing the winter in the wild reaches of the Nipmuck country and beyond the Connecticut River. Some of the river Indians were encamped in the neighborhood of Squakeag, while other groups were located near Mount Wachusett, some twelve miles west of Lancaster. Most of the Nipmucks were concentrated in the vicinity of Menameset on the Ware River, and the Narragansetts, greatly reduced in strength but still dangerous, were trekking northward into the same area. Thus the bulk of the enemy was located at various points in the region bounded by

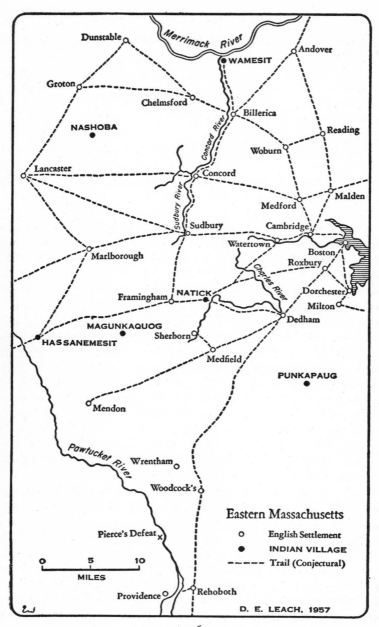

Eastern Massachusetts

○ English Settlement
● INDIAN VILLAGE
--------- Trail (Conjectural)

D. E. LEACH, 1957

156

Squakeag, Mount Wachusett, Quabaug, and the Connecticut River. This was the hornets' nest.

During the long weeks of midwinter, the Indians lived on whatever supplies of meat and corn they were able to accumulate. They had obtained some of their food from abandoned English settlements whose only function now was to be a gleaning ground for the savages. Huddled around their campfires, the warriors nursed their weapons, and laid their plans for the coming months when they hoped to drive the English out of the land.

As early as the 24th of January the English had received the first distinct hint of what was in store for them. Two Christian Indians, James Quannapohit and Job Kattenanit, had previously been sent into the Nipmuck country as spies, and now James, traveling hard on snowshoes, returned from his adventure bearing ominous news. He and Job had actually gone among the enemy Indians at Menameset under the pretext of being hostile to the English. One of the sachems had talked rather freely to these spies, boasting that within three weeks the Indians would attack the town of Lancaster. The bridge leading to the settlement was to be destroyed, so that the inhabitants would be unable to retreat and help would be unable to reach them. Following the destruction of Lancaster, there would be a series of attacks upon the exposed frontier towns of Groton, Marlborough, Sudbury, and Medfield. Despite this clear warning, however, the government of Massachusetts seems to have felt that the enemy's boasting did not call for any drastic countermeasures.[1] Some additional emphasis was given to James' testimony when, on the first of February, the enemy fell upon an isolated farm several miles from Sudbury, burning the farmhouse, and killing or carrying away the inhabitants. News of this event stimulated the authorities to order two mounted patrols to cover the frontier line from Groton down to Medfield.[2] Even yet, however, the government seems to have been unaware of the immediate danger.

Captain Daniel Gookin had already retired to bed in his Cambridge home on the evening of February 9th when there came a pounding at the door. It was the second Indian spy, Job Kattenanit, just arrived from the Nipmuck country with additional information. The news brought by this weary messenger was such as to bring Gookin bounding out of his warm bed. A party of the enemy, four hundred strong, was even now on its way to attack Lancaster, just as James had warned a fortnight earlier. The assault was due the next morning, and so whatever action should be taken must be started at once. After discussing the situation briefly with Thomas Danforth, his near neighbor and fellow magistrate, Gookin dispatched messengers to Concord, Marlborough, and Lancaster with orders for a hasty converging of troops upon the threatened town.[3] Had Gookin acted with less speed and determination, the ensuing event might have had a far different ending.

At daybreak of the 10th Captain Samuel Wadsworth, commander of a small military force which had been stationed at Marlborough when Winslow's army was demobilized, learned of the impending attack on Lancaster. Quickly assembling his men, Wadsworth led about forty of them northward to the scene of action. As he neared Lancaster, he knew that the enemy was there before him. The climbing columns of gray smoke, the hideous din of Indian yelling, and the sporadic crack of musket fire prepared him and his men for the scene ahead. Reaching the bridge leading across the Nashua River and into the main part of town, Wadsworth's company found it partially destroyed by the enemy, just as James Quannapohit had warned it would be. Nevertheless, the soldiers forced their way across the bridge and into the town.[4]

The arrival of Wadsworth helped turn the tide, and the Indians ultimately withdrew, but not until they had destroyed most of the deserted homes and outbuildings in the town. Fortunately, the inhabitants of Lancaster had taken shelter in six garrison houses, five of which had managed to hold out successfully against the enemy's onslaught. Only at one of the houses, that of the town's minister, Mr. Joseph Rowlandson, did the Indians have their way. As it happened, because Mr. Rowlandson had gone to Boston to plead with the Council for more adequate protection for his town, he escaped the disaster at his own home. Returning from his mission shortly after the attack, the horrified pastor found his home in ruins. Sadly the neighbors told him how his wife and children and other relatives had been seized and taken away by the enemy. "In such a Junction of Affairs a Man had need have a God to go to for Support, and an Interest in Christ to yield him Consolation," was the solemn comment of one contemporary writer.[5] Altogether about a dozen inhabitants had been killed at this one house, and perhaps twenty or more taken prisoner. Total casualties for the entire community were probably more than fifty. Six weeks later the town was abandoned.

After the attack on Lancaster, in all the frontier towns as well as many less exposed communities there was a renewed flurry of excitement and tension as the inhabitants sought to increase their meager security against the ruthless foe. People stayed closer to the designated garrison houses; guards were more alert. Some towns such as Wrentham and Medfield apprised the government of their weak condition, and begged for military aid or advice; others busied themselves about their fortifications in an attempt to strengthen the town defenses. Chelmsford reported hostile Indians in the vicinity, and told of travelers being waylaid on the road from Groton.[6] Five days after the attack on Lancaster the government of Massachusetts ordered Captain Moseley to Sudbury for the purpose of strengthening the endangered frontier area.[7] It began to look as though the outer ring of towns from Chelmsford and Groton down to Medfield and Wrentham might be like a giant string of firecrackers, with Lancaster being only the first to be lit by the enemy.

The next blow fell upon Medfield, a settlement less than twenty miles southwest of Boston. The inhabitants had gone to bed on the evening of February 20th feeling reasonably secure, for within the town there were now quartered about a hundred colony soldiers in addition to the local trainband of approximately the same number. These troops, except for a small force of some thirty men on duty at the principal fortification near the meetinghouse, were quartered at various houses throughout the town rather than at one place. Sometime before daybreak on the 21st, while the townspeople slept in their beds and the guard force doubtless grumbled about the length of the night, several hundred Indians crept silently into the town, and dispersed to various hiding places under fences and behind barns. If a dog sniffed the cold night air and growled at the coming of the intruders, no-one seemed to pay much attention.

The silent enemy, well-equipped with guns, ammunition, and combustible material, waited patiently in their various coverts until the first gray light of dawn began to steal across the fields. Then as sleepy farmers and soldiers stepped out of their doors they were met by deadly musket fire. At Goodman Dwight's house the Indians bounced missiles against the building, and when the wondering Dwight peered out to learn what was going on, they shot him through the shoulder. At another place Lieutenant Henry Adams, hearing the alarm, hastened out to do his duty, but as he stepped over the threshold he was struck in the neck by a bullet, and fell down dead. While the startled community was trying to organize its defenses and bring the scattered troops into some kind of order, the savages hastened to set fire to as many of the buildings as possible. Altogether some forty or fifty houses and barns were put to the torch. As one contemporary later remarked, "The sight of this poor people was very astonishing in the morning, fires being kindled round about them, the enemy numerous and shouting so as the earth seemd to tremble, and the cry of terrifyed persons very dreadful. . . . Few when they Lay downe thought of such a dolefull morning." [8]

Meanwhile, the soldiers stationed at the main fortification had fired cannon to warn Dedham, the nearest town toward Boston. The loud reports of this weapon, plus the awareness that there were an unexpectedly large number of soldiers in Medfield, seemed to persuade the savages that the time for retreat had come. Loaded with plunder, they withdrew across the Charles River by way of the bridge leading to Sherborn, and then set the bridge on fire to prevent pursuit. As a consequence, the English attempt to follow after them was completely foiled, and the exulting savages were able to stand on the far side of the stream, hurling taunts and insults at the settlers. Later, after the warriors had gone, someone found attached to the ruined bridge a note which read as follows:

Know by this paper, that the Indians that thou hast provoked to wrath and anger, will war this twenty one years if you will; there are many Indians yet, we come three hundred at this time. You must consider the Indians lost nothing but their life; you must lose your fair houses and cattle.[9]

Four nights after the burning of Medfield some marauding Indians fired a number of buildings at Weymouth, thereby carrying the offensive to the very coast of Massachusetts.

The latest depredations only served to emphasize once more that the war was entering a new and terrible phase. Men spoke solemnly of God's wrath, while at the same time public suspicion and hatred of all Indians, even those who professed to be loyal to the English, mounted to new heights. The General Court hastened to tighten up the regulations governing scouting and other defensive activity along the frontier, ordered that brush be cleared away along the roads, and offered a substantial reward for enemy Indians killed or captured by English scouts.[10] On February 23rd, while a solemn Day of Humiliation was being observed in the meetinghouse at Boston, the people were startled by an alarm caused by rumors that the Indians were less than ten miles away. Within the next few days the land along the southern shore of Boston Bay from Milton to Hingham was said to be infested with the enemy, and a small military force under Captains Wadsworth and John Jacob was ordered to the area. Plymouth Colony, fearing that the raiding parties would cross the line into its territory, ordered the establishment of a garrison at Scituate, directed that a group of local Indians be transferred to Clark's Island, and tightened the rules for watching and warding in the towns.[11]

Elsewhere, too, the English were hastening to improve their local defenses. The government of Connecticut ordered completion of fortifications in Hartford, New Haven, and other towns of the colony, the work to be done by all inhabitants capable of physical labor. The people of New Haven, assembled in town meeting, commandeered all available teams to haul wood for the local fortifications, and forbade the planting of corn within two rods of the stockade line.[12] Thus did the various settlements from Maine to Plymouth and from Hadley to New Haven look to their safety. By now all of New England was alive to the dreadful threat of a renewed Indian offensive.

*   *   *

Following the return and demobilization of Winslow's army at the end of the campaign against the Narragansetts, the Commissioners of the United Colonies had immediately started to lay plans for a new offensive operation. On February 8th they issued orders for the assembling of an intercolonial force of about six hundred mounted men, to rendezvous at Brookfield on the last day of the month. Command of the expedition was given to Major Thomas Savage, who had gained his experience during the fighting of the previous summer. Connecticut, which for some time now had been fretting over the lack of real offensive operations by the United Colonies, received the new orders with unconcealed enthusiasm, and proceeded at once to make the necessary arrangements. Massachusetts raised a contingent of about three hundred men, plus six friendly Indians to serve as guides and scouts. Among the latter were the two former spies, James Quannapohit and Job Kattenanit. Plymouth failed to contribute any men to the expedition.[13]

In connection with the new venture, the government of Massachusetts decided to make Marlborough the main supply base between Boston and the Connecticut Valley. The town was well situated for such a purpose, lying, as it did, about a third of the way from Boston to Springfield. Within a radius of twenty miles lay Groton, Lancaster, Medfield, Watertown, Sudbury, and Concord. On February 14th the authorities ordered that a supply of food, clothing, and ammunition be deposited at Marlborough, and later appointed James Braiden as commissary. Mr. Rowlandson was offered the post of chaplain to the expedition, but he felt unable to accept, probably because of his deep concern over the welfare of his missing wife and children. In his place was chosen the Reverend Samuel Nowell of Boston, who had served with the army in the Narragansett country at the time of the Great Swamp Fight.[14]

Job Kattenanit had secured from the government of the colony permission to proceed on his own to seek out his three children whom he had left in the Nipmuck country. Now, however, when Savage concurred in this decision and allowed the Indian scout to precede the army into the wilderness, a storm of protest blew up among the soldiers. Many of the troops had nothing but contempt and hatred for all Indians, and were ready to believe that Job's only intent was to betray the army, perhaps causing its annihilation. Captain Moseley, learning of Job's departure from Marlborough, became infuriated, and created a most unpleasant scene in the presence of the assembled troops at Savage's headquarters there, so that from the very beginning the expedition started out under a cloud of discord.[15] In view of all that had happened in the past half-year, one can understand the apprehension of Moseley and his faction, unjustified though it was. If nothing else, the episode is interesting as an indication of the sharp division which had come to exist among the English over the question of how far the Christian Indians ought to be trusted.

Major Savage led his force on to Brookfield, where they were joined by the Connecticut contingent of English and friendly Indians under Major Treat. According to one contemporary observer, Savage knew from information given by an escaped captive girl that the enemy was located in three villages beyond Brookfield.[16] This undoubtedly referred to the area of Menameset. Accordingly, the expedition now moved northward into the wilderness, but the Nipmucks, of course, knew that the English were coming, and fled before them. It must have been an agonizing experience for Mrs. Rowlandson and other English prisoners to know that their countrymen were approaching, and yet be forced to move with their captors farther and farther northward to avoid an encounter. Reaching the banks of the swollen Miller's River shortly after the Indians had crossed it on rafts, Savage's army decided to give up the chase. For one thing, their supplies were getting low, and then too, the deeper they went into the wilderness, the greater became the danger of defeat. So they marched down to Hadley, and found quarters in the river towns. Extant reports of the army's operations since leaving Brookfield suggest that the enterprise had been carried out with something less than ordinary skill.[17]

By this time Philip and his party, having been driven out of New York by the Mohawks, had returned to the upper Connecticut Valley. Now the warriors started down the river to launch an attack upon the settlers below. They chose as their victim the palisaded town of Northampton, striking their blow just about daybreak on March 14th. Fortunately for the English, two companies of Connecticut soldiers under Major Treat and a company of Massachusetts men under Captain William Turner were at that time stationed in the town, so that the warriors, having penetrated the fortifications in three places, were completely taken aback by the stout resistance which they encountered. The Indians were soon driven back into the forest with considerable loss to them, whereas the English suffered relatively light casualties. On this occasion, at least, the enemy had "found such warm Entertainment, that though they had kindled their Fire, they durst not stay to roast their Breakfast, but were forced to fly with great Confusion." [18] The retreating warriors did manage to take with them some captured horses and sheep, a welcome addition to their depleted stores.

The total absence of Indian records makes it impossible for the historian to describe the plans and movements of the Indians with anything approaching accuracy or thoroughness. One cannot even be sure that the Indians were consistently following any one master plan of strategy, and no-one has yet been able to say which sachem, if any, was acting as commander in chief. At best we can only cite the Indians who were known to be in positions of leadership. Among the Wampanoags, of course, Philip was supreme. Supporting him were his uncle and chief counselor, Unkompoin; his chief captain, Annawon; his brother-in-law, Tuspaquin; and the squaw sachems Awashonks and Weetamoo. The latter, incidentally, was now the wife of sachem Quinnapin of the Narragansett tribe. Other important leaders of the Narragansetts included the elder sachems Pomham and Pessacus, and the old squaw sachem Quaiapen. But undoubtedly the most vigorous leader of the Narragansetts at this time was the sturdy young warrior-sachem Canonchet, a man with a proud fighting heart, and a relentless foe of the English. Prominent among the Nipmuck war leaders were old Matoonas; Monoco, alias One-Eyed John; Shoshanim, alias Sagamore Sam; and Muttaump of Quabaug.[19]

The greatest military asset possessed by the Indians was their ability to move through the forest undetected. Utilizing this skill to the utmost, they were able to surprise the English again and again. Obviously it was impossible for the English to maintain adequate forces at every possible target along the far-flung frontier, and so they were constantly faced with the difficult choice of stationing garrison forces in the frontier towns and letting the Indians strike where they would, or going after the Indians in the field and leaving the exposed settlements open to attack. Almost never did the authorities know where the enemy would aim his next blow, and for a time the English seemed hopelessly bewildered by the widely scattered attacks. In all probability some of these attacks, in the form of nuisance raids, were made solely on the initiative of small groups of local Indians, without reference to any master plan. On the other hand, there is reason to believe that sometime in February the main body of the enemy divided into two or more groups, which then began to conduct separate and simultaneous raiding operations. One of these groups, probably composed mostly of Nipmucks, continued

its activities along the Massachusetts frontier east of Mount Wachusett. Another group or groups, probably consisting of Wampanoags
and Narragansetts, moved southeastward into Plymouth Colony and
Rhode Island. Other Indians continued to lurk in the Connecticut
Valley, giving rise to occasional alarms in that area during the month
of March. Finally, too, there may have been hostile Indians from
the north operating along the Merrimack frontier. Here suspicion
naturally fell upon the Indians of Wamesit who, fearing for their
safety under the English, had previously fled into the northern
wilderness.[20]

Early in March trouble developed at Groton. At first there were
one or two marauding episodes which cost the life of at least one
person. Then on March 13th the Indians, led by One-Eyed John,
launched a major attack on the town, during which they managed
to burn the meetinghouse and a large number of dwellings. Fortunately, most of the inhabited garrison houses successfully withstood
the assault, but soon afterward the people abandoned the settlement,
and took refuge at Concord.[21] This latest eruption of violence caused
the government of Massachusetts to divert some mounted troops
which had been scheduled to reinforce Savage's army in the Connecticut Valley, sending them instead to Groton and to Lancaster.
At the same time new orders were sent to Savage. If, after thorough
search, he should fail to locate the enemy in that area, he was to
bring his army back to the now threatened eastern part of the
colony.[22]

It was at this time also that the government of Massachusetts
was sponsoring the idea of building a line of fortifications, including
an eight-foot palisade, all the way from the head of navigation on
the Charles River to a point on the Concord River in the town of
Billerica, a distance of some twelve miles. According to the plan,
large ponds along the way would form natural barriers for much of
this distance. Unfortunately, such a wall would lie *behind* the towns
of Chelmsford, Groton, Lancaster, Concord, Sudbury, and Marlborough. Unfortunately, too, the project would be very expensive,
and even when completed would be no guarantee against the stealthy
and resourceful enemy. Apparently a number of towns in northern
Massachusetts conferred about this proposal, and were almost unani-

mous in their opposition to it.[23] That such an idea could be entertained even for a moment shows how confused and desperate the
English had become.

On March 18th and 19th signs of the enemy were discovered south
of the Merrimack River, bringing anguished cries for aid from
Chelmsford, Andover, and Haverhill. Major-General Denison, then
at Ipswich, hurriedly dispatched troops to the threatened area, but
the expected trouble failed to develop. Meanwhile, the enemy had
appeared in Plymouth Colony on March 12th, successfully attacking
William Clark's isolated garrison house at Eel River, less than three
miles south of the town of Plymouth. In this well-planned assault
Totoson and a handful of warriors killed eleven defenseless people.
Shortly afterward the flames of war again spread to the western shore
of Narragansett Bay, when most of the remaining houses in Warwick and Wickford were burned. The garrison house at Smith's had
previously been abandoned, so that by the end of March the whole
area south of the Pawtuxet River had been largely deserted by the
English.[24]

March 26th proved to be a day of multiple disaster for New England. It was a Sunday, and the people were rejoicing in the early
signs of the long-awaited springtime. At Longmeadow, just a short
distance below Springfield, a small party of settlers was riding up to
town to attend public worship, anticipating, no doubt, a pleasantly
long sermon and a chance to meet old friends. Suddenly they found
themselves beset by the savages, and although most of the group
managed to escape with their lives, a man and a girl were killed, and
two women, each with a small child, were seized and carried off.
Later the Indians, upon being overtaken by a rescue party, killed the
children and severely wounded the two mothers before fleeing.[25] On
the same afternoon another band of savages fell upon Marlborough
at a time when the people were attending worship in the meetinghouse. It is said that the approaching Indians were discovered by
the pastor who, because of the severe pain of a toothache, had left
the meeting for a moment and stepped to the door of the building.
The enemy's attack was effective, and this important town was partially destroyed. That night the daring Ephraim Curtis, at the head
of a special force of about forty men from Sudbury and Marlborough,
came upon the place where the attackers were encamped. In the

ensuing melee the Indians managed to make their escape after suffering an undetermined number of casualties. Most of the inhabitants
of Marlborough subsequently abandoned the settlement, but because
of its strategic location and its importance as a base the authorities
continued to maintain a garrison there. On the night of March 26th,
far to the westward, some Indians were amusing themselves by burning the deserted settlement of Simsbury in Connecticut.[26]

The greatest single disaster of that black day, however, occurred
on the banks of the Pawtucket River about five miles north of
Providence. Some days earlier a company of Plymouth Colony men,
many of them from the town of Scituate, together with some twenty
friendly Indians, all under the command of Captain Michael Pierce,
had taken the field in search of the enemy. On the night of March
25th they quartered in Rehoboth. The next morning Pierce, who now
had information that a band of Indians was located near the Pawtucket River, assembled his men for what he hoped would be a
highly successful mission. He added some Rehoboth men to his company to serve as guides, and took the additional precaution of sending
a messenger to Providence with a request for help. Then he started
northward along the eastern bank of the Pawtucket River with his
small force of about sixty-five English plus the Indian auxiliaries. The
messenger to Providence arrived there at the time of public worship,
and for some reason chose to wait until the service was over before
delivering Pierce's request. Once the situation became known, however, Captain Andrew Edmunds hurriedly set out with a party of
armed men to join Pierce, but by then it was too late. The ill-fated
Plymouth company had unwittingly engaged an extremely strong
force of Narragansetts, who were soon able to surround them. The
courageous Pierce hastily formed his men into a ring, and there they
fought, back to back, against overwhelming numbers. Their situation
was hopeless, and soon there was no sound in the forest except the
groans of the dying and the victory yells of the savages. Scarcely a
handful of English and Indian survivors staggered into Woodcock's
to announce the disaster. Within the next few days some forty-two
English bodies were buried at the scene by men who came from
Rehoboth, Medfield, and Dedham. It was obvious that the peril
which had struck down Hutchinson, Beers, and Lathrop was still very
much alive. "We see now plainly that it is one thing to drill a Com-

pany in a plain Champagne and another to drive an enemy through the desert woods," ruefully admitted one Massachusetts preacher.[27]

On the morning of March 28th the Indians fell upon Rehoboth itself. Since most of the inhabitants remained tightly buttoned up in a few garrison houses, the savages indulged in an orgy of destruction, burning deserted houses and mills, digging up hidden stores of food, and driving off cattle, sheep, and horses. They left the town a smoking wreck. On the following day, despite a personal appeal by the venerable Roger Williams, the Narragansetts struck at Providence, which at that time was held by less than thirty men. Many of the houses along the town street, including the dwelling of Williams himself, were burned in this attack.[28] The Puritan poet Benjamin Thompson could not resist the temptation to pen a grim jest about the burning of Providence, that notorious center of heresy:

> But of a solitary town I write,
> A place of darkness yet receiving light
> From pagan hands, a miscellanious nest
> Of errors Hectors, where they sought a rest
> Out of the reach of Lawes but not of God,
> Since they have felt the smart of common rod.[29]

Much to its credit the government of Massachusetts, learning of the disaster at Providence, immediately rescinded the years-old ban on Roger Williams, and granted him permission to seek refuge in one of the Bay towns. The old patriarch who had weathered so many storms in his lifetime did not take advantage of the offer. In the meantime the authorities at Newport, finding the war painfully close once more, took additional measures to ensure the safety of Aquidneck Island, which now contained almost all the people remaining in the colony. Among other things, they arranged for a boat patrol in the waters around the island, while to the small group of men who were still holding on at Providence they promised some help.[30]

Meanwhile, the successful Indian offensive had caused the government at Boston to advise the people in the weaker frontier settlements to abandon their homes and seek refuge in stronger towns. By the first week of April, Groton, Lancaster, Mendon, and Wrentham were depopulated, and Marlborough was nearly so. This meant that almost the entire outer ring of the frontier had crumbled. The official plan for the upper Connecticut Valley called for the people of Hatfield and Northampton to withdraw into Hadley, while the inhabitants of the small outpost settlement of Westfield were to move into partially ruined Springfield. Despite the danger of the hour, the plan was not well received by the people in those towns, who were being asked to abandon the farms and homes they had acquired with so much labor. To make matters worse, the official pressure for the abandonment of Westfield became an issue of inter-colonial politics between Massachusetts and Connecticut. Doubtless the real roots of the controversy run back into the old boundary disputes between the two colonies. Pastor Russell of Hadley warned the authorities at Boston that many in Westfield, if forced to re-move, would rather go down into Connecticut than over to Spring-field. Hartford, meanwhile, was advising the Westfield people to remain where they were. Within a few weeks, under the pressure of adverse criticism from Hartford and from the river towns them-selves, Massachusetts decided to let the matter drop, and so none of the Massachusetts settlements below Deerfield were abandoned during the war.[31]

In Plymouth Colony the exposed towns of Rehoboth, Taunton, and Bridgewater were given an opportunity to withdraw to more secure surroundings, but all stoutly declined the offer. Conversely, however, when the colony government tried to organize a military expedition to reinforce the frontier towns, many men from less ex-posed communities failed to respond to the call, and the whole at-tempt ended as a fiasco. "I am exceedingly afflicted to thinke," re-marked one concerned observer, "that wee should soe reele and stagger in our counsells as drunken men, and that soe pretious a people as Rehoboth should be soe forsaken by us for our owne selfish-interests."[32] It is clear that under the heavy blows of the past few weeks the public morale of Plymouth was beginning to crack.

In the meantime the Indians were continuing to harass the settlers at widely scattered points. Near Hadley three people were killed and one taken prisoner while attempting to carry on agricultural work. There were rumors of skulking Indians below Middletown, Connecti-cut. In Massachusetts and Plymouth the towns of Andover, Chelms-ford, Billerica, Braintree, Woburn, and Bridgewater were raided or otherwise molested. At their worst such depredations were tragic, at the very least, annoying; and no-one really knew how they could be prevented.[33]

Many people argued that the only effective answer to Indian power was a strong offensive in the heart of the enemy's territory, but the early spring offensive of the United Colonies had already become bogged down in a morass of intercolonial wrangling. A dispute over the size of colony contingents had occurred, whereupon Connecticut withdrew her troops, and Massachusetts turned with accusing eyes on Plymouth, which had failed to furnish a single man for the expedition. Early in April Major Savage, after leaving some men under Captain Turner to garrison the river towns, led the Massachusetts contingent back toward Boston. So ended another hopeful enterprise.[34]

By mid-April, then, the English were faced with a number of extremely difficult problems. The new Indian offensive which had started early in February was enjoying great success over a vast area, while leaving in its wake a growing accumulation of smoking ruins and mutilated bodies. At various points the line of English settlement had been pushed back toward the coast, and people in all but the largest and best-defended seaports were in a state of almost constant apprehension. The colonies were finding that they simply did not have enough men to guard all towns at once while still maintaining offensive operations. Furthermore, the planting season was upon them, and much labor was needed in the fields. If too many men were kept on military duty, famine might be the result. There were clear signs of a decline in public morale. The recent avalanche of defeats and disasters had led to much grumbling; many people were questioning the wisdom of their leaders. As one clergyman remarked in a sermon, "The minister the magistrate the souldier can do nothing but it is murmured at by some." [35]

Added to these troubles was the advent of epidemical disease throughout southern New England, which proved fatal to many people. The deaths of Major Simon Willard and Mr. Richard Russell, both of them prominent leaders in Massachusetts, were probably due to this epidemic. But New England's greatest single loss from sickness occurred on April 5th when Connecticut's eminent governor, the well-beloved John Winthrop, Jr., succumbed at Boston. He was succeeded as governor by William Leete. Winthrop's passing was a blow not only to his own colony, but also to the New England Confederation, whose affairs he was serving at the time of his death. A pioneer colonial scientist and a Fellow of the Royal Society, he was famous among his friends for his medical prescriptions, and only a few weeks before his own death he had sent a supply of "Rubila" back to Hartford to be used for the relief of the sick in that town. New England would miss his kindly ministrations as well as his firm leadership.[36]

*   *   *

All during the spring of 1676 Connecticut was conducting independent military operations of her own, mostly in the Narragansett country. From time to time during this period parties of Narragansetts made their way down into their home territory in search of hidden caches of food, and it was these Indians who became the objects of Connecticut's military efforts east of the Pawcatuck. Typically these expeditions included some English volunteers together with Indian auxiliaries from the Mohegan, Pequot, and Niantic tribes. That the expeditions were well manned, aggressive, and successful can be attributed largely to a decree by the Connecticut Council allotting proceeds from captives and other plunder to the volunteers themselves. On the other hand, certain difficulties also appeared. For one thing, it proved to be virtually impossible to keep all of the participating Indian groups satisfied, because of long-standing rivalries among them. In addition, the English who had volunteered for duty refused to obey any officers except those under whom they had enlisted, and there were quarrels between the pressed soldiers and the volunteers over the distribution of plunder. But despite these difficulties, the Connecticut expeditions performed about as effectively as any during the war.[37]

Early in April one of these expeditions, commanded by Captain George Denison of Stonington, surprised a party of the Indians who had recently participated in the massacre of Pierce's company and the burning of Rehoboth and Providence. In the midst of the excitement Denison's men spotted an enemy warrior dashing through the woods at full speed as he attempted to escape the trap. At once the soldiers gave chase, and they were spurred to even greater speed when they saw the flying quarry fling off first his blanket, then a fancy coat and a belt of wampum. Obviously this was an Indian of considerable importance—perhaps even the great Canonchet himself. He ran well until, dashing through a small stream, his foot slipped on a wet rock, and he stumbled in the water, wetting the pan of his gun. The accident seemed to take all of the heart out of him, for now he sloshed across the stream and staggered onto the opposite bank as though drained of all hope. A speedy Pequot made the capture. It was indeed Canonchet, one of the greatest prizes of the entire war. He had come down into the Narragansett country to obtain seed corn for the future sustenance of his people.

So manfully did the royal prisoner behave from the moment of his capture that the English could not help but be impressed, and their grudging admiration filters through contemporary accounts of the episode. Canonchet was led on to Stonington, where apparently he was offered his life on conditions which were totally unacceptable to him. His old enemies among the Connecticut Indians clamored for immediate execution, whereupon the English yielded to their urging. The actual killing was done at Stonington by the Indians themselves, thereby assuring the continued enmity of the Narragansetts toward those tribes. Canonchet's head was sent on to the Council at Hartford as evidence of the victory. Later in April another Connecticut expedition killed about twenty-five Indians and took fifty-one prisoners, all without the loss of a man.[38]

Despite occasional successes by the English, the enemy continued to strike effectively at various points along the frontier. Single violent deaths were recorded at Hingham and Weymouth, while at Marlborough the Indians managed to destroy most of the remaining houses. In Plymouth Colony, Scituate was attacked. A few days later some Indians fired upon a small party of the people who still lived at Woodcock's isolated plantation on the trail from Boston to Rehoboth. Two persons, including Woodcock's own son, were killed; Woodcock himself and another son were wounded.[39]

Again, out of a whole series of encounters one stands out as being of the first importance. Since the total evacuation of Groton and Lancaster, and the partial abandonment of Marlborough, the town of Sudbury, about seventeen miles west of Boston, had become one of the most exposed frontier outposts of English civilization. Here, despite the very real danger of attack, the English population continued to cling to its area of settlement, most of which lay on the eastern side of the Sudbury River. About the 19th of April the enemy Indians based in the neighborhood of Mount Wachusett consulted the spirit world through their *powaws*, and then went off in great strength, perhaps as many as five hundred of them, to attack Sudbury.[40] They seem to have invested the town on the evening of the 20th, commencing their attack early the next morning. The inhabitants were well sheltered and ably organized in their garrisons, and for a time the savages busied themselves setting fire to unoccupied buildings.

At Concord, a few miles downriver from Sudbury, the people soon learned of the assault. Thereupon a brave but foolhardy group of about a dozen armed men hastened toward the stricken town to give assistance. All the previous experience of the war should have prevented this futile foray by such a small number, but the Concord men defied the peril. Arriving at the river meadow in Sudbury, they were surprised by a strong party of the enemy, and were wiped out almost to a man. It is said that some were taken alive and held for later torture.

Another group of rescuers, meanwhile, had marched from Watertown.[41] These men reached Sudbury safely and, joining with some of the townsmen, managed to drive the savages back to the western side of the Sudbury River, thereby freeing the main part of the settlement from the enemy. While this was going on, still another force of soldiers led by Captain Samuel Wadsworth, accompanied by Captain Samuel Brocklebank of Rowley, hastened in from Marlborough on the other side of Sudbury. About a mile from the town this force of perhaps fifty or sixty men sighted a small party of the enemy, who at once began to retreat before them. The English, believing themselves strong enough to deal with the retreating Indians, followed closely for some distance, when suddenly they found themselves confronted by several hundred savages. Again an overaudacious spirit had led the English into a trap. As the howling warriors moved to surround them, Wadsworth's soldiers quickly fought their way to the top of a nearby hill which offered some possibility of defense. Here during the course of the afternoon the English, fighting desperately for their lives, held off the swarming enemy. The Watertown men, hearing the unmistakable sounds of battle coming from Green Hill, crossed the river to lend assistance, and quickly became involved in the struggle. But despite their best efforts, they were unable to join forces with Wadsworth's group, and eventually retreated to the Goodnow garrison.

Other groups also had become enmeshed in the wild battle for Sudbury. News of the attack had reached Charlestown about mid-day, causing the immediate dispatch of some troopers under Corporal Solomon Phipps, and a company of about forty Christian Indians under Captain Samuel Hunting. This latter group had originally been destined for patrol duty in the Chelmsford-Billerica area, but was now diverted to meet the emergency. Because Hunting's Indians were on foot, they were soon left behind by Phipps' troopers, and did not reach Sudbury until night. The troopers, on the other hand, arrived in plenty of time to join the fray. Earlier in the day Captain Edward Cowell with eighteen troopers en route from Brookfield to Boston had been attacked by the enemy about three miles from Sudbury. Four of Cowell's men were killed and one wounded in this attack. Nevertheless, Cowell's group remained operative, and may have been instrumental in helping Phipps and his men to extricate themselves from an enemy trap. Still another military group coming from Marlborough, this one under the command of Captain John Cutler of Charlestown, also had a narrow escape from the enemy.[42]

By late afternoon the confused and tragic battle was approaching its climax. At Green Hill the Indians set fire to the dry brush, thereby further confusing the defenders, who were now choked by the billowing smoke. Some of the terrified soldiers began trying to escape from their desperate situation, and this movement caused all the others to follow, with the result that a confused and disorganized retreat began. Hereupon the triumphant enemy "came on upon them like so many Tigers, and dulling their active Swords with excessive Numbers, obtained the Dishonour of a Victory." [43] The death toll of Wadsworth's company reached some thirty or more, including Brocklebank and Wadsworth himself. Thirteen or fourteen of Wadsworth's men managed to make their way to an abandoned but fortified mill. Here they were later found by a rescue party, and taken into the town. Following the slaughter at Green Hill, the enemy withdrew from Sudbury, leaving the stricken town to wait out the long dark night, and count its losses.

Early the next day the company of Christian Indians, stripped and

painted to resemble the enemy, crossed the Sudbury River to reconnoiter. They returned with the report that the enemy was nowhere to
be found, but that a large number of English bodies lay strewn over
the ground where they had fallen. Accordingly these Indians, together with a force of English soldiers, crossed over the river once
more to bury the dead. It was later said that the good service performed by the Christian Indians at Sudbury did much to soften the
blind prejudice of some settlers against them.

While the sad task of recovering the dead was under way on the
day after the battle, the Council at Boston was issuing orders for a
mounted reconnaissance of the frontier zone. One group of forty
troopers was to proceed to Dedham, Medfield, and then up to Sudbury, while another group of equal size was to go to Concord, Sudbury, and Medfield.[44] Lieutenant Richard Jacob, in charge of the
garrison force at Marlborough, knew where the Indians were on the
morning after Sudbury Fight. They were in Marlborough, whooping
to signify their triumph over the English, setting fire to deserted
houses, and driving off cattle. After passing through the town in this
fashion, they went on back to their lair at Wachusett where Mrs.
Rowlandson, still a captive, noted their return. Her impression was
that the homecoming warriors showed little of the jubilation that had
characterized their return from other victories.[45] Possibly their own
great losses were now weighing heavily upon them.

Jolted into action by the disaster at Sudbury, the government of
Massachusetts hastened to organize a new expedition to set out from
Concord on April 27th. Although Captain Gookin seems to have
had nominal oversight of the operation, actual command in the field
was in the hands of Captain Daniel Henchman. During the first week
of May, Henchman fell upon a group of Indians in the vicinity of
Hassanemesit, killing or capturing more than a dozen of them. This
little skirmish proved to be the high point of the operation, for
shortly afterward Henchman's troops, many of whom had become
sick, were released from service, and the expedition came to an end.[46]
Thus closed another episode in the long search for victory.

*   *   *

The war confronted the New England colonies with many difficult
problems which were more diplomatic than military in nature, and
of course these problems necessarily occupied a considerable portion

of the time and energy of the colonial authorities. One of the more difficult of these issues concerned the role to be played in King Philip's War by the royal province of New York and its powerful Mohawk tribe. Long-time enemies of the New England Algonkins, the Mohawks would be a powerful factor in assuring victory for the English if only their aggressive inclinations could be properly channeled. Obviously, little or nothing could be accomplished in this direction without the help of Governor Andros, whose own territorial ambitions have been previously noted. All during the war the United Colonies, especially Connecticut, were negotiating with Andros concerning the possible use of the Mohawks, but unfortunately all relations between New York and Connecticut at this time were colored by the bitterness of their boundary dispute.[47]

By springtime the pattern of Connecticut thought with respect to the Mohawks was becoming clear. She earnestly wanted them as allies, but she wanted them on her own terms, and without the interference of the Andros regime. To this end the authorities at Hartford tried to secure permission for their own agents to negotiate directly with the New York Indians. However, on this point Andros remained immovable. There is some evidence to indicate that the Mohawks did make one or two raids against the enemy in the upper Connecticut Valley during the spring of 1676, but this must have been done on their own initiative. Officially, New York never allowed itself to become an active participant in King Philip's War.[48]

An additional source of irritation between the United Colonies and New York was the question of whether or not the enemy Indians were obtaining powder from Albany merchants. The New Englanders were convinced that it was so, basing their opinion largely on evidence from enemy sources. Again and again enemy Indians testified that they had obtained their powder from Albany Dutchmen. Even allowing due weight to the argument that such testimony was given under duress, and that the witnesses themselves were highly unreliable, the evidence is far too plentiful to be completely discounted. There can be little doubt that some channel of illegal trade did lead eastward from Albany. However, Andros apparently was doing everything in his power to enforce the laws prohibiting the sale of munitions to enemy Indians, and he naturally tended to view the repeated complaints of the United Colonies as a slanderous aspersion against his regime. When the government of Massachusetts gave official backing to the charge against New York in December, 1675, Andros' wrath knew no bounds. In a blunt reply he cited the severe laws enforced by his government against the alleged traffic, and demanded that Massachusetts either name the guilty merchants, or punish the originators of these false rumors.[49]

Inevitably the quarrel reached the ears of the English government. Andros now suspected that the persistent charges being leveled against his colony were part of a malicious plot of the New Englanders to destroy his reputation, thus removing him as a threat to their own position. It is perhaps worthy of notice that certain Massachusetts gentlemen were casting hungry eyes on the land at Martha's Vineyard and Nantucket, then under New York jurisdiction. After the war in New England was over, Andros had an opportunity to defend himself before the Lords of Trade. The affair was subsequently argued before the King and the Privy Council, following which the King took the only logical course to end a bootless controversy. Asserting that he found no cause to believe the allegations against the Albany merchants, Charles forbade the authorities at Boston to continue their imputations unless they were prepared to take definite legal action against particular persons within one year. Thus, for all practical purposes, the subject was closed.[50]

Although Andros played politics with hardheaded realism, he showed a genuine concern not only for the people of New York, but for the distressed of other colonies as well. When the depredations of the Narragansetts turned the mainland people of Rhode Island into homeless refugees, the government of New York offered them a haven. In May, 1676, Andros actually dispatched several sloops to Newport, and they returned bearing a number of refugees, some of whom settled at New York, while many others joined a community of former Rhode Islanders at Musceta Cove (Glen Cove) on Long Island.[51] It is unfortunate that the more creditable aspects of Andros' policy during King Philip's War were sometimes overshadowed by his penchant for power politics.

Most difficult of all diplomatic negotiations during the war were those with the Indians themselves. We have already followed the futile attempts of the English to keep the Nipmucks and the Narragansetts out of the conflict. These frustrating experiences only served to confirm the settlers in their belief that Indians were shifty and untrustworthy. Nevertheless, a spark of hope that somehow peace could still be restored through negotiation remained alive. For a time the English toyed with the idea that peace might be procured through the good offices of Ninigret, the Niantic sachem, plus the Pequots and Mohegans, but nothing ever came of this. There is some evidence that by March, at least, considerable numbers of the enemy were sickening of the war, and would eagerly accept an easy way out if such could be made to appear. Despite all obstacles, negotiations between the two sides were actually begun in March, and continued for a number of weeks.[52]

Although peace was the long-range objective of the colonial negotiators, they had a more immediate goal as well—the recovery of English settlers held prisoner by the Indians. As we have seen, both the Indians and the English made a practice of taking prisoners in battle. The English did so for the price that Indian captives would bring in the slave markets of the Western World. The Indians, on the other hand, wanted victims upon whom they could later inflict the most horrible and revolting tortures, a practice not uncommon in Indian warfare. Fortunately, however, many of the English captives were spared, being allowed to accompany the tribe as it moved from place to place. There is reason to believe that as the impending failure of their own cause became evident to the Indian leaders, they saw in the English prisoners a possible means of buying concessions from the colonial governments.[53]

On March 28th the government of Connecticut opened a peace offensive in the upper Connecticut Valley by proposing to the enemy sachems a conference to discuss Indian grievances. At the same time, Connecticut suggested an exchange of prisoners, promising that as soon as the English captives reached Hadley, Indian prisoners would be set free. It is apparent that the English still had not grasped the real meaning of the war. They still thought of it in terms of possible grievances and wrongs done to various Indians, all of which presumably could be settled to satisfaction through negotiation. Instead, as we now realize, the war was actually a struggle for survival between two mutually antagonistic civilizations, and only a total victory of one side or the other would be likely to settle the matter. Nevertheless, toward the end of April Pessacus and other sachems then at

Squakeag sent a special emissary bearing their reply to the English. Encouraged by this evidence of the enemy's readiness to negotiate, the authorities at Hartford now bent every effort to the end of securing a formal conference with the sachems. They proposed that such a meeting be held at Hadley within eight days, and urged the people of that town to avoid action against the Indians while the matter of a treaty was under consideration. But beyond this point the records are bare. The peace conference never met.[54]

Meanwhile, Massachusetts had begun her own negotiations with the Indians clustered around Mount Wachusett. Early in April a Christian Indian named Nepanet, alias Tom Dublet, was sent to the sachems with a preliminary letter asking whether the English captives would be exchanged for Indian prisoners, or whether a ransom would be demanded. The answer, written by an Indian scribe at the dictation of the enemy leaders, was returned to the Council on April 12th. It assured the English that the captives were in good condition, and requested another communication on the matter. Accordingly, the authorities dispatched Tom Dublet and another Indian called Peter Conway with a second letter. Steps were also taken to strengthen the government's bargaining position, for on April 25th Daniel Gookin was ordered to make raids against enemy groups in an effort to take prisoners, who could be used for purposes of exchange. The sachems' answer to the second letter, brought to the Council on April 27th, included a demand for £20 ransom for the release of Mrs. Rowlandson. This message was considered unsatisfactory on the grounds that it was neither signed nor dated, and was actually no real answer to the Council's previous letter. Tom and Peter were sent out again in an effort to obtain a proper reply, this time accompanied by John Hoar of Concord. On May 2nd, after much haggling, Hoar was able to obtain the release of Mrs. Rowlandson. He took her back to Concord, and on Election Day, May 3rd, she arrived at Boston for a joyful reunion with her husband.[55]

The redemption of Pastor Rowlandson's wife was a signal victory for the English in the negotiations, but many other unfortunate persons remained in captivity, serving various Indian masters in a number of different places. On May 5th a new letter was written to the enemy sachems, and carried into the wilderness beyond Lancaster by a Boston man named Seth Perry and the faithful Tom Dublet. In this letter the government chided the Indians for trying to bargain about the captives on an individual basis. "Our minde is not to make bargaine with you for one and one, but for altogether. Unto this, which was our cheife buisnes, you send us no answer, which wee doe not take kindly, for this way spends much time." [56] The message went on to urge that the sachems come to meet with the English at Boston or Concord or Sudbury for the purpose of discussing peace. Just as happened in the Connecticut Valley, the proposed meeting was never held. Massachusetts concluded that the Indians were negotiating merely to gain time. [57]

Released or escaped captives, however, began to appear at various towns during the spring and summer. Shortly after Mrs. Rowlandson's return to civilization, her sister, Hannah Divoll, and a neighbor woman, Goodwife Kettle, were freed upon payment of ransom. Similarly, the Indians released John Morse of Groton. At Norwich, Connecticut, a group of surrendering Indians brought in with them two young lads belonging to Sudbury and Lancaster. By the middle of June it was estimated that over twenty of the English prisoners had been safely returned. Still they continued to straggle in. While the Reverend and Mrs. Rowlandson were traveling between Ipswich and Rowley they met the Reverend William Hubbard, who bore the glad news that their son, Joseph, had been brought in to civilization at Dover, New Hampshire. On the very next day their joy was doubled when they learned that their daughter, Mary, had appeared at Providence, Rhode Island. [58]

Many of those who emerged from captivity were greatly in need of immediate aid. In many cases their homes were destroyed, their families broken and scattered forever. They had shared the near starvation of the Indians, and were pitifully hungry and ill-clad. Mrs. Rowlandson during her captivity was sometimes so hungry that she could relish a meal of boiled horses' hoofs. Everywhere the released captives went they found sympathetic help. The Reverend Thomas Shepard of Charlestown entertained the Rowlandsons in his home for eleven weeks, treating them like his own kin. When the family was all together again, the South Church in Boston hired a house for them, where they lived for about nine months. Mrs. Rowlandson remarked that she "thought it somewhat strange to set up House-keeping with bare walls; but as Solomon sayes, *Mony answers all things;* and that we had through the benevolence of Christian-friends, some in this Town, and some in that, and others: And some from England, that in a little time we might look, and see the House furnished with love." [59] This is but one example of the way in which sympathetic neighbors and loving Christians tried to help the victims of King Philip's War piece together their broken lives.

How were the Indians faring in the meantime? To the keen observer the basic weaknesses of the enemy were now becoming apparent. Sharp divisions were coming to the fore, even among those Indians who were supposedly united in their opposition to the English. Earlier in the spring there seems to have been a dispute over basic strategy—the older and more prudent Indians favoring a program of numerous scattered raids on English dwellings, and the avoidance of battle with strong colonial forces, while the younger and more ardent warriors insisted on a program which included pitched battles with the English. Certainly the second policy was in effect at Sudbury. Later, dissension arose over the question of negotiating with the English. It is obvious that the willingness of the Indians to negotiate concerning prisoners and peace stemmed from a growing realization on the part of many of them that total victory was impossible. The most ardent foes of the English, including Philip himself, were opposed to the negotiations, but were overruled by the growing faction of moderates. In fact, with disillusionment about Philip's cause came growing opposition to Philip himself, and a tendency on the part of some Indians to blame him for all their troubles.[60]

Ever since winter the Indians had been extremely short of food, and their only real hope for a future supply lay in the prospect of successful fishing in May at the falls of the rivers, plus the possibility of raising some crops at remote places where English raiding parties would not be likely to venture. Therefore, toward the end of April, Indian military activity began to slacken as the tribes turned their attention to these important projects.[61]

CHAPTER X

The Spirit of Zion

UNDER the severe strains of wartime conditions, public morale in New England showed alarming signs of deterioration. If we were to plot the morale line on a graph, it would begin at an arbitrarily chosen point of normality, and would drop almost constantly for the first five months of the war. Then there would be perhaps a slight upswing during December when the armies were making their drive against the Narragansetts. This temporary improvement, however, would quickly reverse itself, and the downward trend would continue for another four months before showing any substantial signs of a change. The low state of civilian morale during the first ten or eleven months of the struggle can be directly attributed to the astounding successes of the enemy, together with the attendant suffering experienced by the colonists.

Conditions in the fortified garrison houses were difficult, to say the least. Imagine fifty or sixty men, women, and children living together in a house designed for ten or twelve. Not only the people themselves but also their most prized possessions, and probably some of their food supply as well, were squeezed into the garrison house to preserve them from the torches of the enemy. In the daytime the inhabitants might be so bold as to attempt some work outside the house, but at night they were crowded together inside, sleeping on straw or blankets strewn over the floor. The sleepers were frequently awakened by the crying of small children and the changing of the guards at shuttered windows and doors. The sudden sharp barking of a dog out in the darkness would startle everyone into scalp-prickled wakefulness. Were the bloodthirsty savages upon them? Thanks be to God, a false alarm, and so back once more to a troubled sleep. Under these conditions it is no wonder that tempers sometimes grew short, and the days and nights seemed interminably long.

In the army also, morale was the victim of Indian successes and tactics. The men were dismayed by the enemy's ability to strike without warning, and evade pursuit by hiding in snake-infested swamps. As ambush followed ambush, the English soldiers, with their heavy, cumbersome equipment, began to doubt their own ability to stand up to the Indians, man for man. Their earlier enthusiasm for going after the renegade redskins was now rapidly waning. The silent arrow, the sudden deadly volley from the brush, were playing havoc with the fighting spirit of men trained in the traditions of civilized warfare.

For long periods of time military units were kept on garrison duty in the frontier towns, a situation which further added to the problem of public morale. In theory all military matters on the local level were supposed to be under the control of the selectmen and militia officers of the town, who together constituted the town's own council of war. Now with colony troops brought into the local community, there was danger that the real control would fall into the hands of the "strangers." It must be remembered that in any well-laid plan for defending a typical frontier town, a few strong houses, strategically located, would be selected to serve as the nuclei of the town's defensive works, while many other homes would have to be written off as undefendable. Naturally, if such a bitter decision had to be made, the townsmen preferred to have it made by their own chosen representatives, not some outsider. On the other hand it seems likely that the colony soldiers, in turn, would feel some resentment at being placed under the command of men whose interests and vision were limited to the boundaries of their own towns. In this way mutual resentment grew.[1]

Many of the soldiers, bored and irritated by garrison duty on the frontier, did little to endear themselves to the townspeople. Doubtless they complained frequently about their quarters and food, blaming all of their woes upon the unhappy inhabitants. Some of the troops were indentured servants who were finding in garrison life an unaccustomed chance to swagger as they had never been able to do at home. Their roughness and arrogance must have contributed to the irritation felt by the local people.

In general the colony governments felt that the towns which were given the added protection of garrison soldiers ought to be willing to feed them. As the Council of Massachusetts remarked, "It is enough for the country to pay wages and find ammunition." [2] Yet oftentimes the towns resented the imposition of this additional burden at a time when they were having trouble feeding their own people. However, the authorities insisted on the point. In September, 1675, when Massachusetts was allotting garrison soldiers to the newly threatened towns of Dunstable, Groton, and Lancaster, the officers in charge of the operation were ordered to leave no soldiers in any town which refused to furnish their provisions.[3]

Before the depredations of the war became widespread, the towns made little attempt to conceal their resentment of the garrison forces quartered upon them, but this attitude tended to change in remarkable fashion as the enemy drew near. The burning of Springfield on October 5, 1675, did much to produce a new appreciation of the garrison forces in the towns of the upper Connecticut Valley. Whereas formerly the people had groaned whenever the numbers of troops in the towns were increased, now they hated to see the soldiers called out on an expedition, for fear the Indians would come in their absence. The townsmen of Northampton actually wrote to Boston, begging that a garrison of forty men be left in the town, and promising to feed them. Later the same town requested additional men, even offering to pay their wages.[4] The garrison soldier in King Philip's War—unwanted when the enemy was far away, grudgingly accepted as danger mounted, eagerly sought after when the warwhoops began to sound—would have read Kipling's *Tommy* with real appreciation.

The usual inactivity of garrison life gave the men an opportunity to brood over the distress of their families at home. Many a family was made desperate by the absence of its breadwinner, and beyond this there was always the possibility that the undefended family would become the victim of a sudden sharp Indian raid. The colonial governments were constantly bombarded with petitions requesting the release of some father, son, or indentured servant desperately needed by his family. More than one lonely soldier in some faraway outpost was brought to the verge of desertion by the knowledge of how much his loved ones were suffering at home. The growing prevalence of this situation naturally made those men who still remained at home ever more reluctant to go into the army.

Efforts to recruit additional men for military service encountered increasing resistance as the war dragged on. Towns which believed themselves to be in danger of attack tried to retain their own men for local defense, a tactic which became increasingly serious as the enemy expanded his operations. As early as September, 1675, Woburn requested blanket exemption from the draft.[5] Eastham, when presented with a new quota, judged that some mistake had been made, and resolved "to send our full Complement of men and no more." [6] A petition of February 26, 1675/6, informed Governor Leverett that the towns of Milton, Braintree, Weymouth, and Hingham were now infested with the enemy, and asked to be freed from the press. Weymouth even requested that its ten men then in garrison on the Connecticut River be allowed to come home to defend their own town.[7]

Cases of resistance to the draft occurred from the very beginning of the war, but not until morale began to tumble appreciably did the problem assume serious proportions. In September Secretary Rawson, in a letter to Major Pynchon, confided that enemy successes were having an adverse effect upon recruiting. "Some escape away from the press and others hide away after they are impressed," Rawson complained.[8] In one town a warrant of impressment came open, so that its contents became generally known. As a result, when the constable made his rounds he was unable to find any of the men wanted. Other cases simply confirm the situation.[9]

The appalling hardships of the winter campaign in the Narragansett country brought military morale to a new low, making even more difficult the raising of sorely needed reinforcements. Men sought to dodge the draft by "sculking from one Toune to Another," which caused the government of Massachusetts to announce that any town apprehending such fly-by-nights could apply them against its own quota. Some towns apparently placed a broad interpretation on this decree, for one Joshua Ray complained that he had been snapped up in the press while visiting another town on business. Similar complaints were heard from Connecticut, where inhabitants of some of the inland towns were drafted by the seaside towns when they arrived there to carry on necessary affairs.[10]

By February, coincidental with the start of the enemy's new offensive, the recruiting program of the United Colonies was entering its period of greatest difficulty. Increasingly the towns were falling far short of their quotas, and all too often the men actually sent were physically unfit for combat duty. April was the blackest month of all. People in eastern Massachusetts, Plymouth, and the Rhode Island mainland were in a state of near panic because of the successful Indian assaults on Providence, Rehoboth, Clark's garrison, and many other settlements. When five men were impressed in Boston, one of them said he was going home to get some clothes, but never came back. Of the others, three could not be found. John Pittam and Robert Miller, when ordered to report for military service, defiantly replied that they would be "hanged drawne and quartered rather than goe." [11] One man relied on his ingenuity rather than his feet in a bid to escape the draft, favoring the Council with this remarkable document:

The Petition of Nathaniell Byfield Humbly Sheweth that your Petitionour is a Stranger in the Country: and Lately married and is now Prest to goe out to Warr against the Indians: And where as the Law of God is plaine: in 24 Dewter: 5: That when a man hath taken a new wife he shall not goe out to warr neither shall he be charged with any business but he shall be free at home one yeare

Your Petitionour doth humbly request the favour of your Honours to grant him the Privilidge and benefit of the said Law: and to grant him a discharge from this present service. . . . [12]

There can be no doubt as to what the Bible says in the matter, and the archives have played a cruel trick in failing to reveal how the Puritan authorities dealt with this provocative petition.

Late in April the government of Plymouth Colony was forced to admit its inability to place any large body of soldiers in the field, and so could do little more than conduct scouting operations around the various settlements. Massachusetts soon yielded to the clamor of its own exposed frontier commmunities by ordering that all soldiers from Medfield, Sudbury, Concord, Chelmsford, Andover, Haverhill, and Exeter be released from the army to go home and defend those towns. The released men were granted immunity from further impressment so long as they remained active in local defense. To all appearances the whole war effort of the United Colonies was being undermined by men's reluctance to leave their own concerns and unite for offensive action against the savages.[13]

All during the war, increased enemy activity usually sent droves of frightened settlers straggling along the trails toward the safer towns. These unfortunate refugees often were not welcome in the places to which they fled. Generally speaking, New England towns were closed corporations which tended to view outsiders with suspicion. Under ordinary conditions, such strangers would not be allowed to remain long in town without an affirmative vote of the inhabitants assembled in town meeting. The war, of course, tended to break down the rigidity of these standards, but the influx of refugees was still viewed with a certain amount of apprehension by the local people. The reason for this apparently selfish attitude was that the arrival of considerable numbers of destitute strangers threatened to unsettle the closely knit moral and economic life of the town, creating a host of new problems for the already heavily burdened community.[14]

In Massachusetts the major responsibility for providing financial aid for needy refugees was assumed by the colony treasury, thereby relieving the towns of one great worry. Later the Council issued a special proclamation designed to assure a proper disciplinary control over the incomers. The selectmen of each town containing such people were ordered to make a special survey or census of refugees, in order that they might be known and closely observed. Moreover, the local officials were authorized to see that these refugees were kept busy at some suitable work for their own support, with particular attention being paid to young unmarried people who might otherwise get into trouble.[15]

The official attitude of the colonial governments toward the people who fled the frontier towns was conditioned by two opposite interests. Naturally, the authorities were concerned for the safety of individuals, but they were also concerned for the preservation of established townships and the maintenance of the frontier lines of defense. If the increasing tendency of the people in outlying districts to abandon their homes should become a stampede, there was real danger that the area of English settlement would be pushed back to the seacoast. When Massachusetts ordered the smaller frontier towns to evacuate all women and children not actually needed there, she also declared that persons who abandoned their homes without authorization were to lose their property and right in those places. In Plymouth Colony the government took a similar stand. Rhode Island, on the contrary, admitted her inability to protect the mainland people living at Providence and Warwick, and consequently urged them to take refuge on Aquidneck Island.[16]

Even before the Narragansetts were brought into open hostility in the fall of 1675, the people at Pettaquamscut, Wickford, and Warwick foresaw the danger that was facing them, and began to look for shelter in other places. "Many people in these partes are like soules distracted, running hither and thither for shelter, and no where at ease; whole families together not leaving there houses only, but goods and livelihood also," wrote Samuel Gorton.[17] Aquidneck Island, site of the towns of Portsmouth and Newport, became a secure refuge for hundreds of people from Plymouth Colony, Massachusetts, and the mainland of Rhode Island. By the spring of 1676 there was scarcely a house left standing along the western shores of Narragansett Bay from Pawtuxet to Point Judith. In the other colonies such towns as Simsbury, Northfield, Deerfield, Lancaster, Groton, and Middleborough were left to the enemy. Some of the Rhode Island refugees were scattered as far away as Nantucket, Long Island, and New York.[18]

The acute scarcity of food in some towns unfortunately led to profiteering. In Andover, people who had corn to sell insisted on cash in return, an impossible condition for many hungry purchasers at that time. John Kingsley of Rehoboth begged his friends in Connecticut to send some meal, "for if wee send . . . [to] road island there is won wolf in the way, and hee wil have money, which won of 40 hath not it to pay, tho thay starve; yea 1 sh for 1 bushel, caring and Bringing. There is unother, that is the miller, and hee takes an 8 part." [19]

The flail of war created a multitude of other human problems as well. What should be done with the aging widows of men killed in the country's service? Who would take care of the little girls and boys deprived of their parents by Indian tomahawks? For the most part such cases were quietly handled, often by relatives and friends, without recourse to the government. It was always possible to put homeless children, even as young as six years old, into articled service to learn a trade and earn their keep. The records of the county court at Northampton describe a case in which both the mother and the father of three small children had been slain by the Indians. The court appointed two uncles to take care of the children and look after the estate.[20] Tragedies such as this were a bitter everyday reality in King Philip's War.

In viewing the whole tragic picture of the suffering and distress caused by the conflict, we cannot fail to be impressed by the tremendous scope of the problem. A sizable proportion of New England's relatively small population had been demoralized and cut adrift in a world of confusion, danger, and want. There was no adequate organization ready and able to channel the efforts of all who wanted to help. The colonial governments were chiefly occupied with other affairs which seemed to be more important. Moreover, the colonies were far from wealthy, and the expense of military operations was a very heavy burden for the people, without adding to it the costs of relief for unfortunate victims of the conflict. For all of these reasons the relief afforded was, to say the least, inadequate. Administration of the relief program, if indeed there was any such effort worthy of the name, was haphazard. Private charity did its best to fill in the gaps left by official inadequacies.[21] The sacrificial giving of Christian people both here and abroad deserves all due honor, but these efforts were simply swamped by the tremendous size of the disaster. New England's inability to take care of herself adequately in such a crisis was a humbling experience, and a somber warning that the price of this land had not been fully paid by the labor and suffering of the first generation.

* * *

The public spirit of the New England colonies derived much of its strength from religious faith, and so it is relevant to inquire into the state of religion under the impact of Indian war. During the 1660's and 1670's Puritans on both sides of the Atlantic believed that sin was making dangerous advances in their own society. In England the Puritan clergy were shocked at the worldliness and frivolity which had returned with the Stuarts. Despite oppression they lifted their voices to denounce the current sins and call the people back to the godly ways of their fathers. Similarly in Puritan New England there was developing an earnest campaign against the supposed growth of immorality and religious indifference. In 1670 the government of Massachusetts conducted a special investigation to determine why God was afflicting the people with sickness, poor crops, and shipping losses. But despite the constant warnings of the clergy, New England continued to follow its wonted way of life until struck by the scourge of Indian war in 1675.[22]

Almost as soon as the first couriers arrived in the capital towns with news of the Wampanoag uprising, proclamations for special days of humiliation and prayer were hastily drafted and published. The Council of Plymouth Colony recommended that June 24th be set apart as a day "wherin to humble our soules before the Lord for all those sins whereby wee have provoked our good God soe sadly to interrupt our peace and comforts, and also humbly to seeke his face and favour in the gratious continuance of our peace and priveledges. . . ." [23] All of Massachusetts observed June 29th as a day of public humiliation, and invoked the blessing of God on the colony's troops in the field. Connecticut even established a regular rotating system of days for public humiliation, with each of the four counties taking its turn on successive Wednesdays.[24] Never since the days of the Founding Fathers had New England been in such mortal danger. With a dogged persistence the people again and again prostrated themselves before the Lord, begging for present salvation.

Special days of humiliation were not in themselves the answer to God's anger, although it was believed that the edge of His wrath might be somewhat dulled by a sufficiently intense volume of public prayer. The real answer, as every orthodox clergyman knew, was to launch a great movement of public and private reformation. First of all it was imperative to search out the sins or "provoking evils" which had kindled the anger of God. Once these had been recognized, steps could be taken to obliterate them. It is not easy for the modern generation to imagine such a public self-examination as the Puritan colonies imposed upon themselves during King Philip's War. In our day the emphasis is at the opposite extreme. Thinking of our wars as crusades for righteousness, we feed ourselves on lists of the enemy's sins rather than our own.

From the pulpit the Puritan divines repeatedly uttered damning indictments of their own civilization, listing and describing in great detail the various sins for which New England was now suffering.

Contentiousness, drunkenness, profanity, Sabbath breaking, love of the world and its treasures, disrespect for parents, formality in worship, inadequate financial support of clergymen, and personal vanity were included in the catalogue of evils. "A proud Fashion no sooner comes into the Country," complained one prominent minister, "but *the haughty Daughters of Zion* in this place are taking it up, and thereby the whole land is at last infected. What shall we say when men are seen in the Streets with monstrous and horrid *Perriwigs,* and Women with their *Borders and False Locks* and such like whorish Fashions, whereby the anger of the Lord is kindled against this sinfull Land!" [25]

Even poetry was summoned to aid the cause, and indeed, the cause of moral reformation came to dominate what little poetry was written. A few selections will serve to indicate the mood and manner of this reformation verse. Deacon Philip Walker of Rehoboth grimly dipped pen in ink to spur on the hunt for provoking evils:

> Lets search the Cort the Cuntry toun and Sitty
> the Tribe the house the person find tis pity
> to mis the knowledg of the thing or things
> for which gods angry and his Judgment brings. . . .[26]

At Boston in 1676 the press was turning out copies of a poem called *New-England's Crisis,* written by Benjamin Thompson. In the prologue Thompson suggests in some detail the kinds of sin which had brought the country to its present low condition after the virtuous days of the first generation.

> Deep-skirted doublets, *puritanick* capes
> Which now would render men like upright Apes,
> Was comlier wear our *wiser* Fathers thought
> Than the cast fashions from all *Europe* brought.
> Twas in those dayes an honest *Grace* would hold
> Till an hot puddin grew at heart a cold.
> And men had better stomachs to religion
> Than I to capon, turkey-cock or pigeon.
> When honest Sisters met to pray not prate
> About their own and not their neighbours state.
>
> .   .   .   .
>
> Twas ere the neighbouring *Virgin-land* had broke
> The Hogsheads of her worse than hellish smoak.

Twas ere the Islands sent their Presents in,
Which but to use was counted next to sin.
Twas ere a *Barge* had made so rich a fraight
As *Chocholatte*, dust-gold and bitts of eight.
Ere wines from *France* and *Moscovadoe* too
Without the which the drink will scarsly doe,
From western Isles, ere fruits and dilicacies,
Did rot maids teeth and spoil their hansome faces.

Nor were such sentiments limited to visionary stay-at-homes and professional prophets of doom. Late in December, 1675, Captain Wait Winthrop composed a poem which he called *Some Meditations.* After describing the agony of the Great Swamp Fight, and sending up a prayer to God for salvation, he says:

O *New-England,* I understand, with thee God is offended:
And therefore He doth humble thee, till thou thy ways hast mended.

Repent therefore, and do no more, advance thy self so High,
But humbled be, and thou shalt see these Indians soon will dy.

A Swarm of Flies, they may arise, a Nation to Annoy,
Yea Rats and Mice, or Swarms of Lice a Nation may destroy.

Do thou not boast, it is God's Host, and He before doth go,
To humble thee and make thee see, that He His Works will show.

And now I shall my Neighbours all give one word of Advice,
in Love and Care do you prepare for War, if you be wise.

Get Ammunition with Expedition your Selves for to defend,
And Pray to God that He His Rod will please for to suspend.

Thus in poetry and prose the people of New England speculated concerning the sins which had led them to the brink of disaster, and groped for a way to salvation. The idea that God might be angry because of previous mistreatment of the Indians apparently occurred to none of the sin searchers.

Interestingly enough, in Massachusetts there was a certain undercover tension between the orthodox clergy and the higher governmental officials over the question of how far the humiliation and reformation theme ought to be pressed. On this issue the Deputies in the General Court tended to uphold the opinions of the clergy, while the governor and the Assistants were inclined toward a more moderate position. Generally speaking, however, New England officialdom stood solidly behind the clergy in their program of reform.

Church and state promoted the reformation movement by a number of methods of which two have already been mentioned—the setting apart of special days for public humiliation, and constant exhortation from the pulpit for a return to righteousness. These methods were implemented by the full power of the law. Early in November, 1675, the General Court of Massachusetts made a thorough review of the provoking evils in the colony, listed them by name, and provided stringent remedies and penalties for each. Connecticut's assembly hesitated longer, but in May of 1676, following the military disasters of winter and early spring, it too passed a series of preventive laws.[27] No loophole where Satan might enter was left unguarded. Even military commanders sometimes found in their official orders a warning to prevent and punish irreverent language and other sins in the army. How well these measures worked, there is no way of telling. Court records show that the government was vigorous in its prosecutions, but it is perhaps significant that the complaints of the ministers concerning the prevalence of sin never abated as the months went by, and every disaster evoked new sermons on the continued existence of provoking evils.

There can be no doubt that the majority of the people heard of the crying need for reformation, understood its relationship to the war, and believed that God's future attitude toward New England would depend upon the completeness of the reform achieved. It was unthinkable to suppose that God would not relent when the sincerity of the people's repentance became evident. Therefore it would seem that the final triumph of the Christians over the Indians depended not so much upon military resources, although they were certainly important, as upon a great moral victory over sin. In this battle all of the people were engaged, and they could win it only by relentless opposition to sin. Thus was the difficult path to victory clearly marked. With such an outlook on the war, the people had a long-range basis for common optimism, unrelated to the vicissitudes of military affairs in the field. The call to reformation made a wonderful rallying cry, challenging civilians as well as soldiers to play a vital role in winning the war.

Indian victories did not really mean that God was fighting on the side of the Indians, the Puritans argued, for surely the brutal savages deserved even less of God than did the colonists. Indeed, many of the settlers were convinced that the Indians were actually tools of Satan, temporarily unleashed by God to punish His erring children, but nonetheless legitimate objects for all the hatred and destruction which the English could bring to bear upon them. This explains, in part at least, the fierce exultation displayed by colonial troops whenever they were able to overwhelm an enemy group, as in the Great Swamp Fight.

The Quaker movement had begun to make its first serious inroads upon New England about twenty years before the outbreak of King Philip's War. In Puritan Massachusetts the Quakers had been severely persecuted, but in Plymouth Colony the authorities tended to be somewhat more tolerant. After the outbreak of the war, the general search for provoking evils led many sincere people to question the lenient policy. They argued that only Puritan orthodoxy was pleasing to God, and that consequently any government which failed to enforce that one true way was remiss in its duty. The Quakers, on the other hand, took every opportunity to harp on the opposite theme, asserting that the war was God's way of punishing the colonies for their cruel treatment of the Quakers. In short, the country was damned if it did and damned if it didn't! The Reverend Thomas Walley of Barnstable, in speaking of the cause of God's wrath, said, "A Quaker told me it was for saying in my sermon they were blasphemers and idolators and for the persecution they have had from us but I judg we may as well feare its our suffering the publik exercise of their false worship. . . ." A short time later he wrote, "I am not for cruelty yet I judg there should at lest be a restraint of all publik false worship." [28] Many a puzzled Christian was forced to face up to this issue.

From Barbados the Quaker William Edmundson analyzed the calamities in New England, writing that "the Lord hath given them Blood to drink. . . . Thus Persecution makes men blind, that they run headlong to their own Destruction; but many of the People are dissatisfied, and believe, it is *the Killing and Persecuting of the* QUAKERS *that is the Cause of their distress.* . . ." [29] Peter Folger, who later became the grandfather of Benjamin Franklin, wrote a poem called *A Looking Glass for the Times* in which he declared:

If we then truly turn to God,
  he will remove his Ire,
And will forthwith take this his Rod
  And cast it into Fire.
Let us then search what is the Sin
  that God doth punish for;
And when found out cast it away,
  and ever it abhor.

Folger then went on to identify this provoking sin as religious persecution, predicting an early end to the war if the policy were abandoned by the Puritan colonies. The town of Sandwich on Cape Cod contained a number of Quakers. In March, 1676, one Edward Perry of Sandwich proclaimed that he had received a message from God, and with magnificent assurance demanded that this message be published by the governments of Plymouth and Massachusetts.[30] According to this latter-day prophet, the sufferings of New England were caused both by general sin and by the persecution of the Quakers. With regard to the first of these, Perry could have won the wholehearted approval of the orthodox ministers, and he was just as vigorous as they in listing and denouncing the sins of the people. But when he spoke of the persecution of Quakers, he was on dangerous ground. We can safely assume that Perry's grandiose manifesto was afforded a chilly reception by the governmental authorities, and of course was never published by them.

The early Quakers seemed to take grim satisfaction in shocking and infuriating the Puritans by daring acts of defiance. In wartime such flaunting in the face of authority is especially dangerous; nevertheless, the bold Quakers were still willing to take great chances in order to witness for their faith. On a July day in 1676, for example, the citizens of Boston were treated to the startling spectacle of a Quaker marching through the streets shouting "Repent!" [31] But the most intriguing Quaker demonstration that occurred during the war was organized on a much more elaborate scale. It was typical of the pranks that have often been attempted by underground movements in times of oppression. Out by the Boston gallows were the lonely graves of two Quakers who had been executed during the persecutions. Nearby was a military outpost where a guard of soldiers was stationed for the protection of the town. One dark night three men carrying some sort of heavy wooden frame slipped furtively up to the place of burial, listening all the while for sounds of alarm from the nearby outpost. Carefully they set their burden down upon the graves, and then quietly disappeared into the night. Early in the morning someone, probably one of the soldiers, noticed the strange wooden framework, and soon the news of its appearance was all over town.[32] Crowds flocked out to the gallows to see the mysterious handiwork, and to read the inscription found upon it:

> Although our Bodyes here
>   in silent Earth do lie,
> Yet are our Righteous Souls at Rest,
>   our Blood for Vengance cry.

Even though the authorities angrily ordered the framework to be knocked down, the lesson perhaps was not entirely lost upon the common people.

In peacetime the Quakers had been a threat to orthodoxy mainly because of their religious beliefs and practices; in wartime their pacifism constituted a further affront to authority. One reason why Rhode Island was so unprepared to defend itself in 1675 was that the strong Quaker element in the colony had previously managed to gain exemption from military service. A Quaker meeting held at Joshua Coggeshall's house on August 24, 1675, even as the Indian terror was spreading over New England, issued a manifesto condemning the use of weapons. Such sentiments were bitter gall to the settlers in neighboring colonies who were fighting for their lives. When William Edmundson visited Rhode Island toward the end of the war, he found the colony still sharply divided on the issue. Apparently the blanket exemption of conscientious objectors had become the refuge of any who, because of cowardice or self-interest, wanted to escape military service. Taking note of this situation, the General Assembly revoked the exemption on June 30, 1676.[33] In the other colonies, of course, the Quakers never received any special privileges, and were subject to all the laws concerning military training and impressment. Individual Quakers sought to uphold their principles as best they could in the face of overwhelming hostility. It is said that in some cases they refused to take any measures to protect themselves from the savages, even declining to leave their houses for the shelter of defended garrisons.[34] Thus throughout the war the attitudes and actions of the Quakers were a constant source of irritation to all who were faced with the terribly difficult problem of saving New England from the Indian terror.

*   *   *

Even as the morale of the colonies seemed to be reaching its lowest ebb in the spring of 1676, signs of a change in spirit were becoming evident. The new optimism appeared first in the Connecticut Valley, which had enjoyed a period of relative peace while the savages were concentrating on eastern Massachusetts and Plymouth. On April 29th the leading men of Hadley reported that "it is strange to see how much spirit (more than formerly) appears in our men to be out against the enemy. A great part of the inhabitants here would our committees of militia but permitt; would be going forth: They are daily moving for it and would fain have liberty to be going forth this night." [35] In May Massachusetts began strenuous preparations for a new offensive against the enemy, a further sign that the people had recovered some of their old confidence. Plymouth men also were beginning to spoil for a fight. Here and there the New Englanders were even getting a taste of victory, and it stirred their blood. Having learned the hard lessons of earlier defeats, the colonists now were developing new tactics suitable to the enemy's mode of warfare. The increasingly successful use of loyal Indians helped minimize the old fear of enemy ambuscades, giving to the English troops a new sense of buoyant confidence as they moved through the forest. In battle the soldiers had the encouragement of a new and more liberal policy with respect to plunder and captives. The colonial governments were now more inclined to grant such spoils of war to the men who, by forwardness and bravery, were able to seize them.[36] Captives, especially, were eagerly sought by the soldiers, for they could be sold into slavery at a good profit.

Meanwhile, the church-led movement for reconciliation with God was approaching a climax. The orthodox clergy of New England had come to feel that all of the repentance and reform which God demanded of His people could be drawn together in terms of a single definitive religious act. This act they called "renewal of covenant." Behind it lay the theory that the early settlers in the land had made

a solemn covenant with God when they carried the true religion to
its haven in the New World and established their churches here.
Subsequent generations had violated this sacred covenant by their
backsliding and apostasy. Now a successful movement of reformation
should be climaxed and sealed with formal renewal of covenant in
the various churches. This was the ultimate act of reformation demanded by God. As one pastor expressed it, "Wee intende (God
willing) . . . solemnlye to renew our Covenant in our church state
according to the example in Ezra's time. . . . this is a time wherin
the Providence of God does in a knocking and terrible maner call
for it." [37]

The extant records of the church at Plymouth together with a
letter from the pastor's own hand give an excellent picture of how
one church handled this solemn matter of renewing its covenant. At
a special meeting of the congregation on June 29, 1676, the church
covenant was read aloud, and then inquiry was made as to how it
had been violated. After a speech by the elder, the pastor read an
engagement for reformation, which was then adopted by the people.
At a subsequent meeting held on July 18th the congregation completed the solemn process. The pastor read a paper acknowledging
the various sins of the congregation and pledging future obedience
to the will of the Almighty. Thereupon the men and women of the
church indicated their consent by standing. Then a similar paper was
read to the children, and they likewise rose to their feet. Thus was
the new bargain with God signed and sealed in an atmosphere heavy
with the earnest solemnity of war-weary adults and wide-eyed children.[38]

Despite signs of improving morale and morality, however, New
England knew that the war was still far from over, and that the
weary search for peace and security must be continued unabated.
Shaken by the awareness of their own revealed weaknesses, yet feeling stronger by virtue of their increasing successes, the people looked
ahead to the warmer days of late spring and summer, with a hope
that God in His own good time would grant them the victory they
so much desired.

CHAPTER XI

The Waning of Indian Strength

ON the first of May the enemy Indians at Wachusett held a great dance in a specially built wigwam near the southern end of Wachusett Lake.[1] The participants were dressed in their most colorful and elaborate finery, and they danced their ceremonial dance as though the whole world were theirs. Perhaps, intoxicated by the excitement of group activity and the rhythm of the drum, they still thought so. But in truth the long shadows of defeat were already upon the great wigwam, and the time was coming when the fire of Indian strength would be reduced to embers. Then even those would be quenched by the power of a mightier civilization whose destiny was to conquer and rule the land which had once belonged to the red men.

By the first week of May, in fact, the tide of victory was slowly beginning to shift toward the English. Of course, an awful awareness of tragedy and danger still hung heavy on the hearts of many settlers, for their losses had been great, and the end was not yet in sight. Nevertheless, conditions were definitely improving. For a long time the Indians had been carrying on the war in spite of a rapidly accumulating series of handicaps whose combined weight was now starting to have a decisive effect in the struggle. Long periods of hunger, the ravages of disease, severe losses in battle, and divided counsels were draining the enemy's power with a slow but deliberate sureness which could not long remain hidden even from the war-weary English. From Maine to Connecticut small groups of disillusioned Indians were plodding in from the wilderness and giving themselves up to the colonists or their Indian allies. The English, by contrast, were beginning to feel the warmth of a reviving optimism based upon the growing superiority of their military forces operating in conjunction with friendly Indians. Obviously, the colonists had a depth of resources—human, material, financial— which would enable them to carry on the war almost indefinitely while the Indians continued to use up their very limited resources.

As we have seen, following the attack upon Sudbury on April 21st the Indians turned their attention to the pressing problem of food for the coming year, and large numbers of them moved toward the old favorite fishing places at the falls of the rivers. One of the most promising of these was located at Peskeompscut on the Connecticut River about five miles above Deerfield, a place not unfamiliar to the English of the river valley. Here the river was encased in banks of rough slabbing rock, while the normally smooth flow of the water was broken by a chain of rocks and rocky islets. Forced between the narrowing rocky banks and the small islands in the channel, the flowing water built up speed, and then plunged over a forty- or fifty-foot drop which set it tumbling and swirling as it resumed its way toward Deerfield and the sea. On the northern side of the river the terrain rose rather steeply to wooded ridges, except where the high land parted to admit the shallow Fall River, which entered the Connecticut just below the drop.

Various groups of hungry Indians now established their camps along both banks of the river at Peskeompscut and on an island some distance below the falls. Having erected their wigwams, they busied themselves about the matter of food. Some of them turned to fishing, and soon there was a growing hoard of good fish to be cured. Others made their way down the river to the site of Deerfield, where they took over the abandoned fields, planting them with carefully accumulated seed in hope of a crop. They also took the opportunity to visit the river towns below for the purpose of stealing English cattle. On the night of May 13th they raided the Hatfield herd, making off with a large number of cows, which they drove along the trail ahead of them to Deerfield. The local inhabitants, already chafing under the confinement and boredom of garrison life, were vastly irritated by these sneaking forays, and longed for a good opportunity to strike back at their tormentors.

On Monday, May 15th, as the sun was coming up, the watch at Hatfield spied a lone figure emerging from the woods. It proved to be Thomas Reed, a soldier who had been captured by the enemy near Hadley on the 1st of April, only to escape from his captors at Peskeompscut. Reed had much to tell. He spoke of the large numbers of the enemy congregated at the falls, and assured his eager listeners that these Indians would be easy prey. Their actual strength in warriors probably was not great, yet they felt so secure at their fishing place that they were not taking even the normal precautions against surprise. Captain William Turner, who at this time was in command of the garrison troops in the river towns, heard this news with the greatest interest, for it seemed to place in his hands a golden opportunity to strike a stunning blow.[2]

The chance was there, but there were difficulties to be overcome. In the river towns there was no organized military force ready to take the field. The garrison troops alone were not capable of such an enterprise. So the matter was placed before the male inhabitants of the three towns, and word of the opportunity was sent down to Hartford in the hope that reinforcements might be sent from there. Many of the able-bodied men of Hatfield, Northampton, and Hadley declared themselves ready to march against the Indians who had caused them so much woe, especially since Reed had given them to understand that a large number of the natives at Peskeompscut were women, children, and old men. When it became clear that the hoped-for reinforcements from Connecticut were not coming immediately, Turner and the other men decided to proceed with whatever strength they themselves could muster, rather than delay the project, and perhaps lose the opportunity which beckoned so enticingly.

Turner at this time was weak from sickness, but he felt the call of duty, and placed himself at the head of the expedition. On the 18th of May upward of 150 men and boys—some of them garrison soldiers, the remainder local inhabitants from as far south as Springfield—gathered in Hatfield with their knapsacks and muskets. Most of them, perhaps all of them, were mounted on horseback, knowing that a horse's speed might mean the difference between life and death. The whole venture was a huge gamble, for the company was far too small and inexperienced to engage a major force of the enemy, and if any whisper of their coming should go ahead of them the savages would surely gather their strength and prepare a deadly trap. Afterthoughts of this nature may well have caused more than one of the volunteers to regret his rashness at the last moment, but with all the villagers assembled to see them off who would confess himself a coward by dropping out of ranks?

Probably it was after supper when Turner and his men rode out of Hatfield, and took the well-known trail leading up to Deerfield. They proceeded through the fields and woods as quietly as possible, hoping that no enemy scouts were in the vicinity. A few miles above Hatfield they passed by Hopewell Swamp below Sugarloaf Hill, and crossed Bloody Brook—places fraught with evil memories. In darkness they rode silently through the ghost town of Deerfield, whose once busy homes were now gutted and black. They forded the Deerfield River, and swung around to the northeastward, tensing now with the strange queasiness that creeps upon men as they approach the time of battle.

Reaching a suitable place about half a mile from the falls, Turner gave the word to dismount. The company tethered their horses to young trees and, leaving a few men behind as guards, moved ahead on foot. Like silent wraiths they stole along the northern side of the great river, thankful that the crackling of branches underfoot and the occasional clank of weapons were swallowed up in the roar of the water as it hurled itself over the rocky drop. Dawn was rapidly approaching as they waded across the shallow Fall River, and moved in among the silent wigwams of the first Indian camp. Miraculously, there were no sentries to challenge them. The Indians, having feasted the previous evening on roast beef and milk from the stolen English cattle, and knowing that no field army was in the upper valley to disturb them, were all asleep.

Scattering through the camp, the attackers aimed their muskets directly into the wigwams, and opened fire upon the huddled figures inside. Instantly, with the first crashing shots, there began a scene of wildest confusion. Wounded Indians writhed and screamed in the wigwams, while others leaped to their feet and dashed for the riverbank. There were startled cries of "Mohawks! Mohawks!" until the savages saw their assailants, and knew that it was the English who were upon them.

Turner's highly excited men were ruthless in their murderous attack. They shot the fleeing Indians down like wild game. Many of the savages sought escape in the river by leaping into canoes or hurling themselves into the rushing stream, but the English followed them to the riverbank, and poured their shot into the panic-stricken enemy. Canoes upset, throwing their occupants into the turbulent water. The river swept on, carrying dozens of struggling swimmers over the falls. Like ferrets the English scoured through the camp and along the riverbank, flushing terror-stricken Indians out of their hiding places, and dispatching them with sword or gun. Women and children were considered fair prey along with the men, and there was no thought of quarter. Some of the soldiers found two forges which the Indians had set up for the repairing of guns. These the English destroyed, along with quantities of ammunition and provisions. Among the plunder thrown into the river were two great pigs of lead.

If all was confusion and slaughter at the falls, it was not so in the other nearby camps, and strong groups of warriors were already beginning to form and move toward the scene of action. One party crossed to the northern shore from the island below the falls, thereby placing itself between the English and Deerfield. Apparently Turner had neglected to take precautions against such a move. Reveling in destruction, the soldiers had remained at the falls far too long, and it was almost as an afterthought that they now turned their attention to the problem of withdrawal. The word spread quickly among the men, and soon they were all hurrying back toward the place where they had left their horses.

By all standards the attack had been a smashing victory. There was reason to believe that well over a hundred Indians, perhaps several hundred, had met their destruction during the assault, while the English had had only one man killed and a very few wounded. But now was no time for rejoicing. The retreating soldiers were becoming aware that other Indians were closing in upon them, and the rumor spread that Philip and a thousand of his warriors were drawing near. One band of Indians reached the tethered horses before the English got there, but a group of twenty soldiers arrived in time to recover at least some of the mounts. By now the retreat was taking on the characteristics of a disorganized rout. Panic-stricken groups of soldiers, some mounted and some scurrying along on foot, plunged through the woods toward Deerfield, while the enemy circled along the flank, inflicting casualties at every opportunity. Turner himself was shot as he attempted to get across the Green River, and there he was left to die.[3] Samuel Holyoke of Springfield, Turner's second-in-command, performed valiantly in attempting to direct the retreat, and by his courageous leadership did much to prevent a massacre.

The horrible experience of the rout brought out the best in some men, and the worst in others. There was the case of John Belcher who, straggling along on foot, was permitted by Isaac Harrison to climb up behind him on his horse. After they had ridden together some distance Harrison, who was wounded, fell part way off and let himself slip to the ground, saying that he would like to rest there for a little while. Upon hearing this, Belcher whipped up the horse, and rode away to save his own skin, heedless of Harrison's pleading cries. Some of the retreating soldiers became separated from their comrades, and, losing the way, stumbled through the woods alone, perhaps to fall prey to the pursuing savages or starvation. Sixteen-year-old Jonathan Wells survived such an experience. Although wounded in the leg, he wandered along by himself for two days, and on one occasion saved himself from prowling Indians only by hiding under a pile of brush. He eventually found his way back to Hatfield.[4]

Not until the retreating company had passed through Deerfield were they completely free of the Indians. Exhausted, they reached Hatfield later that day. A few lone survivors straggled in during the next three days. All told, at least forty men, or about one-quarter of those participating, had met death on this venture. But although the English had lost heavily, the Indians had suffered far greater casualties, and there can be no doubt that Turner's attack was a severe blow to the enemy's strength.

The news of the action caused the government of Connecticut to send a company of eighty men under Captain Benjamin Newbury to strengthen the towns in the upper valley. Newbury left three of his men to reinforce Westfield, and then proceeded to Northampton with the remainder. This additional strength more than made up for the losses of May 19th.[5]

Several days after the battle, scouts reported that the enemy appeared to be still encamped at the same places near the falls. On May 30th the Indians returned to Hatfield in force, and proceeded to fire some outlying buildings while rounding up more cattle and sheep for their roasting-fires. Learning of the attack, Newbury's company started to the relief of Hatfield by crossing the river to Hadley, thus avoiding a possible ambush between Northampton and Hatfield. They next tried to recross the river to gain their objective, but a thick concentration of Indians on the Hatfield shore thwarted the attempt. Fortunately, however, a daring group of twenty-five men from Hadley had earlier made a crossing despite enemy opposition, and the vigorous attack of this group helped convince the savages that it was time to depart.[6]

Meanwhile, the government of Massachusetts had been formulating plans for a new intercolonial expedition. The Massachusetts contingent, five hundred strong, was to begin by raiding the enemy's headquarters at Mount Wachusett, and then proceed to Hadley for a rendezvous with the Connecticut forces. Together, the troops of the two colonies would seek out the enemy in the upper Connecticut Valley, while the independent forces of Plymouth Colony maintained a close watch along the approaches to Philip's home territory.[7] The date proposed for the beginning of the operation was June 1st.

In accordance with this plan the Connecticut contingent, consisting of some 440 English and Indians under Major Talcott, departed from Norwich about the 2nd of June. They marched north to Wabaquasset, where they found an Indian fort and some growing corn, but no Indians. Later, however, they encountered a large group of the enemy, and managed to kill or capture fifty-two of them. After this easy victory, Talcott proceeded to Quabaug, only to learn that the Massachusetts troops, under the command of Major Daniel Henchman, had not yet made their appearance. Irked by Henchman's tardiness, Talcott immediately wrote him a letter urging him to hurry along. For added effect, the tactless Talcott sent this billet-doux unsealed, so that its contents would become known in every way town from Quabaug eastward, and the Massachusetts forces would be speeded on "by the cry of the people where it should come. . . ."[8] Then the Connecticut troops marched on to Hadley, where they arrived on June 8th. Newbury's company was now brought under Talcott's command, giving him a force of well over five hundred men.

During this interval of time Henchman had not been completely idle. Using Concord as a base, he had led his troops westward toward Mount Wachusett, and, thanks to the tracking ability of Tom Dublet, had found a party of Indians fishing at Washaccum Pond, some five miles from the ruins of Lancaster. In short order the soldiers killed seven of the enemy, captured twenty-nine, and rescued a captive English boy. After this exploit Henchman found it necessary to march to Marlborough, where additional ammunition could be obtained. He was still there on June 11th.[9]

Talcott, waiting impatiently on the Connecticut River, knew that Henchman was coming, but failed to appreciate the delay. On June 12th a large number of enemy Indians assaulted the town of Hadley, which gave the Connecticut men a chance to work off their pent-up energy. They and the townsmen beat off the savages rather readily.[10] Later there was a report that while the Indians were engaged in attacking Hadley, a band of Mohawks had fallen upon their camp and killed many of their women and children. If true, this was another serious blow to the enemy.

Within two or three days after the attack on Hadley the Massachusetts contingent arrived, and on June 16th the combined forces headed upriver to seek the Indians. Their advance covered both sides of the river, Henchman moving along the eastern shore, while Talcott proceeded along the opposite bank. Almost from the beginning the operation was hampered by foul weather which dampened not only the spirits of the men, but their provisions and ammunition as well. Nevertheless, the cold and miserable soldiers continued on up to the falls, sending scouts as far north as Squakeag, but discovered none of the enemy. Apparently they had left for other regions. Thoroughly soaked by the persistent northeast storm, the army headed back down the river, all the while speculating on the enemy's whereabouts, and grumbling at the discomforts which they seemed to have suffered for nothing. As one officer later remarked, "Exsperienc teacheth that if the enimy bee ether alaramed or have intelligenc, great bodyes must be content with littell suckses." [11]

Since there was no immediate prospect of action in the upper valley, Talcott now led his troops back to Hartford. At the time of his departure it was believed that he would return after a brief period of rest and recruitment, but such was not to be. The Connecticut Council advised Henchman not to wait for Talcott's return, and urged him to proceed against the Indians in the Nipmuck country. Henchman himself realized that there was more to be accomplished elsewhere. Leaving the river towns in the care of the usual garrison forces, he led the Massachusetts troops back along the trail leading to Marlborough. At Quinsigamond Henchman left a strong detachment with orders to investigate the vicinity of Mount Wachusett and Lancaster. Then he and the remaining troops proceeded on to Marlborough, where they arrived during the evening of June 29th.[12]

* * *

Ever since April the Indians had been on the move, shifting in groups from place to place like the restless pieces in a kaleidoscope. Hunger was driving them to the choice fishing spots on rivers or ponds, and to the abandoned fields of colonial villages. The English, being well aware of how greatly the Indians needed food, were now directing much of their effort to the destruction of Indian crops and caches. The savages scarcely knew from which direction the next attack might come, for to their fear of English expeditions was now added the threat of Mohawk raiding parties. Worse yet, Philip's followers and confederates were now arguing among themselves. Apparently some of the tribal groups which had been brought together under the excitement of Philip's revolt were now becoming disillusioned with his cause, and were beginning to go their own separate ways.

For some time now enemy Indians in considerable numbers had been filtering across the border into Plymouth Colony. Early in May they had killed four men at Taunton, and had conducted raids on several of the towns, including Bridgewater. Indians were reported in the vicinity of Cohasset and, a little later, at Titicut on the Taunton River. There were signs of enemy movement in the direction of Assawompsett Pond and Dartmouth. That still more Indians might be dangerously near the colony was indicated on May 24th when a party of troopers under the command of Captain Thomas Brattle fell upon a group of Indians at the falls of the Pawtucket River, killing a number of them, and spoiling their catch of fish.[13]

Early in June the government of Plymouth Colony was considering the possibility of organizing a force of about 150 English plus fifty friendly Indians to patrol the frontier area. Just as these plans were being formulated, Benjamin Church arrived in Plymouth. Ever since the campaign against the Narragansetts, Church had been out of military service, and in March he and his wife, who then was expecting another child, had taken up residence on Aquidneck Island. Following the birth of this second son, however, the old fighting spirit had got the better of Church, and he had talked his tearfully reluctant wife into letting him journey to Plymouth to see if the government could use his services as leader of an independent company of English and Indians. Needless to say, his proposal was immediately and gladly accepted.[14]

Church at once started back for Aquidneck to recruit men from among the Plymouth Colony refugees on the island. His route lay southward to Sokonesset on the Cape, and thence by water to the eastern shore of Aquidneck. Having reached Sokonesset, he secured two Indians to paddle him in a canoe the rest of the way. They were passing close by Sakonnet Point when Church saw some Indians fishing from rocks along the shore. These were Sakonnet Indians belonging to Awashonks, and thus enemies, but Church had long believed that the Sakonnets were not overly enthusiastic about Philip's cause, and might possibly be persuaded to make peace with the English. Therefore he had the canoe brought in closer to the rocks, and after some shouting back and forth, Church took his life in his hands and stepped onto the shore. Soon he was engaged in a peaceful conversation with one of the Indians, whom he knew. During the course of their talk Church learned that Awashonks herself was in a swamp only a few miles away, and that she was inclined toward peace. Accordingly, it was agreed that Church and Awashonks should meet in two days for a conference at a certain large rock near the eastern shore of the Sakonnet River about four miles above Sakonnet Point. Having concluded his conversation in this satisfactory manner, Church continued on to his destination.[15]

Not only Church's wife but the authorities at Newport as well tried to dissuade him from keeping the rendezvous, but the daring Church believed that he had before him one of the great opportunities of the war, and was loath to abandon it. So he finally persuaded even his "tender, and now almost broken hearted Wife" to let him go on the dangerous mission. The appointed day came, and Church, accompanied by one companion and his two Indian paddlers, departed from green and peaceful Aquidneck in two light canoes. He took with him a bottle of rum and a small quantity of tobacco, items well-calculated to smooth over any rough spots in the negotiations.

Going ashore at the appointed place, Church found Awashonks waiting for him. Years later he could still recall how they

walk'd together about a Gunshot from the water to a convenient place to sit down. Where at once a-rose up a great body of *Indians*, who had lain hid in the grass, (that was as high as a Mans waste) and gathered round them, till they had clos'd them in; being arm'd with Guns, Spears, Hatchets, &c. with their hair trim'd and faces painted, in their Warlike appearance.[16]

Church offered Awashonks some of his rum; but, fearing poison, she insisted that he drink first. Accordingly, as Church later remarked, he "drank a good Swig which indeed was no more than he needed." Then Awashonks and her attendants willingly tasted the rum, and afterward shared the tobacco as well. There was another tense moment when one of the braves advanced to attack the lone Englishman, but others restrained him, and the parley proceeded.

It became evident that Awashonks and her people were eager to abandon Philip's cause, if only they could be sure that the English would permit them to reoccupy and enjoy their old territory. Church was quick to fan their hope, and finally persuaded them to seek terms from the government of the colony. Carried away now by enthusiasm, the warriors even promised to fight against the enemies of the English. It was arranged that a small delegation of the Indians, including Awashonks' son, Peter, should go to Plymouth to see if the authorities were willing to grant them the easy terms which Church had endorsed. Thus it was that on the 28th of June Peter and two others appeared before the Council, and presented their case.[17]

In the meantime the new Plymouth expedition, under the command of Major William Bradford, had arrived at Pocasset. Here Church conferred with Bradford on June 27th, informing him of his dealings with Awashonks, and expressing the hope that a mass surrender could soon be effected. After this, Church visited the Sakonnet

Indians again to tell them that Bradford knew of their resolution, and to give them instructions for surrendering themselves safely to the army. As a result of Church's efforts Awashonks and her people, totaling about eighty or ninety, came in to Bradford on the morning of June 30th, despite the fact that they had not yet learned how their emissaries had fared at Plymouth. Church immediately asked that the warriors be released into his custody to serve under him in the field. Bradford, however, considering this an unwarranted risk, insisted that all of the prisoners proceed to the town of Sandwich, there to await further orders. So they went trudging off to the eastward behind a flag of truce.[18]

Now the army turned its entire attention to the search for the enemy. A captured Pocasset Indian had informed Bradford that a large number of enemy Indians were clamming at the mouth of the Kickamuit River, and that Philip himself was expected there within three or four days. By prearrangement some boats from Aquidneck came to Pocasset, where they picked up Bradford's army on the evening of July 1st. As the troop-laden boats moved northward toward the tip of Aquidneck Island, the men could see Indian fires on the far shore of Mount Hope Bay at Waypoiset, three miles ahead of them. But instead of proceeding directly to the spot, the boats turned westward, and unloaded the army on the shore of the Mount Hope peninsula as Bradford desired. From there the expedition advanced up the peninsula to Swansea, where recently the enemy had slain young Hezekiah Willet and made off with his Negro servant Jethro. After some further activity beyond Swansea, the troops marched into Rehoboth for a brief rest.

Church, who was with the army at this time, was sure that Bradford had made a mistake in not going directly to Waypoiset, and undoubtedly told him so. Bradford's plan may have been to intercept Philip as he approached Waypoiset, but if so, the tactic was futile. Better success was promised for the future, however, as the expedition was now greatly strengthened by the arrival of about eighty troopers under Captain Brattle. Possibly also at this time, or a little later, there arrived a company of foot under Captain Moseley, and some detachments from Henchman's army.[19]

Connecticut, meanwhile, had been continuing her profitable military activities in the Narragansett country. During the first three weeks of June, volunteers from New London, Norwich, and Stonington made two separate forays east of the Pawcatuck River, each time encountering and defeating considerable numbers of the enemy. In fact, the war-ravaged land of the Narragansetts might now be called a happy hunting ground for the Connecticut men and their Indian allies. By the 22nd of June Talcott was back in Connecticut after his joint operation with Henchman, and within a week he was on his way to the Narragansett country at the head of some three hundred English soldiers plus Indian auxiliaries.

In accordance with instructions from the Council, Talcott's new expedition went first to Wabaquasset, and then turned eastward into northern Rhode Island. After capturing four Indians at Nipsachuck, they continued their search for the enemy, and on the morning of July 2nd they came upon the place where a large body of Narragansetts was encamped. As soon as the attack began, the startled Indians scattered like quail, many of them dashing into a spruce swamp nearby, but Talcott had planned his attack with businesslike efficiency, and his men were deployed so as to encompass the area. The Narragansetts must have been very short of guns and powder, for the Connecticut men were able to push into the swamp almost with impunity, and before long the last signs of resistance were ended. After the tumult was over, it was found that 171 enemy Indians, including women and children, had been killed or taken prisoner. Among the dead lay the body of the old saunk squaw Quaiapen, Ninigret's sister, a gruesome picture of Indian majesty laid low.[20]

Meanwhile, another party of about eighty Narragansetts had arrived in the vicinity of Providence, and their leader, Potuck, had made so bold as to enter the town and inquire how he might get to Boston safely in order to make peace. Several of the Providence men persuaded him to go to Newport instead, assuring him that he would be allowed to rejoin his followers at Warwick Neck. Accordingly, Potuck's party trekked on down to Warwick to wait for their leader's return. It was some time after their departure from Providence that Talcott and his men, fresh from their victory over the Narragansetts, arrived. From Bradford, whose army was then operating in the vicinity of Swansea, Talcott now received a message asking him to come over and help in the search for Philip. The

Connecticut commander and his officers were more than ready to link up with the Plymouth expedition, but Talcott's Indians, loaded with plunder from the skirmish, insisted on returning homeward. Because it was considered unwise to proceed without them, Bradford's invitation was declined with regret.

Whatever disappointment Talcott may have felt because of this situation was considerably diluted by the news that Potuck's Indians were down at Warwick Neck. Talcott cared not a fig for any peace talks that might be going on at Newport, and even less for the unofficial promise of safe conduct given to Potuck by some of the Providence men. Therefore, on July 3rd, the Connecticut troops headed down the trail toward Warwick, where they had no trouble finding and overwhelming the waiting Narragansetts. They killed or captured 67 of them, making a grand total of 238 in two days. Talcott's total casualties for the same period consisted of one Connecticut Indian killed and a few men wounded. Potuck, incidentally, was never released by the English, on the grounds that the Providence men had no authority to grant him a safe conduct. He was subsequently executed as a war criminal.[21]

After the victory at Warwick, Talcott led his men along the Pequot Path toward home. Below the ruins of Wickford they scoured the area east of the Pettaquamscut River, and beyond that the vicinity of Point Judith, but found only one old squaw. Then the troops continued on to Stonington, and dispersed to their own communities. The history of this expedition clearly shows how ruthless the English had become in their prosecution of the war. Apparently men who themselves had loving wives and children waiting for them at home could stain their swords with the blood of Indian women and children almost without a qualm. Moreover, they had actually permitted the Connecticut Indians to wreak vengeance on one of the captives by torturing him to death in an unbelievably savage manner, while they themselves looked on.[22] To such an extent had the war brutalized men who called themselves Christians.

* * *

With the continued decline of Indian strength, more and more of Philip's former allies sought to save their lives by making peace with the colonial governments. Late in May the Narragansett sachems began to sound out the government of Massachusetts on the question of peace. In an effort to shift blame from themselves, they tried to give the impression that it was not they but the dead Canonchet who had led their people in the war. The authorities at Boston were sufficiently interested to send Peter Ephraim, one of the loyal Indians, back to the sachems to hear their proposals. By a trick of fate this faithful emissary, while with the Narragansetts, was captured by Connecticut troops during the first week of June, thus ending his mission. The government of Connecticut, not having been previously informed of the undertaking, showed some resentment at the fact that Massachusetts was conducting separate negotiations with the enemy, but the incident was quickly smoothed over without serious recrimination.[23] On the whole, in the delicate matter of negotiating for peace with various Indian groups, the United Colonies were able to keep friction among themselves at a minimum.

Also early in June, at Dover, New Hampshire, the neutral Pennacook sachem Wannalancet, accompanied by certain other Indians and also several English captives whom he had managed to acquire, came in to reestablish his former good relationship with the English. The result was a treaty of peace and amity signed on July 3rd by Major Richard Waldron of Dover for the English, and Wannalancet for the Indians. This agreement pledged the fidelity of a large number of Indians in the area between the Merrimack and Kennebec rivers, so that at one stroke the English seemed to have made a most advantageous settlement.[24]

Seeking to encourage mass surrenders of Indians who had become disillusioned with Philip's cause, the government of Massachusetts on June 19th issued a special declaration of mercy. Some hope of leniency was held out to the rank and file of the enemy if they would surrender within a stated period of time. Many hungry and heartsick Indians shuffled in to take advantage of this offer, a further sign of the now rapid disintegration of enemy power. Among those who yielded to the inevitable was the educated Indian known as James the Printer, who came into Cambridge with others on the 2nd of July. He is believed to have served as scribe for the enemy sachems during the negotiations leading to the release of Mrs.

Rowlandson. The penitent James now told the authorities that during the past year more Indians had died of disease than had been killed by the English—a most significant fact, if true.[25]

It was also in the opening days of July that Shoshanim, usually known as Sagamore Sam, and certain other Nipmuck leaders began a new and pathetic correspondence with the Massachusetts authorities. In the most humble and pleading words they tried to exonerate themselves, and begged for terms. But the English remained unmoved by late repentance, telling the Indians that those who had begun the war or engaged in atrocities must expect to die. However, mercy would be extended to those who had been drawn into the war by others and who had not participated in notorious atrocities. Two Indians representing Shoshanim even came into Boston to see if terms of peace could not be arranged, but the authorities haughtily refused to discuss peace until all English captives had been released. The humble pleading of the frightened Nipmuck sachems was music in the ears of the Massachusetts Puritans, and they exulted in it. "Thus doth the Lord Jesus make them to bow before him, and to lick the Dust," was the disdainful comment of one contemporary observer.[26]

The English had additional cause for rejoicing, meanwhile, in the news of Mohawk attacks against the enemy Indians. Possibly this news was exaggerated, but there is much evidence to indicate that ever since spring the Mohawks had been anxious to strike at the New England Indians, their old enemies. There can be no doubt that the Nipmucks and other enemy groups were now extremely apprehensive of Mohawk raids. In July the governments of New York and Connecticut were again discussing the advisability of allowing a Mohawk expedition to enter Connecticut territory. However, the authorities at Hartford were still reluctant to encourage such a move, and suggested that the Mohawks turn their attention to the area above Squakeag and around Mount Wachusett, thereby saving Connecticut from the disagreeable prospect of playing host to the fierce warriors from New York. But Connecticut's fears were needless; the Mohawks carried out their activities elsewhere, and in their own way.[27]

Even as the leaders of Massachusetts were rejoicing over the growing discomfiture of their Indian enemies, they themselves began to writhe under a new affliction in the person of one Edward Randolph, special agent of the Crown. Randolph's mission was to investigate charges that the New England colonies, especially Massachusetts, were not conforming to the rules and regulations of the British imperial system. He was also concerned with the question of whether or not Maine and New Hampshire should be separated from the Bay Colony. Randolph was strongly prejudiced against the Massachusetts Puritans, and from the moment when he stepped ashore at Boston on June 10th and showed his credentials to the authorities trouble began to brew. A situation which at best would have been difficult and unpleasant in a time of peace was ten times more irritating in a time of suffering and war. Randolph seems to have been completely without tact, and he showed little or no appreciation of the ordeal through which the Bay Colony was passing. His reports to the home government on the conduct of the war were not only derogatory; they were shot through with false and misleading statements. For example, he informed the King that the Indians had been overcome mostly by the efforts of Plymouth Colony. He also stated that in Boston the majority of the people were hoping for the establishment of royal government in their colony.[28] The shortness of tempers in Massachusetts during July of 1676 can be explained largely in terms of three things—Indians, drought, and Edward Randolph.

Meanwhile, in the western part of Plymouth Colony the grim game of hunting down the enemy was continuing. Bradford knew that there were plenty of Indians around; the problem was to catch them. On July 6th the army had the good fortune to rescue Jethro, the Negro servant who had been taken prisoner at Swansea the previous week. While in captivity Jethro had kept his wits about him and, having some knowledge of the Indian tongue, had been able to learn that the savages were planning an attack on Taunton. Acting on this information, Bradford assigned a detail of soldiers to guard the threatened town, with the result that when the Indians did attack Taunton on July 11th they met with a warm reception, and quickly fled.[29]

Five days earlier Bradford's troops had marched out of Taunton for a further probing of the great empty area west of the Taunton River. They were out for about a week, during which time they visited Swansea and then Mattapoiset, where they encountered a considerable party of the enemy, and captured about twenty or thirty of them. Heading northward again, they seized an Indian who promised to take them to Philip's place of concealment. He led them into a swamp where the Wampanoag sachem had been lurking that very morning, but by now the bird had flown. The disappointed soldiers began a search which led them on for many a rough mile, and they did manage to kill a dozen or more straggling Indians, mostly old people who had not been able to keep up with the rapidly moving fugitive bands. On the following day the chase was resumed, and the English found a party of several hundred Indians deep in a swamp. Bradford launched a vigorous attack in which the soldiers killed or captured a large number of the Indians, while the survivors fled in all directions. Philip, however, apparently was not with this group at the time. After this action, the army returned to Taunton on July 15th and 16th.[30] In terms of total casualties inflicted, the week's work could hardly be reckoned a failure, but Bradford and his men were, of course, chagrined at having missed Philip so closely.

While Bradford was thus combing the woods between Taunton and Swansea, Benjamin Church was off on an adventure of his own. He had taken leave of the army at Rehoboth about the 5th of July, and had ridden to Plymouth, where he gave Governor Winslow the latest news from the front. The governor, in turn, informed Church of his decision to grant to the Sakonnets the terms which Church had proposed for them. This meant that Awashonks' warriors were now eligible for special military service under Church's command. With this good news to spur him on, Church with a few companions hurried on down to Sandwich to find the Sakonnets. The surrendered Indians, however, had not yet arrived there, so Church decided to head westward to meet them. Not finding them at Agawam, Church and about half a dozen of his companions pushed on, and finally located the Indians on the shore of Buzzards Bay some distance beyond the Sippican River. The English were cordially received, and soon were feasting on flatfish, shellfish, and eels which the Indians had caught. That night the warriors danced around the campfire, pledging themselves to fight for the English. Church selected the braves whom he wanted, and next day took them back to Plymouth.

Here the governor commissioned Church for the special type of service he had in mind. Thus at last Church found himself the captain of an independent company of English and Indian volunteers, a force specially designed to search out the remnants of the enemy wherever they might lurk, and beat them at their own tricks of forest warfare. As in the case of the Connecticut volunteer bands, men were attracted to the service by the prospect of booty and the profits to be made from the sale of prisoners.

About July 11th Church's new company had its first action near Middleborough, where they surrounded and captured a party of enemy Indians. The prisoners informed them of another party located at Monponsett Pond. After dropping off his first batch of prisoners at Plymouth, Church hurried out to the pond, and gathered up this second group without losing a single Indian from his net. This was to be the pattern of Church's operations for the next few weeks; he later boasted that he never returned from one of these forays empty-handed. The unbroken string of successes now being enjoyed by the English wherever they encountered Indians, especially the fact that again and again large numbers of the enemy were seized or killed with virtually no loss to the English, indicates most clearly the weak and demoralized condition to which Philip's followers had now come.

On July 17th the ever-busy Church and his company of about forty English and Indians started forth from Plymouth on a new adventure. Their first assignment was a rather tame one—that of convoying some carts loaded with hogsheads of bread for the army at Taunton. While engaged in this duty, Church permitted some of his men to scout around Middleborough, and as a result they surprised a group of Indians there, taking several of them captive. They also learned that Tuspaquin, the sachem of Assawompsett, was back in his own territory. Very likely it was this Indian who had been leading the recent raids against Bridgewater and Taunton. As soon as Church had delivered the provision carts safely at Taunton, he and his eager company returned to the hunt. Entering the narrow neck of land which lies between Assawompsett Pond and Long Pond, they were fired upon by hidden Indians, but suffered no casualties. They then continued on southward toward Buzzards Bay, and entered the country west of the Acushnet River, where they captured some hostile Sakonnets. Finding an old canoe, they transported the prisoners to an island in the river, and left them there under the care of one of Church's Indians.[31]

The company spent the next night hidden in a thicket not far from the site of Russell's garrison house in Dartmouth. In the morning they found traces of Indians, and tracks indicating the direction they had taken. Church followed these tracks northward for about three miles to a place where the enemy group had split into two separate parties. It was decided that Church's Indians should follow the left-hand track, which led toward the western end of the Great Cedar Swamp, while the English soldiers followed the right-hand track leading toward the eastern end of the same swamp. The fact that Church would let his Indians go off by themselves at a time like this shows how much he trusted them, and they appreciated his confidence. His willingness to divide his already small force indicates his contempt for the remnants of the once-powerful enemy.

The track which the English followed led them to where a group of Indians could be seen peacefully gathering berries on the far side of a swamp. Capturing these Indians, Church learned that they were a mixed group, some belonging to the Narragansett sachem Quinnapin, and others to Philip. One of the prisoners, an old squaw, revealed that these two sachems and many of their followers were then in the Great Cedar Swamp only about two miles away. Even Church realized that it would be foolhardy to attack such a strong party of the enemy in its lair. So he withdrew to the eastward, picking up his prisoners from the island, and then waiting beyond the Mattapoiset River until he was rejoined by his own Indians. They, too, had taken some prisoners, including the wife and son of Tiashk, one of Philip's principal war leaders. Rejoicing in their successes, Church's men headed for Plymouth by way of Sippican, and arrived there safely with their captives and plunder.

In the meantime Bradford's army had been continuing its patrol activity out of Taunton. By July 24th, however, part of the Massachusetts contingent and some of the Plymouth Colony men as well were withdrawing from Bradford's command, thereby greatly reducing his striking power. At this time, too, Bradford was feeling the sting of the comparison now being made between the audacious and highly successful operations of Benjamin Church and his own more cautious tactics. The modest but sensitive Bradford was the first to admit his own shortcomings as a military commander, and he was generous in his praise of the Massachusetts officers who had served under him.[32] It is true that Bradford's successes were not as spectacular as those of Church who, like many other memorable commanders in history, had not only great ability as a leader of men, but also a flair for the dramatic. Nevertheless, by guarding the line of the Taunton River, Bradford was performing a very important function—that of keeping large numbers of the enemy concentrated in the area south of that river, where they might the more easily be disposed of.

As the war passed into its second year, and the power of the Indians continued to decline, a strange, almost symmetrical pattern began to appear in the broad fabric of developments. The bitter conflict which had started as a sudden explosion in the extreme western part of Plymouth Colony, and had then sent leaping flames all through Massachusetts, Rhode Island, and parts of Connecticut, now seemed to be contracting again. In fact, its center of activity was definitely shifting back toward the very region where it had all started. One could almost believe that some master dramatist was shaping the trend of events to produce a grand climax, a climax in which all the vast scope of developments should be drawn irresistibly back into the narrow confine of its origin, thus completing a perfect cycle.

There was no longer any doubt that Philip, the archenemy of the English, had returned from the Nipmuck country to the wild and shaggy southwestern reaches of Plymouth Colony. With him had come considerable numbers of Wampanoags, and also some of the Narragansetts who dared not venture into their own country because of the scourge of the Connecticut expeditions there. These weary and disheartened Indians had elected to take their chances on familiar ground rather than remain in the much larger region of the Nipmuck country, or migrate beyond the Connecticut River where they might become a prey to the Mohawks. But they must have known that in the relatively confined area of Plymouth Colony their situation would be next to hopeless, for their warriors were now few, their supplies of guns and ammunition were dangerously low, and the English were relentless in their pursuit.

The fugitive Indians were now organized in migratory bands

which included many women and children. This meant that movement from place to place was a slow and cumbersome operation easily detected by the English and their Indian scouts. Philip himself and his closest associates were with these wandering bands, moving from one location to another in search of sustenance and security. Whenever the English appeared, the Indians would plunge into the nearest swamp, hoping that the soldiers would not be able to root them out. But the English now had the invaluable assistance of Indian auxiliaries who were used to swamps. Furthermore, because the enemy was now so weak, the English had lost much of that fear of swamp fighting which had gripped them in the summer of 1675.

Day after day the English ranged the woods, rounding up the wandering fugitives. Frightened prisoners, hoping for mercy, were oftentimes willing to reveal the location of groups of Indians, and even to tell where Philip himself could be found. In this way the colonial forces kept close on the trail of the elusive sachem, but every time they closed in for the kill Philip managed to slip through their fingers. He was still on the loose, and as long as he was alive and free he was dangerous. Therefore Bradford's army watched the line of the Taunton River, and Church's company relentlessly prowled through the woods south of that line. It was simply a question of how long the game would continue.

CHAPTER XII

Philipus Exit

DESPITE drought, disease, and the terrible ravages of war, by mid-summer of 1676 the English settlers had considerable cause for optimism. Signs of impending Indian defeat were mounting on every hand, and the countryside was becoming noticeably safer even for relatively small groups. The colonists, who only a few months before had been terror-stricken by Indian successes, now went boldly forth to sweep the woods in search of fleeing enemy bands.

The Narragansett sachem Pomham, for many years a thorn in the side of the English, fell a victim to one such expedition in the last days of July. The old sachem did not die without a fight. His party of hungry Indians had been discovered in the vicinity of Dedham, and a group of men from that town, together with some others from nearby Medfield and a few of the Christian Indians, hastened in pursuit. They fell upon their quarry with cold fury, and inflicted a considerable number of casualties, with little or no loss to the English. Pomham himself was knocked to the ground by a bullet, but managed to crawl off to one side while the fight swirled on nearby. Suddenly one of the English soldiers spotted the wounded sachem, and ran over for a closer look, whereupon Pomham summoned his last reserves of strength, seized his unwary opponent in a death grip, and sought to kill him with his hatchet. The shouts of the surprised and frightened victim quickly attracted a companion, who wasted no time in dispatching the old chief and releasing the gasping soldier from that unwelcome embrace. Among the prisoners taken in this brief skirmish was one described as "a very likely Youth . . . whose Countenance would have bespoke Favour for him, had he not be-

longed to so bloody and barbarous an *Indian* as his Father was." [1]
This was Pomham's son. He, a prisoner, looking down upon the
dead body of his father, perfectly symbolized the bitter defeat which
was now descending upon the followers of King Philip everywhere.

On August 10th a report from Marlborough told of valuable information obtained from a newly captured Indian, information which
gave further cause for optimism. The enemy had lost their will to
fight, and were now dispersing in various directions. Some remnants,
however, were still lingering in the vicinity of Mount Wachusett,
where their supply of corn was located. Accordingly, Captain Samuel
Hunting and his company were sent toward that area to destroy the
enemy's corn and mop up any Indian groups encountered. [2]

The English also found themselves complete masters of the situation in the upper Connecticut Valley. Captain Jeremiah Swain, with
a force made up of garrison soldiers from the Massachusetts river
towns, was detailed to scour the valley from Deerfield clear up to
Squakeag. This was territory which had been abandoned to the enemy
long since, but now the English dared move into that region with a
boldness unknown four months earlier. One important objective of
this expedition was to destroy any corn which the Indians might
have been growing at Squakeag, for the English realized that starvation was now one of their most important allies. Swain completed
his exploration without sighting a single enemy Indian. [3] About thirty
men were also sent to reconnoiter at Paquoag, on Miller's River about
twenty miles northwest of Mount Wachusett. The fact that such a
small party could now be sent so far into hostile country without un-
due hazard is eloquent evidence of the growing weakness of the
enemy. To the south, in the vicinity of Springfield, only a few
skulking Indians were reported, and these were objectionable mainly
because they killed English cattle and horses to appease their hunger.

One of the clearest indications of the enemy's fast-waning power
was the number of Indian surrenders in these hot midsummer days.
"God be thanked, many Indians come in daily, and submit themselves with much Dejection, crying out against King Philip, and other
ill Counsellors, as the Causes of their Misfortunes," reported one
contemporary observer. [4] Many of these discouraged and half-starved
Indians—men, women, and children—had been only lukewarm in
their support of Philip's cause, and now that the preponderance of

power was clearly swinging to the side of the English they wanted to be found on the right side of the battlelines when the day of reckoning came. Once surrendered, many of them felt a sense of relief, knowing full well that if they had been caught up in the iron-meshed dragnets of the English expeditions their hope of mercy would have been slight indeed. So the disillusioned Indians hastened in voluntarily in the hope of saving their skins.

Some merely presented themselves at an English settlement and surrendered to the first white men who would take them into custody; others took refuge with some of their own kind who had remained loyal to the English during the war. The powerful Mohegan chieftain Uncas was viewed as a possible savior by many surrendering Indians, and Mohegan villages in eastern Connecticut became a Mecca for swarms of these frightened fugitives. Uncas apparently welcomed the surrendering Indians in the hope that he could absorb them into his own tribe and thereby increase his strength. Their presence in the Mohegan villages became a source of no little concern to the neighboring settlers.

On July 27th a spectacular mass surrender occurred at Boston. Sagamore John, a prominent Nipmuck, led about 180 of his people into the hands of the English, and as a further sign of his submission he brought with him, securely bound with rope, the much-wanted sachem Matoonas and his son. The authorities must have rubbed their hands at the sight of this prize catch, for Matoonas was notorious as the leader of the first attack against a Massachusetts town soon after the outbreak of the war. Hubbard undoubtedly expressed the opinion of all Bostonians when he called this prisoner an "old malicious Villian" and a "malicious Caitiff." [5] The authorities wasted little time on Matoonas. They marched him onto Boston Common, tied him to a tree, and had him shot by Sagamore John and his men.[6]

What act of treachery had led to Matoonas' capture and ignominious death? Had Sagamore John and his men come to Matoonas with fair words and concealed weapons, sitting with him around the campfire until the signal was given, and then seizing the old chief as the ransom for their own lives? The records do not say. But however effected, the betrayal of Matoonas well illustrates how the element of treachery was now eating into the very heart of Indian resistance, Many Indians, eager to abandon a lost cause and secure their own safety, were willing to betray their old comrades into the hands of the English. This kind of shameless treachery became so widespread that Philip and his loyal followers could never again feel completely secure, even in their own secret retreats. The English, of course, recognized the tremendous possibilities of such betrayals among the enemy, and sought to encourage and promote them. Thus by casualties in battle, disease, starvation, and treachery the strength of the enemy waned with every passing week.

From the very beginning of the war the colonial authorities had been faced with the question of what to do with Indian prisoners. Four possible solutions presented themselves. The most simple and direct was to execute the captives, under the theory that a dead Indian could cause no further trouble. But the second and third possible courses of action offered the advantage of financial gain to help defray the cost of the war. The captives could be either shipped out of the country and sold into perpetual slavery, or else sold into local servitude for a stated period of time. The fourth and final possibility was simply to settle the Indians on designated tracts of land under English supervision, thereby allowing them to continue their old way of life. The latter method offered neither profit nor future security to the English settlers, and so was not given much consideration until later.

In all the New England colonies, including Rhode Island, the death penalty was freely meted out to enemy prisoners who had stained their hands with English blood through wanton acts of violence. During the closing weeks of the war and for some time afterward Boston Common was the scene of frequent executions of notorious Indians. Sometimes they were hanged; sometimes they were shot. The records mention eight Indians shot in Boston on September 13th, three hanged there several days later, four more executed on the 26th, and two others put to death on October 12th.[7] Rhode Island executed four enemy Indians at Newport, among them the Narragansett sachem Quinnapin.[8] In most cases the death sentence was not imposed until the prisoner had been afforded at least the form of a legal trial, but in some instances military commanders were officially authorized to kill prisoners at their own discretion. King Philip's War was neither glorious nor humane, and both sides on many occasions violated the noble concept of mercy.

If we are tempted to condemn the English settlers for being bloodthirsty and vindictive in their treatment of enemy prisoners, we must remember that to the people who had experienced the horror of the war every enemy leader represented a living menace which had to be obliterated in order to assure the future security of homes and families. Furthermore, the authorities in the Puritan colonies tended to the view that King Philip's War was an internal rebellion rather than a war between sovereign powers, and for rebels the customary penalty was death. So great a humanitarian as Roger Williams not only played an active role in the military defense of his community, but helped bring about the speedy and perhaps unjust execution of a wounded enemy prisoner. In the dying days of the war there staggered into the little settlement at the head of Narragansett Bay a badly wounded Indian known as Chuff ("so called in time of peace, because of his Surlines against the English").[9] The inhabitants, believing him to have been a ringleader in the enemy raids on Providence and vicinity, clamored for his execution, and threatened to take matters into their own hands if the authorities would not condemn him. Emotions were running high; a lynch mob could have been assembled at the click of a firelock. Under this kind of public pressure, Roger Williams had the Town Council and the Council of War summoned by the beating of a drum. Public sentiment was accurately reflected in these official bodies, sentence of death was duly passed, and the wounded Indian was accordingly shot.

Many Indian prisoners, instead of being executed, were condemned to be sold into foreign slavery. Although the colonial authorities looked upon this as an act of mercy, the matter is open to argument. Of course, there was plenty of legal precedent for sentencing criminals to distant servitude—such might even be the fate of a colonist unable to pay a fine for some offense—but to sell a prisoner of war into perpetual slavery was certainly a long step beyond ordinary practice. Again, the authorities would justify their action by insisting that the Indians were traitorous rebels, not prisoners of war. By sending such culprits out of New England, the conquerors spared their lives, while at the same time satisfying the demands of criminal justice and protecting society against further trouble.

The Reverend John Eliot, the well-known apostle to the Indians, was one who early in the war voiced a strong objection to this practice. He argued that Indian prisoners sold out of the country would lose all chance of being converted to the true Protestant religion. Furthermore, he wisely pointed out that such a harsh policy was likely to prolong the war, because the Indians would fight more desperately if they knew that slavery and death were the only alternatives to victory. In war the most ruthless policy, such as "unconditional surrender," is not always the wisest. But Eliot argued in vain, and only brought upon himself the suspicion and hatred of those who favored the iron fist for all Indians.[10]

Thus during the war and for some time afterward, Indians believed to be hostile or dangerous were shipped away to the slave markets of the West Indies, Spain, and the Mediterranean coasts. North American Indians were temperamentally unsuited to slavery, and lands which had long been receptive to the African slave trade seemed to shun the stolid and intractable captives from New England. Both Jamaica and Barbados legislated against their admittance. John Eliot knew of a case in which a vessel filled with Indian prisoners tried in vain to unload its human cargo at one market after another. She finally managed to get rid of them at Tangier in North Africa, where they were still living in 1683.[11] Probably many a black man today in North Africa and the islands of the West Indies carries some traces of the blood which once surged through the veins of Philip's defeated warriors.

Canny New Englanders also saw in the hordes of surrendering Indians a cheap source of labor at home, and many of the less dangerous captives were turned over to responsible colonists as bound servants for a stated period of time. This merciful alternative to the horror of transportation was especially useful in dealing with Indian children, who by every standard must be regarded as the innocent victims of the war. On July 22, 1676, the government of Plymouth Colony stipulated that the magistrates must assign such children only to families which would use them well, and declared that their term of service would end when they reached the age of twenty-four or twenty-five years. Massachusetts appointed a committee to deal with the same problem in that jurisdiction.[12]

During the summer of 1676 the islands in Narragansett Bay became a favorite refuge for Indians trying to escape the fury of the United Colonies. The fact that the Rhode Islanders were not entirely in sympathy with the war effort of the United Colonies, and might not be so vindictive toward fugitives, was of course well known to the Indians. Massachusetts and Plymouth, mindful of the cash value of prisoners, were greatly disturbed by the situation, for it appeared to them that Rhode Island, which had remained officially neutral during the war, was now reaping the benefits which others had sowed in blood and treasure. Therefore they lodged a united protest with the authorities at Newport. Officially, the government of Rhode Island seemed willing to cooperate in the matter, but insisted that the accounts of enemy Indians on the islands were considerably exaggerated, as indeed they probably were.[13]

Rhode Island people, like their Puritan neighbors, engaged in the business of selling Indians, and did so with the approval of their colony government. For example, the inhabitants of Providence, finding themselves in possession of a number of surrendered Indians, formed themselves into two trading companies which then disposed of the captives for a total of more than £21 in money, plus various commodities. These Indians, incidentally, were sold for specified periods of service, and many if not all of them remained within the colony. Roger Williams was an active participant in the venture.[14]

Connecticut, which throughout the war had shown the greatest skill of all the colonies in dealing with friendly Indians, now produced the most systematic program for the rehabilitation of former enemies. The October session of the General Court established a list of rules governing the disposal of the colony's many Indian captives. Prisoners who could not be convicted as murderers were not to be sold into foreign slavery. Instead, they were to be assigned to service among the English settlers, where they would receive good treatment. At the end of ten years, all such Indians over sixteen years of age were to be free to work for themselves under English jurisdiction. The others were to continue their service until they reached the age of twenty-six. Under this system the Indians could look forward to a day when they might once again be free, and would then be able to make a living by the skills learned during their period of service. Despite the apparent leniency of this program, many of the Indians were dissatisfied with the restraints imposed upon them, and took the first opportunity to run away. On these the authorities wasted little sympathy. By an act of May 15, 1677, the General Court decreed that recaptured runaways could be sold into foreign slavery if their masters so desired.[15]

Few today would care to defend *in toto* the policies of the New England colonies with respect to their prisoners of war. On the other hand, we ought to remember that if the colonies were ruthless in dealing with their enemies, so were other governments and other societies of that day. It was an age in which cruel repression was often considered to be justified, especially in the case of group rebellion against authority in church or state. Such episodes as the persecution of heretics in Spain and France, or the "Bloody Assizes" in England, are cases in point. When the colonial authorities executed enemy Indians they sincerely believed that they were justified in doing so, just as the victorious powers believed that they were justified in putting to death certain notorious enemy leaders at the end of the Second World War. Having suffered so greatly, the settlers were determined to make a repetition of the uprising impossible. Once they had gained the upper hand, they set out to crush the military power of the natives beyond any hope of resurrection. The ruthless executions, the cruel sentences of transportation, and the more enlightened programs for settling large numbers of the Indians under close English supervision were all aimed at the same goal— unchallengeable white supremacy in southern New England. That the program succeeded is convincingly demonstrated by the almost complete docility of the local natives ever since.

* * *

The name most frequently associated with the ending of King Philip's War is that of Captain Benjamin Church. This man's fame as an Indian fighter, although much enhanced by his own memoirs written many years later, had developed into large proportions even as the conflict raged in 1676. People admired his daring exploits in the summer campaign of 1675 around Mount Hope and Pocasset, his role in the wintertime attack against the Narragansett fort in the Great Swamp, and especially his accomplishments in Plymouth Colony during the month of July, 1676. Church had discovered the perfect kind of military unit for dealing with the scattered remnants of the enemy—a small, cohesive, volunteer company including both Indians and English. Even captured enemy Indians were sometimes given the opportunity to join Church's band, and these turncoats proved to be excellent scouts and soldiers. Their knowledge of the plans and habits of their former comrades on more than one occasion enabled Church to make daring and successful strokes at little or no cost to his own men. Cotton Mather, writing a number of years later, summed up Church's general reputation in New England when he said that some of the old Indian fighter's achievements were so extraordinary that "my reader will suspect me to be transcribing the silly old *romances*, where the *knights* do conquer so many *giants*, if I should proceed unto the particular commemoration of them." [16]

Toward the end of July the Massachusetts forces operating in Plymouth Colony had been withdrawn, which meant that the only organized field forces now available in that area were those under the command of Major Bradford, plus Church's small company. Connecticut's Major Talcott was also temporarily in the vicinity of Taunton with a strong body of men, but his support could not be counted upon indefinitely.

On the 24th of July, Governor Winslow issued to Church a new commission which granted him broad discretionary powers in the conduct of his subsequent operations. Under the terms of this commission Church was authorized to appoint his own officers, pursue the enemy anywhere within the bounds of the United Colonies, and make treaties with Indians who wanted to abandon Philip's cause. He could even grant mercy to all except notorious enemy leaders, if he so desired.[17]

Captain Church was at worship on Sunday morning, July 30th, when Governor Winslow and a small party of horsemen rode into Plymouth town, and summoned him from the meetinghouse. Quickly the governor explained the reason for this intrusion. Two messengers from Bridgewater, who were now here with the governor, had brought news that the enemy had been sighted near their town.[18] Winslow wanted Church to assemble as many of his company as possible without delay to march against the Indians. Church needed no urging, and bustled about the town in great haste trying to gather his men and furnish them with the necessary provisions. During these feverish preparations Church, no doubt, was pleasantly aware of the admiring eyes of the local inhabitants fixed upon him, the man of the hour. He loved the role of popular hero. By afternoon all was ready, and Church gave the order to march. The trail led them to the shore of Monponsett Pond, where Church decided to camp for the night. The two messengers from Bridgewater, who had come out from Plymouth with the troops, continued on ahead to tell their people that Church's company was on the way.

The next day twenty-one of the Bridgewater men marched out of their town to meet the approaching force from Plymouth. On the way they encountered a party of hostile Indians trying to cross the Taunton River on a great tree which they had felled across the stream to serve as a bridge. A brief skirmish ensued, and the "brisk *Bridgwater* Lads" managed to inflict a number of casualties and seize some enemy guns and ammunition without loss to themselves. Among the slain was old Unkompoin, Philip's uncle. Church, meanwhile, advancing from Monponsett Pond, heard the noise of this skirmish, but was unable to locate the scene of action in time to participate, and so came into Bridgewater that night.

The English were now excited by the knowledge that Philip himself was in the neighborhood. Apparently he and his people, together with a group of Narragansetts, had come down from the Nipmuck country into the eastern part of Plymouth Colony, and were now trying to cross to the western side of the Taunton River. The Bridgewater men had foiled one such attempt; now Church was on hand and eager to finish the job. Early on the morning of August 1st a well-armed party, consisting of Church's company and some of the local men, carefully approached the place where the tree lay across the narrow stream. There on the far bank, sitting on the very stump of the fallen tree, was a lone Indian warrior. Church raised his gun to fire, but at that instant one of the Indians in Church's party called out that the warrior across the river was one of his own men, whereupon Church held his fire. At the same time, the Indian on the stump heard the commotion, and threw a quick look in Church's direction. It was Philip himself. Before anyone could take an effective shot, the Wampanoag sachem had scrambled out of sight like a field mouse discovered by the barnyard cat. The warning cry which had prevented Church's shot may well have been a genuine mistake, rather than an act of treachery, for Church himself, although bitterly disappointed at the lost opportunity, apparently did not call the loyalty of the erring Indian into question.

Trying to seize every possible advantage, Church and his men raced across the tree trunk, and fanned out in search of the quarry. They did manage to capture some Indians, but the most desired prize had made good his escape. Still there was cause for rejoicing, for when the prisoners were examined it was found that among them were Philip's own wife and little son. This was prime prey indeed! Roger Williams many years before had written that the Indians' "*affections*, especially to their children, are very strong; so that I have knowne a *Father* take so grievously the losse of his *childe*, that hee hath cut and stob'd himselfe with *griefe* and *rage*." [19] There was cruel satisfaction to the English in imagining how the hated Philip must now be suffering in the knowledge that his own wife and beloved little son were in the hands of the white men.

The capture of Philip's son posed a difficult problem for the government. What should be done with the boy? Even though a mere youngster, he was considered a dangerous symbol of insurrection. The authorities turned to the clergy for advice. Would it be proper to put the child to death? The question became a lively issue in the next few weeks, and the Scriptures were searched to find precedents for and against the execution of children for the crimes of their parents. [20] Some of the ministers did actually recommend death for the boy, but the authorities finally decided against execution, and instead sent him out of the colony to be sold as a slave. At that point the unfortunate lad drops from the view of History.

After the capture of Philip's wife and son, Church continued for another day or two in pursuit of the enemy, during which time his men killed or captured a large number of Indians, many of them women and children. It is clear that by this time the remnants of Philip's followers who had returned with him to Plymouth Colony were no longer capable of any organized resistance in a military sense, and were really nothing but wandering fugitives fleeing before the English like wild animals. A more enlightened and merciful policy on the part of the colonial governments might have brought the struggle to an end at this point without further bloodshed, but the English were in no mood to compromise now. Philip himself still managed to evade capture, although Church nearly had him in his clutches again on August 3rd. After this, Church returned to Bridgewater, where he spent the night of the 3rd, and on the next day proceeded with his drove of prisoners toward Plymouth.

Even after the departure of Church's spirited company, the local people continued their vigorous mopping-up operations in the area west of the Taunton River. On August 6th an enemy deserter came into Taunton and revealed the location of an enemy group nearby. Twenty men from the town went out to take advantage of this information, returning with more than two dozen prisoners. The squaw sachem Weetamoo had made a successful escape during this encounter, but soon thereafter her body was found near the mouth of the Taunton River. Apparently she had been drowned in a desperate attempt to escape across the river to her own country. Thus ended another episode in the lengthening tale of Indian tragedy and defeat. One by one the great leaders of the uprising were falling—Canonchet, Quaiapen, Pomham, and now Weetamoo. Philip himself might be next.

* * *

Captain Church had little rest after his arrival at Plymouth, for a few days later he led a raiding expedition to the southern part of the colony. This effort resulted in the death of the Indian known as Sam Barrow, whom Church considered "as noted a Rogue as any among the Enemy." [21] Following this exploit, the authorities at Plymouth once again persuaded Church to go out in the country's service, and so about the 10th of August he and his band of skilled Indian hunters, red men and white, marched into the forest. They moved along the trails leading toward the Pocasset country, constantly alert for any tracks or other signs which would indicate that enemy Indians were in the vicinity. But they saw no enemy Indians nor any signs of them, and arrived at Pocasset without incident. To all appearances, the land south of the Taunton River was clear of Philip's followers.

Because the hike from Plymouth had been long and tiring, Church now led his men across the narrows of the Sakonnet River to Portsmouth on Aquidneck Island, where he knew they would receive rest and refreshment. Church himself, with a small group of companions, rode part way down the island to pay a surprise visit to his wife, who was staying at the home of Major Peleg Sanford. The good woman was so startled to see her husband that she swooned in a fashion scarcely to be equaled by her Victorian descendants. This tender and embarrassing scene of conjugal reunion was soon interrupted by the precipitous arrival of Major Sanford himself, accompanied by Captain Roger Goulding, the man who had rescued Church from the Pocasset shore the preceding summer. They brought exciting news. One of Philip's own men had just arrived on the Portsmouth shore, after having slipped away from Philip's camp and deserted to the English. This Indian had disclosed the fact that Philip was now in his old lair at Mount Hope with a small group of companions. Moreover, the deserter was willing to betray the Wampanoag sachem because Philip had caused the death of his kinsman for daring to suggest that the Indians should now try to make peace with the English. Church knew that this was his big chance. And so his poor wife "must content her self with a short visit, when such game was a-head; they immediately Mounted, set Spurs to their Horses, and away." [22]

The excitement at the little town of Portsmouth must have been intense as Church and his party, including now Sanford and Goulding, galloped into the settlement. There Church's hardy soldiers were awaiting him, ready to go. Church, of course, wanted to talk with the Indian deserter who had provided this opportunity, and was pleased to find him free and frank with his information. The embittered Indian offered to lead the English to the very place where Philip was now encamped, a small piece of upland located in a miry swamp on the southwestern side of Mount Hope. Obviously, this all could be a clever trap, but Church preferred to believe the deserter's story, and decided to act quickly, for night was approaching. He knew he could count on his own experienced company of English and Indians, plus Sanford and Goulding, who were eager to participate in the adventure. The next few hours might well witness the action which would make Church the hero of all New England.

The men piled into boats, which ferried them across the half-mile of water to the shore of the Mount Hope peninsula. The moon, not yet full, was setting beyond the Narragansett country, assuring a mantle of darkness for the dangerous game ahead. With the informer as a guide, Church led his silent company to the edge of the swamp where Philip had his camp. All seemed peaceful and quiet; there was no sound except the normal noises of the woods on a summer's night. Apparently the stealthy approach of Church's men had been undiscovered by the enemy. But the next stage would be the most difficult of all. Unless extreme care were taken, the Indians would scatter and escape at the first sign of the English intrusion. A skillful trap was the thing.

Midnight had passed, and it was now August 12, 1676. All over New England, people were asleep in bed, peacefully unaware of what was transpiring at Mount Hope. Church divided his force, sending a party of men with Captain Goulding to crawl into position within sight of the enemy's camp. Goulding's instructions were to lie hidden until daybreak, and then launch a surprise attack. Presumably the startled Indians would flee in panic before this sudden onslaught, and Goulding's men, following closely, would drive them into the waiting ambush. Church carefully warned Goulding's detachment to make as much noise as possible during the chase, for the men waiting in ambush would have orders to shoot at anyone who came silently through the swamp.

Ideally, the swamp should have been completely ringed with armed men, but Church soon found that he did not have enough soldiers to cover the perimeter completely. He did the best he could with what he had, stationing the men in pairs along the side of the swamp toward which Goulding was to drive the enemy. That this complicated movement in virtual darkness was carried out as efficiently as it was is eloquent testimony to the skill and experience of Church and his entire company.

Goulding's assignment called for cool courage and great patience. Fortunately, he had with him the Indian deserter, who knew the exact location of their objective. Cautiously Goulding and his men moved forward through the swamp, and arrived at the Wampanoag camp without being detected. There before them was the small open-front shelter in which Philip and his companions were sleeping. No Indian sentry kept watch, a sign of almost unbelievable neglect, especially since Philip probably knew that an informer had gone to the English.[23] It almost seems as though the Wampanoag sachem, driven by some great compelling sense of tragic drama, had come back to Mount Hope to die. Here he had first raised the tomahawk against the hated English; here he would meet his end, still defying their pretended authority over him and his people. Yet who can measure a motive? Perhaps Philip had come to Mount Hope in search of food, intending then to escape once more to safer ground where he could spend the winter rallying the red men for another supreme effort.

Goulding's finger tightened on the trigger of his gun as he became aware of a slight stirring in the camp. He saw a dark figure emerge from the crude shelter and walk some distance from it. Did Philip suspect the trap? It was too early to launch the attack, for Church might not yet be ready. Goulding was relieved to see that the Indian was merely out to answer a call of nature. But then the savage glanced about him, and his gaze seemed to fall on the very place where Goulding was concealed, tense with excitement. Believing himself discovered, Goulding fired, and his overeager men immediately poured a volley through the walls of the hut. They fired so soon after Goulding's shot that the Indians inside had not even got to their feet when the bullets came ripping through the shelter, and so the volley had little effect except to warn Church, on the other side of the swamp, that the action had begun. He had just completed the stationing of his men.

The surprised Indians now dashed into the woods with Goulding's men in hot pursuit, just as Church had planned. The ambush party looked once more to their pieces, and peered ahead into the dimly lighted woods to catch the first glimpse of the fleeing enemy. Goulding's onrushing men doubtless made a roaring hullabaloo as they came, for no-one wanted to make himself a target because of his silence. That was the role reserved for the fleeing savages.

Suddenly one of the waiting pairs spotted an Indian racing toward them in silence, running for his very life from the pursuing white men. They stood together in readiness, this pair—one an Englishman, the other an Indian. At the right moment, when their target was within range, the white man pulled his trigger, but the gun failed to function. Thereupon his Indian companion opened fire, and the fleeing enemy spun forward upon his face. Elated, the two men advanced to have a closer look at the twisted and motionless form sprawled there in the mud. When they peered at the begrimed and contorted features, they recognized King Philip—dead.

Elsewhere in the swamp Church's men pursued and killed a few more Indians, while others of the enemy, including the war leader Annawon, made their escape through a gap in the line of ambush. After the area had been thoroughly scoured to make sure that no

Indians were left, Church assembled his battle-grimy men, and informed them of Philip's death. At this news the jubilant company broke into cheers. Some of the friendly Indians in the party hastened down to the place where the sachem's body lay sprawled in the mud, and dragged it ignominiously onto higher ground, where all clustered around for a better look at "that monster." Church's own famous description of Philip's corpse well reflects the feelings of the English soldiers toward their fallen enemy. In the eyes of these men, blind to the deeper tragedy of the moment, Philip only looked like "a doleful, great, naked, dirty beast." [24] As a last act of triumph and vengeance, Church had the body decapitated and quartered. Then the elated party of English and Indians returned to Aquidneck, bearing with them Philip's head.

* * *

With the rapid decline of Indian strength in Massachusetts and Plymouth, many of the despairing natives decided to flee westward in the hope of obtaining food and shelter among distant Indian groups. This migratory movement was first noticed by the English about the middle of July, when a sizable company of Indians crossed the Connecticut River, and slipped past Westfield on their way toward the Housatonic and the Hudson. A second group made a crossing some distance above Springfield on August 11th, the day before Philip's death. These sick and hungry Indians had no desire to fight. Their cause was a lost one, and now they and their women, with children and old folks as well, were desperately trying to get away to some place of safety.

Within a day or two Major Talcott's company, which had been in western Plymouth as recently as August 3rd, arrived at Springfield after having indulged in a corn-destroying operation in the vicinity of Quabaug. Now Talcott led his eager company in pursuit of the westward-fleeing Indians, and overtook them near the Housatonic River. Although he had previously sent a large part of his force back to Springfield, Talcott was able to inflict a sound defeat on the almost helpless Indians. Those who escaped his vengeance staggered on to the westward.[25]

The movement of New England Indians toward New York only served to aggravate still further the already unfriendly relations between Governor Andros and the United Colonies. The New Englanders were quick to jump at any evidence which seemed to confirm their old suspicions about the New York governor. They had not hesitated to charge him with having allowed their enemies to obtain powder in New York, so it is no wonder that they now doubted his diligence in repelling this westward migration. Some people even suspected that Andros was providing sanctuary for fleeing Indians. There was a rather warm exchange of letters about the matter, for Andros deeply resented every implication that he was in any way showing softness toward the defeated enemy.[26] Actually, there was no justification for blaming Andros. The obvious fact is that a beaten and desperate enemy saw a glimmer of hope to the westward, and fled to it. In any case, it is not to be supposed that Andros had such complete control over his vast and sparsely populated territories as to be able to dictate the fate of every Indian who might seek to hide himself there.

After the happenings of August 12th at Mount Hope, the subsequent tragic episodes of King Philip's War seem anticlimactic. Everywhere, the roundup of starving and bewildered Indians continued with a vengeance. Hunting redskins became for the time being a popular sport in New England, especially since prisoners were worth good money, and the personal danger to the hunters was now very slight.

Captain Church had not forgotten that Philip's old trusted companion and war leader, Annawon, had slipped through his fingers at Mount Hope, and was still at large. This prominent Wampanoag was known to be "*a very subtle man, and of great resolution,*" who "*had often said, that he would never be taking* [sic] *alive by the* English." [27] To capture Annawon would add still more luster to Benjamin Church's already brilliant record as an Indian fighter, and would perhaps quench the last lingering sparks of Wampanoag resistance. Church received his chance early in September, when news came that Annawon's company was annoying the inhabitants of Rehoboth by preying upon their cattle and horses.

Church proceeded to organize a small company consisting mostly of friendly Indians, but including a handful of English soldiers as well. They began the now thoroughly familiar task of ranging the woods to discover traces of the enemy's whereabouts. Arriving at Pocasset, they next crossed over to Aquidneck, and thence to the

Mount Hope peninsula. Here they divided to cover more ground, and it was not long before one of the scouting parties picked up ten Wampanoag men who had been sent down onto the peninsula by Annawon to obtain provisions. Church then moved up into Swansea, where he captured another group of Annawon's people, this time women and children. Leaving most of his troops there with the prisoners, Church led a party of about half a dozen scouts, including only one other white man, Caleb Cook, in a northerly direction to a swamp about five miles due north of Mattapoiset. There he had the good fortune to waylay two Indians, an old man and a young woman. These prisoners revealed that Annawon was encamped in Squannakonk Swamp, which was only a few miles north of their present position and about six miles west of Taunton.

Church was now forced to make a crucial decision. The day was drawing to a close, yet by vigorous hiking he and his men might be able to reach Annawon's camp before dark. But they were only a handful of men, while Annawon was thought to be in command of a considerable number of resolute braves. Deciding to act at once, Church easily persuaded his little group to fall in with his dangerous plan, and the two recently acquired prisoners agreed to serve as guides. He sent back orders to his main force to proceed to Taunton with their prisoners, and on the morrow to take the road toward Rehoboth. If all went well, he said, they would meet him somewhere between Squannakonk Swamp and Taunton. This matter taken care of, Church and his party, guided by the old Indian captive, headed north once more.

It was dark when they arrived at the place where Annawon and his company were encamped. Church, having been briefed on the layout of the camp, crawled up a long sloping ledge of rock, and found himself peering over the edge of a fairly steep cliff. There below him was the enemy's camp, backed up against the cliff, and protected on all other sides by difficult swampland. Roasting meat was sizzling above the campfires, while the flames illuminated the scene with an eerie flickering light. A squaw busily pounded corn in a mortar, now and again pausing to turn the grain before resuming her pounding. Church noted that the Indians' guns stood stacked against a crude rack near at hand. At the base of the cliff, below Church's vantage point, lay old Annawon and his son, completely unaware that intruders were above them. Beyond this first camp, Church could see the flickering fires of several other groups a short distance away.

Ascertaining that the steep cliff was the only feasible approach to Annawon's position, Church decided upon a course of action which for sheer daring must stand as one of the greatest individual exploits of the war. He knew that if his two prisoners were seen descending the cliff, no suspicion would be aroused, for they belonged to Annawon's party. Therefore he had them start down first, while he and his men followed close behind, hidden by the first two. Whenever the squaw with the mortar stopped her pounding, Church's men paused in their descent; when she resumed, they continued downward, clinging to bushes and whatever handholds they could find in the face of the rock.

The surprise was complete. Annawon and his immediate party, startled out of their repose, saw that resistance was useless, for Church's first care had been to secure their weapons. Messengers were sent to the other campfires with word of what had happened, and the Indians there readily agreed to submit. Church, on the authority of his commission, promised good treatment to all the prisoners except Annawon. To the latter he could not make such a promise, for Annawon had been a great leader in the war against the English.

Here at Annawon's camp Church spent one of the most unusual nights of his life. The old Wampanoag warrior was not only docile; he was courteous and hospitable. At his command the squaws brought beef and corn to the Plymouth captain, and upon this food Church dined heartily. As a token of submission, Annawon presented to his captor several beautiful bead belts and other regalia which had belonged to Philip. Perhaps the greatest tribute one can pay to Annawon is to say that he was a good loser. His nobility and dignity represents a connecting link with the older, happier age of Osamequin.

Was it so strange that Church and a handful of his companions could keep several scattered camps of Wampanoags in subjection throughout the night in an isolated swamp? Not under the circumstances. For one thing, Church secured the submission of the several groups by sending to them his own Indians, who were former comrades of these Wampanoags. The messengers were able to tell of the good treatment they themselves had experienced at Church's hands. Then too, Church was careful to give the impression that he was accompanied by a much larger force ready to come to his help if the Wampanoags gave him any trouble. Apparently Annawon's Indians now realized that any further resistance would be completely futile. There was no advantage to be gained by running off into the swamp again. The English would be relentless in their pursuit until every unsurrendered Indian was tracked down and killed. Philip was dead, and the war was over. Because obedience to Church offered the only possible hope for peace and life, they submitted and stayed secure during the night.

The next morning Church formed his captives into marching order, and led them northward until they struck the old trail which connected Rehoboth and Taunton. Proceeding eastward along this trail, they soon encountered Church's main force under Lieutenant Jabez Howland, coming out from Taunton as Church had instructed him to do. The entire company, escorting Annawon and the other prisoners, now marched into Taunton, where they were warmly greeted by the people of the town. Church seems to have taken a real liking to his most distinguished prisoner, and apparently hoped that his life would be spared by the authorities. However, despite Church's personal wish, Annawon was subsequently executed at Plymouth. The greatness of the Wampanoags died with him.

In Maine the Indian menace persisted longer, but in southern New England the people at last felt justified in rejoicing. By October, 1676, the Massachusetts legislature was able to proclaim that

. . . of those severall tribes and parties that have hitherto risen up against us, which were not a few, there now scarce remaines a name or family of them in their former habitations but are either slayne, captivated, or fled into remote parts of this wilderness, or lye hid, dispayring of their first intentions against us, at least in these parts.[28]

There were still a few small bands of half-starved Indians wandering through the woods, and the settlers could never feel completely secure until these also were eliminated. For this reason, the fall of 1676 and the following winter saw several minor expeditions against the now helpless savages.[29] These expeditions must be classified either as business ventures or as sport, but certainly not war. The Indian cause of which Philip had been the symbol was now deader than the ashes of a week-old campfire.

* * *

It has long been recognized that Philip was not the great leader he was once assumed to be. The struggle of 1675–1676 bears his name because he started it, and during those fateful months of war he was accepted as the symbol of Indian resistance to the white men, but once the conflict had spread beyond the bounds of Plymouth Colony Philip lost his control of the situation. Other tribes and other leaders began to fight against the English, and they had their own ideas and their own ambitions. There is no evidence that Philip ever exercised supreme command over the various warring tribes. Instead, he seems to have sunk into the position of a leader among many leaders. So far as we can tell, he played no major part in the great battles which occurred after the summer of 1675. Some writers have even charged him with cowardice, although it is difficult to see how a coward could have retained the loyalty of so many brave warriors.

Past estimates of Philip have often gone to extremes. Those antiquarians who are still enchanted by the myth of the noble savage have viewed Philip as a great patriot, heroically striving to preserve his nation against the wiles of the greedy and unscrupulous white men. Other writers, especially those under the spell of New England ancestor worship, have adopted the biased view of the very colonists who were Philip's enemies, scorning him as a cruel and untrustworthy villain who plotted the destruction of the peaceful, home-loving settlers. Neither of these estimates can long survive an impartial examination of all the evidence. The Philip that emerges from such an examination is more futile than heroic, more misguided than villainous.

Philip's whole career as head of the Wampanoags is the story of a proud man embittered by the humiliations imposed upon him through superior strength. He may have been driven to plan his uprising by a final conviction that war was the only chance of salvation for his people, but in taking this course he himself sealed their doom. The uprising began prematurely, was poorly organized, and soon escaped from Philip's control. He had undertaken a project that was far too big for his strength and ability. In effect, he became its victim rather than its leader, swept along on the tide of events which eventually brought him to his own tragic death.

CHAPTER XIII

The Aftermath

WE may well ask ourselves why the Indians were finally defeated in King Philip's War. Although the uprising got off to a slow start in the summer of 1675, within a few months all of southern New England was quaking with fear as town after town went up in smoke. By the late winter and early spring of 1676, the Indians were delivering a powerful and devastating attack which conceivably might have driven the English into a relatively restricted area along the coast. Yet several months later the power of the savages was declining rapidly, and soon their every hope of success was blotted out.

Certainly one important reason for the failure of Philip's uprising was the fact that the Indians of New England were not united in this crisis. The various tribes could not forget their old rivalries and the long years of conflict with one another. Furthermore, the English missionaries such as Eliot had created still a third force within the native civilization—the groups of Indians who had been converted to Christianity and were living in separate communities under English supervision. These Praying Indians, plus warriors from certain loyal tribes such as the Mohegans, performed invaluable service for the colonies during the war. In fact, the English soldiers showed themselves to be almost helpless in the face of Indian forest tactics until they began to take friendly Indians with them as scouts. The English also began to modify their own tactics in imitation of Indian methods, and learned how to protect themselves against the enemy ambushes which had been so successful in the early weeks of the war. If all the Indians of New England had turned upon the white men simultaneously, the outcome of King Philip's War might have been quite different, although it seems very unlikely that the English ever would have been driven completely from the country by Indians alone.

Time was on the side of the colonists. At first they were knocked off balance by the rapid spread of the Indian uprising, but once they had recovered from the first shock the English as a group clearly possessed the greater staying power. Their potential resources in men and supplies were almost limitless compared to those of the Indians. Without doubt, additional help could have been secured from the mother country if necessary, although of course the colonies were anxious to avoid such an expedient for fear of additional English control over their affairs. The Indians, on the other hand, soon used up their accumulated supplies, or else saw them destroyed by the colonial forces. For additional supplies they were dependent upon their own agricultural efforts under increasingly difficult conditions, plus perhaps some uncertain sources at the far ends of very long and tenuous routes through the woods. After the winter of 1675–1676 the Indians were almost always without sufficient food, so that hunger and disease stalked hand in hand through their camps. Under these conditions their downfall became merely a question of time.

The decisive defeat of Philip and his followers brought to New England a great sense of relief and joy, tempered with anguish at the awful destruction which had been wrought. In proportion to population, King Philip's War inflicted greater casualties upon the people than any other war in our history. Several thousand persons had lost their lives; families were scattered; homes and lifetime savings were gone beyond any hope of redemption. The line of English settlement had been pushed more than twenty miles southward in the Connecticut Valley, and an even greater distance eastward from Brookfield toward the coast. A number of communities which had once been thriving centers of human activity now existed only as jumbles of blackened ruins and weed-choked gardens. Northfield, Deerfield, Brookfield, Quinsigamond (Worcester), Lancaster, Groton, Mendon, Wrentham, Middleborough, Dartmouth, Warwick, Wickford, and Simsbury had been almost totally destroyed. Other towns such as Springfield, Westfield, Marlborough, Scituate, Rehoboth, and Providence were partially burned. Here and there in the woods the traveler might stumble upon the rag-clad bones of some colonist or Indian who had died in battle or succumbed to famine. Bereaved pets, fast becoming wild, still haunted the ashes of their former homes, unable to comprehend the disaster which had separated them from human companionship.

Inevitably, too, the war had done serious damage to New England's economy. The important trade in furs was almost completely ruined, while the wartime failure of the fishing industry, owing to a shortage of manpower, had brought hardship to a number of the seaside towns. Similarly, the war had interrupted the export trade to Barbados, which was closely linked with New England's import trade from Virginia. Indeed, the whole structure of New England commerce had been thrown out of balance, chiefly because the usual sources of furs and agricultural products had been partially blocked by the enemy.

On top of all these difficulties must be reckoned the actual cost of the war in terms of pounds sterling. The selectmen of Ipswich indicated the scope of the problem when they spoke of "our late, and sad troubles by the Indians, which have necessarily exposed us to so great and heavy charges, that many of us . . . could not beare, if necessity did not oblidge us thereto." [1] The United Colonies claimed that their war expenses reached a total of some £100,000. This may have been a slight exaggeration, but any figure even approaching it must have been a tremendous burden to be shouldered by such infant states, and one which placed a very heavy load of taxes upon all the people.[2]

The colonies were even deprived of the warming sense of comradeship which normally exists among allies who together have labored and sacrificed to achieve a common goal. The New England Confederation had been founded many years earlier to promote effective intercolonial action in times of crisis. After the outbreak of King Philip's War the member colonies had agreed to work together for victory, and during the course of the struggle a number of military ventures had been organized and to some extent directed by the six Commissioners of the United Colonies. This was especially true of the campaign against the Narragansetts. But, increasingly, intercolonial squabbling had destroyed much of the effectiveness of the organization, while creating an atmosphere of mutual suspicion and jealousy. Notwithstanding the final defeat of Philip's followers in southern New England, the Indians along the coast of Maine continued their resistance, and now when Massachusetts asked Plymouth and Connecticut to help her against these Indians she was told that the northern war was none of their concern. This attitude, of course, infuriated the Bay Colony, and further weakened the cause of intercolonial good will.[3] To add to the difficulties, Deerfield and Hatfield were raided in 1677, apparently by a remnant of enemy Indians en route to Canada.[4]

If the colonists were badly shaken by the effects of King Philip's War, how much greater was the impact of that calamity upon the Indians! In 1675 sachem Philip, consciously or otherwise, risked the whole future of his race on one cast of the dice. History has recorded the outcome of Philip's gamble, and has proved the decisive effect of the English triumph. The Indian failure simply meant the complete breakdown of all the spiritual and physical factors which up to that time had bolstered resistance to the encroachments of European civilization. Henceforth there was to be no doubt as to which race would hold the reins. Those Indians who survived the struggle of 1675–1676 were forced to recognize the stark fact of English supremacy. Even the tribes which shared in the English victory were inevitably dragged down in the general decline of their own race.

The colonies brought all their Indians under close supervision by assigning them to definite places of residence or by otherwise restricting their activities. Massachusetts, for example, required that all Indians who were not family servants live in Natick, Punkapaug, Hassanemesit, or Wamesit, there to be under constant observation. In Rhode Island constables were ordered to prevent Indians from congregating in large numbers, and also to take action against those who carried firearms. Plymouth was likewise concerned about armed Indians, maintaining a stringent prohibition against selling arms and ammunition to the natives. In 1682 all town-dwelling Indians in Plymouth Colony were placed under a biblical tithing system, with every nine Indians being watched by a tenth who was responsible to the authorities. In Connecticut the proud Uncas gave up all his lands to be divided into farms and plantations, and agreed to take advice from the General Court, especially in matters of war and peace.[5]

English greed for Indian land was whetted by the war, and of course the displacement of former enemy groups opened up new territory for exploitation. So great was the pressure of English expansionism that even the loyal tribes found it impossible to retain their lands for long. Under conditions such as these, the Indians rapidly sank to the status of poor tenant farmers and hired servants. Clearly, the red man was now already far along his tragic path of degradation. When a French Huguenot visited New England in 1687 he wrote, "There is Nothing to fear from the Savages, for they are few in Number. The last Wars they had with the English . . . have reduced them to a small Number, and consequently they are incapable of defending themselves." [6] This brief observation, when compared with reports made prior to King Philip's War, indicates how complete was the collapse of Indian power in 1676. The failure of Philip's great gamble sealed the fate of all the tribes from the Merrimack River to Long Island Sound.

Many of the Christian Indians, despite cruel mistreatment during the war, remained firm in the faith, forming a nucleus around which were constructed the Christian Indian communities of the postwar period. John Eliot and Daniel Gookin continued to be pillars of strength to these people, while English philanthropists also contributed to their welfare through the Society for Propagating the Gospel. Thus the war, although a serious blow to the missionary movement in New England, did not prove fatal, and the spark of Christianity remained alive among the native peoples.

As soon as the war was over, New England found itself faced with a gigantic task of reconstruction. The regaining of deserted territory and the rebuilding of burned settlements began almost at once. People who had fled from the Narragansett country to Aquidneck now recrossed the bay, and even were willing to live underground in cellar holes and dugouts until their homes could be rebuilt. In central Massachusetts and the Connecticut Valley, as well as in Plymouth and Rhode Island, the war-scattered populations began to regroup and rebuild. Almost everywhere, new buildings were being constructed upon the foundations of the old. By the spring of 1677, twenty-seven families had returned to the ruined town of Marlborough. In June the former inhabitants of Middleborough held a meeting at Plymouth, and agreed to attempt a resettlement of their lands on the Nemasket River. Similar plans were made for other deserted towns such as Wrentham and Deerfield. In general, there was a strong tendency to insist upon compactness in the planning of post-war communities, a tendency stemming directly from the hard lessons of combat. By 1696 Cotton Mather was able to report that most of the towns which had been destroyed in King Philip's War were now resettled.[7]

Meanwhile, there was the continuing problem of those hundreds of people who had been uprooted or otherwise rendered helpless by the fury of total war. They were like the flotsam and jetsam left floating at sea in the wake of a hurricane. In the areas where the war had left its mark all charitable Christians were concerned with the problem, and indeed, from across the sea as well came tangible help. The churches of Dublin, Ireland, collected funds which they used to send a relief ship with food for the distressed people of New England. Massachusetts alone had over two thousand individuals eligible for such aid.[8] Food was a vital but temporary expedient. The dislocations of war went far deeper than hunger, and it would be years before some of the victims were able to overcome their handicaps. Some could never do it.

King Philip's War produced the first great veteran problem in American history, including the formation of the first active veterans' organizations and pressure groups. Never before had the colonial governments had to deal with such a problem, for this was the first war in English North America which had demanded so many soldiers for such a long period of service. Wounded veterans, obviously, needed immediate and continuing financial help, for many of them were unable to make an adequate living in the ordinary occupations of the day. Cases were handled on an individual basis, either by special committees or by the regular organs of government. Relief usually took the form of a lump sum payment, occasionally supplemented by certain special privileges such as exemption from taxation or the right to operate a tavern. One of the strangest forms of compensation was granted by Plymouth to one Nathaniel Hall, when he was given the privilege of collecting and keeping all fines assessed in the town of Yarmouth for violation of the liquor laws. No doubt the old soldier became an ardent snooper, and probably made more enemies than he had ever killed in the war.[9]

Unwounded veterans also soon began to press for special benefits, usually in the form of land. Various towns accordingly made land grants to their former soldiers in the years following the war.[10] These tokens of gratitude were gratefully accepted, but the men were really interested in bigger things. Finding it difficult to prosper in the old established towns, they had their eyes on the great unsettled tracts beyond the frontier, land which they themselves had helped to free from Indian control. Only the colony governments had authority to grant such lands, so the veterans formed organizations, and began to concentrate their pressure upon the legislatures in Boston and Hartford. As a result, much land was granted over a period of many years, and a number of new townships were founded. More than half a century after the end of the war the veterans and their heirs were still pressing the legislatures for wilderness tracts.[11] By this time, however, other wars had already begun to raise new crops of demanding veterans, and King Philip's War was already slipping into the limbo of half-remembered history.

The postwar years also saw a lively continuation of the long-standing dispute between Connecticut and Rhode Island over the control of the Narragansett country. Both colonies claimed jurisdiction, and tried to enforce their claims, to the bewilderment of the poor inhabitants of the territory. Massachusetts, with many of its prominent citizens being heavy investors in that area, naturally supported the Connecticut case in preference to Rhode Island jurisdiction. The struggle survived even the Andros regime of 1686–1689, and was not finally settled until 1728, when a boundary line between the two contending colonies was actually laid out by mutual agreement.[12] Meanwhile, Plymouth Colony successfully asserted its claim to the Mount Hope peninsula, and then sold the land to four Massachusetts proprietors. Soon the new town of Bristol was established on the territory which had once been the exclusive domain of Osamequin, Alexander, and Philip.[13]

While Connecticut and Rhode Island were enmeshed in the Narragansett controversy, and Plymouth was making good its claim to Mount Hope, Massachusetts was trying to maintain its right of jurisdiction in New Hampshire and Maine, along with its virtual freedom from English control. The King and his ministers were now thoroughly aroused by the independent spirit of the Bay Colony, and were determined to bring that colony to heel. This they succeeded in doing with the establishment of the Dominion of New England in 1686, placing over the Puritan commonwealth as governor none other than Edmund Andros, formerly of New York. Not until 1776 did Massachusetts again have as much independence as she had enjoyed in the years before King Philip's War.

New England orthodoxy, too, was badly shaken by the war. Depending as it did upon a strict system in which the individual was under the constant supervision of both church and state, it was certain to be weakened by the uprooting and dislocating effects of the struggle. The breaking up of families and the scattering of town populations had introduced a serious element of instability and unrest. Men who had never before left the security and tight little orthodoxy of their own towns or counties had marched out with the armies, and been exposed to a crosscurrent of new and radical ideas from Rhode Island and even from overseas. Sensing the danger, but attributing it still to stubbornness against reformation, the orthodox authorities tried to tighten up the controls by which they had always been able to maintain the rigid discipline of Puritan congregationalism. This proved to be futile. The current of restlessness was growing stronger, and the powerful acceleration given it by the dislocations of war continued, until it finally broke forth in the revolts and schisms of the eighteenth century.

The postwar period, then, was characterized not by harmony, but by internal strains and intercolonial quarrels. The fact that the Indians had been reduced to a state of subservience only served to intensify the disputes. Land and power were the real prizes for which the colonies strove, with the rival governments trying to acquire sufficient spoils of war to reimburse themselves for their losses.

Just as in the case of the Indians, so too for the English and their civilization in New England, King Philip's War was a definite turning point. Until 1675 the colonies were in their adolescence, a period which was characterized by youthful self-assurance, a buoyant expansionism, an optimistic seeking after religious and political Utopias. With all the boldness of a God-favored master race, the settlers had busied themselves with state-building and the accumulation of wealth, while trying to make the Indians conform to English standards of law and morality.

In history, societies are tested by crisis, and crisis is often the fulcrum of major change. King Philip's War put an abrupt end to this youthful period of colonial history, for the severe losses suffered by the colonies shook their confidence, weakened their twin structures of church and state, and developed internal strains which were the unmistakable signs of a newer and more diversified order soon to come. The same process of sudden aging has frequently been observed in individuals. Boys who gaily march off to war with all the enthusiasm of immature youth often grow to manhood in a matter of days, under the strain of battle. When they return home they are men, and their own families scarcely know them.

A few intelligent men who lived through King Philip's War, and who later pondered its causes, its development, its outcome, and its effects, sensed the historical significance of that great conflict. They realized that the two races had fought a war of extermination, and they saw that the triumph of the white men had effectively smashed forever the power of the red men in southern New England. Turning to the future, these men might well have been deeply impressed by the magnitude of the problems confronting the colonies. The old Puritan hopes of a true wilderness Zion were dead even in the very moment of English victory. Moreover, not only was the mother country already moving to make effective her authority in this area, but beyond, to the north and west, the growing strength of French colonial enterprise loomed as a future threat. French influence among the more remote tribes was increasing, giving a dark hint as to the nature of coming wars. Despite these clouds on the horizon of the future, however, the colonists still clung to their religious faith and their passion for economic and political development. There was still a moral and a physical vitality impelling New England to pursue its destiny. These intangible assets provided the renewed courage and strength which would enable the colonists to deal effectively with the problems of the future.

Notes

ABBREVIATIONS USED IN CITATIONS

CA   Connecticut State Archives

CCR   J. Hammond Trumbull, ed., *The Public Records of the Colony of Connecticut*

CHC   *Collections of the Connecticut Historical Society*

CSP   *Calendar of State Papers*, Colonial Series, America and the West Indies

MA   Massachusetts State Archives

MCR   Nathaniel B. Shurtleff, ed., *Records of the Governor and Company of the Massachusetts Bay in New England*

MCS   *Publications of the Colonial Society of Massachusetts*

MHC   *Collections of the Massachusetts Historical Society*

MHP   *Proceedings of the Massachusetts Historical Society*

Narratives   Charles H. Lincoln, ed., *Narratives of the Indian Wars*

NCP   *Publications of the Narragansett Club*

NEHGR   *The New England Historical and Genealogical Register*

PCR   Nathaniel B. Shurtleff and David Pulsifer, eds., *Records of the Colony of New Plymouth in New England*

RICR   John Russell Bartlett, ed., *Records of the Colony of Rhode Island and Providence Plantations in New England*

RIHC   *Collections of the Rhode Island Historical Society*

RIHP   *Publications of the Rhode Island Historical Society*

When referring to the accounts of the war written by Church, Hubbard, and Mather, I have used the pagination of the following editions:

Church, *Entertaining Passages Relating to Philip's War*, Boston, 1716

Hubbard, *The Present State of New-England*, London, 1677

Mather, *A Brief History of the War*, Boston and London, 1676

CHAPTER I *THE LAND AND THE PEOPLE*

[1] M. K. Bennett, "The Food Economy of the New England Indians, 1605–75," *Journal of Political Economy*, LXIII, No. 5, pp. 369–97 (Oct., 1955), concludes that corn was the great dietary staple of these Indians, and that agriculture was much more important in their food economy than was hunting.

[2] Roy Harvey Pearce, *The Savages of America*, pp. 19–26.

[3] 1 MHC, I, 223; 3 MHC, IV, 1–23; RICR, II, 135.

[4] My figures for the English population in the three Puritan colonies have been derived from the computations found in Richard LeBaron Bowen, *Early Rehoboth*, I, 15–24, which I believe to be reasonably accurate. Somewhat larger figures are given in Stella H. Sutherland, *Population Distribution in Colonial America*.

[5] Douglas Edward Leach, "The Military System of Plymouth Colony," *New England Quarterly*, XXIV, 342–64 (Sept., 1951).

CHAPTER II *GATHERING CLOUDS*

[1] New London Land Records, III, 131; CCR, I, 337–38, II, 165; *Rhode Island Land Evidences, Abstracts, I* (1648–1696), pp. 145–46; Little Compton Proprietors' Records; Franklin P. Rice, ed., *Records of the Proprietors of Worcester, Massachusetts*, pp. 21ff.; James N. Arnold, ed., *The Records of the Proprietors of the Narragansett, passim*.

[2] Don Gleason Hill, ed., *The Early Records of the Town of Dedham, Massachusetts*, IV, 153–54, 173, 176, 197, 219; Wrentham Records, I.

[3] Arnold, *op. cit.*, pp. 1–16; Rhode Island Court Records, I, 58, 65.

[4] PCR, X, 449; Arnold, *loc. cit.*

[5] Elisha R. Potter, *The Early History of Narragansett*, p. 262; MCR, IV, Part II, 159, 161–62, 175–76, 178, 198; CSP, 1661–1668, p. 199; RICR, II, 59–60, 93–94.

[6] MCR, IV, Part II, 233; RICR, II, 127–29; CSP, 1661–1668, pp. 341–43.

[7] CCR, II, 89–92, 95, 137–38, 146, 156–57, 167, 173–74, 529–30; Clarence W. Bowen, *The Boundary Disputes of Connecticut*, p. 35.

[8] Hampshire County Court Record, I, 63.

[9] RIHP, I, 202–203; RIHC, X, 11–13, 89, 311; RICR, I, 418; *The Early Records of the Town of Providence*, V, 297–305, XV, 162–66; *Rhode Island Historical Tracts*, No. 14; NCP, VI, 387; CSP, 1675–1676, p. 261.

[10] If we may credit the report of one Captain Wyborne, who visited Boston in 1673, the officials of that community were not doing all in their power to promote Indian sobriety. As the story goes, the town of Boston was erecting a fort on one of the islands in the harbor. Wages being high, the magistrates developed an ingenious system for assuring a constant supply of cheap labor—Indian labor. All that was necessary was to change the penalty prescribed for Indians found drunk. Hitherto the besotted redskin could expect no more than

a flogging for his delinquency, but under the new system he found himself wafted over the waters of Boston Harbor under sentence of ten days' labor at the fort. If the town fathers had not been truly ingenious, the culprit would have been released at the end of the ten days, and the fort might never have been completed. Instead, however, arrangements were made to have liquor carried over to the island toward the end of the ten-day period, and those Indians due for release were allowed to get their eager hands on the beverage. Once again they would gulp the fiery liquid, only to find their term of service extended another ten days, and so on indefinitely. Wyborne's report was put forward by an anti-Massachusetts faction, and should be treated with some skepticism. See CSP, 1675–1676, pp. 307–308.

[11] MCR, III, 98; PCR, XI, 60–61; CCR, II, 61, 256–57, 574–76.
[12] NCP, VI, 202–203; 3 MHC, IX, 290; 4 MHC, VI, 283.
[13] PCR, III, 192.
[14] 4 MHC, VIII, 233–34; Increase Mather, A *Relation of the Troubles*, pp. 228–29; William Hubbard, *The Present State of New-England*, pp. 9–10.
[15] PCR, IV, 25–26.
[16] CSP, 1661–1668, p. 380.
[17] PCR, IV, 164–65; RICR, II, 192–99, 205–208.
[18] PCR, IV, 151, 166.
[19] *Letters of and about the Indians*, p. 10; RICR, II, 263–86; CCR, II, 548–51; CA, Indians I, 17; NCP, VI, 332; 5 MHC, I, 414.
[20] 1 MHC, VI, 198–201, 211; Winslow Papers, 65; RICR, II, 370–71. The treaty signed by Philip at Taunton on April 10, 1671, appears in William Hubbard, *The Present State of New-England*, pp. 11–12. See also Increase Mather, A *Relation of the Troubles*, pp. 231–33.
[21] NEHGR, XV, 36; PCR, V, 63–64.
[22] PCR, V, 73–74; 1 MHC, V, 193–97.
[23] PCR, V, 76–77; 1 MHC, VI, 197–98; Winslow Papers, 66.
[24] PCR, V, 77–79, X, 362.

CHAPTER III THE OUTBREAK OF WAR

[1] Increase Mather, A *Relation of the Troubles*, p. 236.
[2] William Hubbard, *The Present State of New-England*, p. 14.
[3] A *Report of the Record Commissioners, Containing the Roxbury Land and Church Records*, p. 193; PCR, X, 362.
[4] PCR, V, 168.
[5] Winslow Papers, 89.
[6] PCR, X, 364; 1 MHC, VI, 94; Winslow Papers, 89.
[7] *Narratives*, p. 9.
[8] PCR, X, 364.
[9] John Callender, *An Historical Discourse*, pp. 126–27n.
[10] MA, LXVII, 202.
[11] Davis Papers, I, 80; Boston Atheneum MSS LI, Vol. I, 17, 18.

[12] Winslow Papers, 90; *Narratives*, p. 12.

[13] MA, XXX, 169; George M. Bodge, *Soldiers in King Philip's War*, p. 104.

[14] MA, LXVII, 200. It is ironical that Roger Williams and Edward Hutchinson should come together in this fashion in the interests of that government which had exiled Williams himself and Hutchinson's mother in the 1630's.

[15] 4 MHC, VI, 299–302; NCP, VI, 366–69.

[16] Callender, *op. cit.*, pp. 127–28n.; *Narratives*, p. 12.

[17] Boston Atheneum MSS LI, Vol. I, 18.

[18] 4 MHC, VI, 302; NCP, VI, 371–72.

[19] Warwick Records, Town Book A-2 (Transcript), 143; CA, War I, 2a; 4 MHC, VI, 302.

[20] CA, War I, 3a.

[21] 3 MHC, X, 119.

[22] Winthrop Papers, XVIII, 137.

[23] Franklin P. Dexter, ed., *Ancient Town Records* [New Haven], II, 338–39.

[24] MA, LXVII, 204, 205; Davis Papers, I, 81.

[25] John Hull's Diary, *Transactions and Collections of the American Antiquarian Society*, III, 162.

[26] MA, LXVII, 206a; CSP, 1675–1676, p. 252; Cotton Mather, *Magnalia Christi Americana*, II, 487.

[27] *Narratives*, p. 28; MA, LXI, 134, 135, 136; Bodge, pp. 59–63.

[28] Boston Atheneum MSS LI, Vol. I, 18; *Narratives*, pp. 12–13.

[29] MA, II, 195; PCR, X, 462–64; Davis Papers, I, 83; 4 MHC, VIII, 299–300; 5 MHC, I, 428–30.

[30] Daniel Gookin, *An Historical Account of the . . . Christian Indians of New England* (*Transactions and Collections of the American Antiquarian Society*, II), 440–41; CHC, XXI, 257–59; RIHC, X, 164.

[31] PCR, X, 462–64.

CHAPTER IV THE JULY CAMPAIGN OF 1675

[1] Winslow Papers, 90; Boston Atheneum MSS LI, Vol. I, 18.

[2] Originally the authorities at Boston had given the command to Major General Daniel Denison, with Savage as his second-in-command, but illness forced Denison to yield actual command in the field to his subordinate. MA, LXVII, 206b, 207, 208.

[3] Thomas Church, *Entertaining Passages Relating to Philip's War*, pp. 5–6. See also William Hubbard, *The Present State of New-England*, p. 18; Winthrop Papers, XVII, 30.

[4] MA, LXVII, 209, 211; *Narratives*, p. 29; George M. Bodge, *Soldiers in King Philip's War*, pp. 88–92.

[5] Church, p. 5.

[6] Winthrop Papers, XVII, 30.

[7] Hubbard, p. 19.

[8] *Narratives*, p. 13; Winthrop Papers, XVII, 30.

[9] Church, p. 6; CSP, 1675–1676, p. 253.

[10] Boston Atheneum MSS LI, Vol. I, 19.

[11] CA, War I, 7, 10; CCR, II, 336–37.

[12] CA, War I, 7; Winthrop Papers, XV, 23, XVII, 30; CHC, XXI, 213–14.

[13] CA, War I, 10; CCR, II, 336; 5 MHC, I, 426–27; 5 MHC, VIII, 401–403.

[14] Hubbard, pp. 20–21; CA, War I, 6; CCR, II, 338; RIHP, VIII, 154–55.

[15] Winslow Papers, 93.

[16] Winthrop Papers, Ia, 155, XVIII, 26; CHC, XXI, 209–11; CA, War I, 6, 6b; CCR, II, 338.

[17] 5 MHC, VIII, 172.

[18] Winthrop Papers, XVIII, 138.

[19] Sources for the dispute between Andros and Connecticut include the following: CA, Colonial Boundaries II, 29–31, 33–37, 40; CA, War I, 4b; CCR, II, 260–63, 334–35, 337, 579–86; Franklin B. Hough, ed., *A Narrative of the Causes Which Led to Philip's Indian War*, pp. 44–47, 49, 51, 54–56; CHC, XXI, 207–209; 6 MHC, V, 3–4; Winthrop Papers, Ia, 155, V, 148, VI, 20, X, 72, XI, 127, XVIII, 138.

[20] Winthrop Papers, Ia, 155, VI, 18, 20; NEHGR, XXIV, 324; 5 MHC, I, 424–26; 5 MHC, VIII, 172–74; 6 MHC, V, 3–4.

[21] Copies of the treaty may be found in CA, War I, 9; and Davis Papers, I. It has been printed in Hubbard, pp. 21–23; Elisha R. Potter, *The Early History of Narragansett*, pp. 167–69; and Richard LeBaron Bowen, *Early Rehoboth*, III, 66–68.

[22] Hough, *op. cit.*, pp. 62–63; *Narratives*, p. 13; CHC, XXI, 212–13.

[23] Winslow Papers, 93, 94, 98; Bowen, III, 73; 1 MHC, VI, 84–85.

[24] Church, p. 7.

[25] Church, p. 8.

[26] Church, p. 9.

[27] Winthrop Papers, XVII, 30.

[28] Davis Papers, I, 84; Winslow Papers, 94, 97; MA, LXVII, 212; *Narratives*, p. 30; Increase Mather, *Diary*, July 12, 1675.

[29] RIHP, VIII, 154–55.

[30] *Narratives*, p. 30; *A Brief and True Narration of the Late Wars Risen in New-England*, p. 5; Winslow Papers, 94.

[31] Winslow Papers, 94, 98; 1 MHC, VI, 84–85; Bowen, III, 73–74; William Bradford, *A Letter from Major William Bradford* (July 21, 1675).

[32] Daniel Gookin, *An Historical Account of the . . . Christian Indians of New England* (*Transactions and Collections of the American Antiquarian Society*, II), 441.

[33] Winslow Papers, 96, 97.

[34] Bradford, *loc. cit.* This swamp country lies just south of the present city of Fall River.

[35] Bradford, *loc. cit.*; Winslow Papers, 98; 1 MHC, VI, 84–85; Bowen, III, 73–74; Winthrop Papers, XIV, 141.

[36] Hubbard, p. 27.

[37] 5 MHC, I, 425.

[88] Bowen, III, 57.

[89] MA, LXVII, 232; Winthrop Papers, XIV, 141; Bodge, pp. 49–50; Bowen, III, 88–89, 94; Davis Papers, I, 87.

CHAPTER V *THE WAR SPREADS*

[1] MA, LXVII, 214, 222; Levi B. Chase, *The Bay Path and Along the Way*, pp. 136–43, 150–63.

[2] This was the attack of July 14th, mentioned previously. See p. 66.

[3] MA, XXX, 172a; Winthrop Papers, XIV, 141; *Narratives*, p. 32; CHC, XXI, 213–14; 6 MHC, III, 447–48; Daniel Gookin, *An Historical Account of the . . . Christian Indians of New England* (*Transactions and Collections of the American Antiquarian Society*, II), 445–47.

[4] The most important documentary sources concerning Philip's flight to the Nipmuck country are found in Richard LeBaron Bowen, *Early Rehoboth*, III, 88–101. Bowen's careful study of this particular phase of the war is the best yet published.

[5] MA, LXVII, 227; George M. Bodge, *Soldiers in King Philip's War*, p. 106.

[6] The principal source for Hutchinson's mission is Captain Wheeler's own account, which has been published in the *Collections of the New-Hampshire Historical Society*, II, 6–23, and in the Old South Leaflets, No. 7. The facts there given are confirmed by numerous other documents.

[7] MA, LXVII, 254.

[8] *A Brief and True Narration of the Late Wars Risen in New-England*, p. 7; Gookin, *op. cit.*, p. 448.

[9] Two places have been suggested as the site of the ambush. Cf. Daniel H. Chamberlain, *Wheeler's Surprise, 1675: Where?*; Grindall Reynolds, "King Philip's War; With Special Reference to the Attack on Brookfield in August, 1675," *Proceedings of the American Antiquarian Society*, New Series, V, 77–95 (Oct., 1887); Lucius R. Paige, "Wheeler's Defeat, 1675: Where?" *ibid.*, pp. 96–106; Lucius R. Paige, "Wickaboag? Or Winnimisset?" NEHGR, XXXVIII, 395–400 (Oct., 1884). Because of changes in terrain during the past two centuries it may never be possible to reach a final decision in the matter. I myself am inclined to favor the southern site. See also 2 MHP, VIII, 280.

[10] Wheeler, *op. cit.*

[11] According to George W. Ellis and John E. Morris, *King Philip's War*, p. 93, Springfield soon learned of Brookfield's plight when one Judah Trumble, having come upon the siege unexpectedly during a journey to Brookfield, managed to get back to Springfield with the news.

[12] It has been thought by some that Willard incurred the extreme displeasure of his superiors for thus abandoning his original mission without orders from higher authority, but there is little or no evidence to support this view. Certainly Increase Mather, who was very close to the top men in the colony government, shows only approval of Willard's action. See Joseph Willard, *Willard Memoir*, pp. 285–303.

[13] Cotton Mather, *Magnalia Christi Americana*, II, 489.

[14] *A Brief and True Narration of the Late Wars Risen in New-England*, p. 7.

[15] MA, LXVII, 239; Bodge, pp. 66–67; NEHGR, XXIII, 324–25.

[16] See below, pp. 148–49.

[17] MA, XXX, 178, 182, LXVII, 252; Gookin, *op. cit.*, pp. 462–63.

[18] Winthrop Papers, XVIII, 138; CA, War I, 11d; CCR, II, 348; Chase, *op. cit.*, pp. 63–64, 67.

[19] CA, War I, 14; CCR, II, 353.

[20] CA, War I, 11c; CCR, II, 349–50; Winthrop Papers, XVII, 12.

[21] CHC, XXI, 222–23; CCR, II, 353–54, 356.

[22] CA, War I, 17; Winthrop Papers, X, 23, XIII, 43; 6 MHC, III, 448–49; CHC, XXI, 222–23.

[23] Winthrop Papers, X, 23, XIV, 85; 6 MHC, III, 448–49.

[24] Winthrop Papers, X, 24, 25; 6 MHC, III, 449–51.

[25] Hubbard, p. 38; MA, LXVII, 262.

[26] CA, War I, 1d, 1e, 1f, 19; PCR, X, 360, 364–65; MA, LXVII, 255; CCR, II, 365–68.

[27] *Narratives*, p. 47.

[28] MA, LXVII, 288.

[29] MA, LXVIII, 2.

[30] MA, LXVII, 282, 286, 290; NEHGR, XLVIII, 317; John Pynchon to Joseph Pynchon, Oct. 20, 1675, Pynchon Papers (Connecticut Valley Historical Museum).

[31] MA, LXVII, 244; NEHGR, X, 245.

[32] Bridgewater Records, I (Transcript), 71; Wallingford Town Records, I (Transcript), 64–65; *Town Records of Topsfield, Massachusetts*, I, 17; Beverly Town Records (Transcript), 32–33; Marshfield Records, I (Transcript), 137; New London Town Records, 1664–1703, p. 69.

[33] MCR, V, 46–51, 55–56.

[34] CCR, II, 360–62.

[35] Franklin B. Hough, ed., *A Narrative of the Causes Which Led to Philip's Indian War*, pp. 74–75, 77–78, 82, 92, 94; Franklin B. Hough, ed., *Papers Relating to the Island of Nantucket*, pp. 88–89.

[36] MCR, V, 49–50; CCR, II, 392–94.

[37] Hubbard, pp. 38–39.

[38] MA, LXVII, 263.

[39] MA, LXVIII, 25.

[40] CA, War I, 15.

[41] MA, LXVII, 263; CCR, II, 368; 4 MHC, VII, 577–78.

[42] See below, pp. 184–85.

[43] Winthrop Papers, X, 24, 25.

[44] MA, LXVII, 286, 290, LXVIII, 6; CA, War I, 1e; NEHGR, XXIII, 23–24.

[45] MA, LXVII, 286. See also MA, LXVII, 246, 280; Bodge, pp. 146–47.

[46] CA, War I, 1e; NEHGR, XXIII, 23–24.

[47] MA, LXVIII, 2. See also MA, LXVII, 285, 298, LXVIII, 10; CCR, II, 374; CHC, XXI, 227–28.

[48] MA, LXVIII, 10, 22; Winthrop Papers, X, 26, XVII, 74, 75.

[49] MA, LXVIII, 11a, 13, 15, 16.

[50] MA, LXVIII, 22.

[51] MA, LXVIII, 18; Bodge, p. 69.

[52] Winthrop Papers, X, 27; *Narratives*, p. 48.

[53] MA, LXVIII, 37; Winthrop Papers, XVII, 31; MCR, V, 66–67; CCR, II, 381.

[54] MA, LXVIII, 47, 47a, 51.

[55] MA, LXVIII, 56; CCR, II, 381.

[56] Gookin, *op. cit.*, pp. 475–80; Winthrop Papers, V, 153; MA, XXX, 188, LXVIII, 40, 41, 42, 43, 46, 50, 57; Bodge, pp. 54, 267–68; NEHGR, XXV, 10–11.

[57] MA, LXVIII, 57, 61, 63, 63a, 66; MCR, V, 52–53.

CHAPTER VI MEN, MATÉRIEL, AND MONEY

[1] MA, LXIX, 35, 237. One servant complained to the government that his master had demanded £10 from him as compensation for his period of military service (MA, LXIX, 40).

[2] Hiring a substitute was not considered dishonorable. One man even sued his hired substitute for avoiding service and thus rendering the bargain invalid. He won his case (MCS, XXX, 683).

[3] 4 MHC, VII, 576.

[4] MA, LXVII, 269; George M. Bodge, *Soldiers in King Philip's War*, p. 53.

[5] MA, LXVIII, 4; Bodge, p. 211.

[6] MA, LXVIII, 166.

[7] MA, LXVIII, 17, 17a, 121; MCR, V, 47–49; *The Early Records of the Town of Providence*, XV, 183.

[8] MA, LXVIII, 211.

[9] For details of one very interesting supply movement, see the following sources: MA, LXVIII, 10, 10d, 19, LXX, 65, 66, 68, 69; John Hull's Letter Book (Typescript copy), I, 282.

[10] Davis Papers, I, 84. George Shove of Taunton estimated that the crop losses suffered by his town in 1675 included 1,500 bushels of corn. See Curwin Papers, III, 77.

[11] Sandwich Records (Transcript), 1651–1691, p. 120.

[12] MA, LXVII, 243, 271, LXVIII, 135b; MCR, V, 66; CCR, II, 410.

[13] MA, LXVII, 285, 290; G. Frederick Robinson and Albert H. Hall, comps., *Watertown Soldiers in the Colonial Wars and the American Revolution*, pp. 17–18.

[14] CA, War I, 31a, 31b; CCR, II, 270–71, 399; MCR, V, 52.

[15] CA, War I, 59, 61; CCR, II, 277–78, 432.

[16] MCR, V, 44–45, 55–56, 81–82; MA, LXVIII, 29a; CCR, II, 401; PCR, V, 191–92.

[17] Scituate Book of Accounts, p. 37; Bridgewater Records, I (Transcript), 71.

[18] *Dorchester Town Records*, pp. 186, 224–25, 245–46.
[19] MCR, V, 71. See also MA, LXVIII, 144, LXIX, 22; MCR, V, 95–96.
[20] John Hull's Letter Book (Typescript copy), I, 282; MCR, V, 50–51; PCR, V, 185–86, 199; CA, War I, 47a; MA, LXVIII, 209, LXIX, *passim.*

CHAPTER VII THE CAMPAIGN AGAINST THE NARRAGANSETTS

[1] CHC, XXI, 217–18, XXIV, 18; 6 MHC, III, 447–48; Winthrop Papers, V, 171, X, 22, XIII, 43; R.I. Historical Society Manuscripts, X, 42; CCR, II, 355–56; Daniel B. Updike, *Richard Smith*, pp. 110–11.
[2] Updike, *op. cit.*, pp. 110–12; Richard LeBaron Bowen, *Early Rehoboth*, III, 67n.
[3] Winthrop Papers, XVIII, 139.
[4] *Loc. cit.*
[5] Winthrop Papers, XVIII, 140.
[6] MA, XXX, 177.
[7] PCR, X, 360–61; *Narratives*, pp. 44–45.
[8] Updike, *op. cit.*, pp. 112–14.
[9] Winthrop Papers, V, 154, 199; Hubbard, p. 48; Mather, p. 19.
[10] MA, XXX, 188–89; Winthrop Papers, XIX, 49; 5 MHC, IX, 99–100.
[11] 5 MHC, I, 105–10; Updike, *op. cit.*, pp. 112–14.
[12] Above, p. 100.
[13] For a more detailed analysis of these events see Douglas Edward Leach, "A New View of the Declaration of War against the Narragansetts, November, 1675," *Rhode Island History*, XV, 33–41 (April, 1956).
[14] MA, II, 363; PCR, X, 456; MCR, V, 66–67; Winthrop Papers, XVII, 31.
[15] Winthrop Papers, X, 28.
[16] MA, LXVII, 247, LXVIII, 39; CA, War I, 24; PCR, X, 357; CSP, 1675–1676, pp. 317–19.
[17] Curwin Papers, III, 47.
[18] MA, LXVIII, 53; CA, War I, 25, 26; PCR, X, 358.
[19] MA, LXVIII, 55; PCR, X, 457–58; R.I. Historical Society Manuscripts, X, 144; *Some Further Papers Relating to King Philip's War*, p. 11; *Narratives*, p. 15.
[20] Winthrop Papers, V, 154, 199, X, 29.
[21] Winthrop Papers, V, 156.
[22] CA, War I, 27; PCR, X, 359.
[23] New London Town Records, 1664–1703, p. 70; CCR, II, 383–84.
[24] Increase Mather, *Diary*; MA, XXX, 185b, 188, 189, LXVIII, 57, 62; Winthrop Papers, XV, 25, XVIII, 141.
[25] MA, LXVII, 247; CSP, 1675–1676, pp. 317–19. See below, p. 185.
[26] John Hull's Commonplace Book, I; Winthrop Papers, X, 29; CCR, II, 387; *Records of the Court of Assistants of the Colony of the Massachusetts Bay*, I, 58; PCR, V, 183.
[27] George M. Bodge, *Soldiers in King Philip's War*, pp. 182–83.
[28] 2 MHP, I, 229–30.

[29] Curwin Papers, III, 6; NEHGR, XCIX, 103–104.

[30] Winslow Papers, 100.

[31] Winthrop Papers, V, 189, XIX, 74; 5 MHC, VIII, 174–75.

[32] Curwin Papers, III, 6; MA, LXVIII, 101; Bodge, p. 192; Church, p. 14; Hubbard, pp. 49–50. Subsequent to the publication of Hubbard's *Narrative*, Governor Winslow stated that Hubbard's account of Moseley's exploits, Dec. 11–13, was not accurate. 4 MHC, VIII, 234–35.

[33] Cotton Papers, Part VII, 2, 3; MA, LXVIII, 101; Bodge, pp. 174–75, 192; *Narratives*, pp. 56–57; Cotton Mather, *Magnalia Christi Americana*, II, 491; Winthrop Papers, V, 189.

[34] Cotton Papers, Part VII, 2, 3; *News from New-England*.

[35] MA, LXVIII, 102a; Bodge, pp. 192–93; Cotton Papers, Part VII, 2, 3. The foundation of Bull's house has been uncovered by scientific excavation. See RIHC, XI, 2–11.

[36] Benjamin Thompson, *New-England's Crisis*.

[37] Hubbard, p. 53.

[38] *Narratives*, p. 65; Cotton Papers, Part VII, 2, 3; Bodge, pp. 174–75, 193–94.

[39] CA, War I, 137.

[40] Cotton Papers, Part VII, 2, 3; Hubbard, pp. 54, 56; Mather, pp. 20–21; 5 MHC, IX, 97.

[41] Cotton Papers, Part VII, 2, 3; Bodge, pp. 174–75, 193–94; *A Farther Brief and True Narration*; *News from New-England*; Hubbard, p. 54.

[42] Church, p. 16.

[43] Church, p. 14.

[44] Winthrop Papers, X, 30, XVII, 76, 77; 4 MHC, VII, 352–53.

[45] Franklin B. Hough, ed., *A Narrative of the Causes Which Led to Philip's Indian War*, pp. 132–35; CA, War I, 72, 137; *A Letter Written by Dr. Simon Cooper*, pp. 19–21; CCR, III, 5–6n.; Winslow Papers, 101; Curwin Papers, III, 75. The James Otis Papers in the library of the Massachusetts Historical Society contain an interesting itemized record of the charges made by one Newport citizen for the care of various wounded men. The same accounts have been published in PCR, VI, edited by Nathaniel B. Shurtleff. The version in the Otis Papers is badly torn on the right-hand side of the page, while Shurtleff's version is incomplete on the opposite side of the page. A comparison of the two gives a fairly complete reconstruction of the original document.

[46] Church, p. 17; Hubbard, pp. 55–57; Bodge, pp. 193–94; CA, War I, 29, 31a; CCR, II, 391–92; Davis Papers, I, 89.

[47] Hubbard, p. 48.

[48] *Narratives*, p. 66; CA, Colonial Boundaries I, 159; CCR, III, 512; PCR, X, 412; *A Farther Brief and True Narration*, p. 11; Cotton Papers, Part VII, 1, 2, 3; Bodge, pp. 174–75; Curwin Papers, III, 75; John Davis, Appendix to Morton's *Memorial*, pp. 434–35.

[49] *Narratives*, pp. 65–66; Curwin Papers, III, 5; Winthrop Papers, V, 138.

[50] MA, LXVIII, 105, 108, 109; CA, War I, 30a; PCR, X, 460.

[51] 4 MHC, VII, 352–53; Winthrop Papers, X, 29, 30, XVII, 76, 77.

[52] CA, War I, 31a.

[53] CA, War I, 34a; CCR, II, 395–96.

[54] CA, War I, 30b; CCR, II, 397–99; Davis Papers, I, 91; 1 MHC, VI, 89–90.

[55] Cotton Papers, Part VII, 2, 3; *Rhode Island Land Evidences, Abstracts*, I (1648–1696), p. 165; Bodge, pp. 193–94.

[56] 4 MHC, VI, 307–11; NCP, VI, 379–84; *Narratives*, p. 67; John Davis, *op. cit.*, pp. 434–35; CA, War I, 37; CCR, II, 401–402; Cotton Papers, Part VII, 2, 3. Much unverifiable legend has grown up around the tragic figure of Joshua Tefft. See James N. Arnold, "Joshua Tefft," *Narragansett Historical Register*, III, 164–69 (1884–1885).

[57] Curwin Papers, III, 5; MA, LXVIII, 111a, 112, 112a, 121; CA, War I, 34b, 37, 38; CCR, II, 401–403, 406; Cotton Papers, Part VII, 2, 3.

[58] Increase Mather, *Diary*.

[59] Curwin Papers, III, 76; *Narratives*, pp. 66–67, 79–80; *News from New-England*.

[60] Curwin Papers, III, 76; *Rhode Island Historical Tracts*, No. 14, pp. 59–62; PCR, X, 394; CCR, III, 494.

[61] Curwin Papers, III, 76; *Narratives*, pp. 68, 112–13; *A True Account of the Most Considerable Occurrences*; Rev. Peter Hobart's Diary; MA, LXVIII, 131; Franklin B. Hough, ed., *A Narrative of the Causes Which Led to Philip's Indian War*, pp. 140–41; CCR, II, 405–406.

[62] Mather, p. 38; Church, pp. 18–19; Daniel Gookin, *An Historical Account of the . . . Christian Indians of New England* (*Transactions and Collections of the American Antiquarian Society*, II), 487; CA, War I, 33; CCR, II, 397; *Documents Relative to the Colonial History of the State of New-York*, III, 254–57, 264–65; CSP, 1677–1680, p. 184.

[63] CA, War I, 91; CA, Colonial Boundaries I, 159; CCR, III, 512; PCR, X, 412; RICR, III, 62.

[64] CSP, 1677–1680, p. 276; John Callender, *An Historical Discourse*, p. 134; *The Early Records of the Town of Providence*, XV, 160; RICR, II, 547–48.

CHAPTER VIII THE PROBLEM OF THE "FRIENDLY INDIANS"

[1] Winthrop Papers, XVI, 65.

[2] CA, War I, 133.

[3] CA, War I, 56.

[4] CA, War I, 69.

[5] CCR, II, 441.

[6] *An Historical Account of the . . . Christian Indians of New England* (*Transactions and Collections of the American Antiquarian Society*, II), 449–50, 454.

[7] *A Report of the Record Commissioners, Containing the Roxbury Land and Church Records*, pp. 194–95.

[8] MA, XXX, 173; PCR, X, 451–53.

[9] Gookin, *op. cit.*, pp. 455–62, 466–67; *Narratives*, pp. 40–41; *Records of the Court of Assistants of the Colony of the Massachusetts Bay*, I, 53–54; Hubbard, p. 30.

[10] Gookin, *op. cit.*, pp. 471–75, 482–84, 491–92; *Records of the Court of Assistants of the Colony of the Massachusetts Bay*, I, 57; 1 MHP, XVII, 252.

[11] Gookin, *op. cit.*, pp. 495–97; MA, XXX, 185a.

[12] A *Report of the Record Commissioners, Containing the Roxbury Land and Church Records*, p. 196; MA, XXX, 185b, 187, 188, 189, 194, 194a, 195, 197; MCR, V, 64, 84; 1 MHP, XVII, 252. Plymouth Colony interned some of her Indians on Clark's Island in Plymouth Harbor (PCR, V, 187).

[13] MA, XXX, 192, 193b, 194, 194a, 196, 197a, LXVIII, 136b, 159; Gookin, *op. cit.*, p. 494; *Records of the Court of Assistants of the Colony of the Massachusetts Bay*, I, 60–61.

[14] MA, XXX, 193, 193a.

[15] Massachusetts Historical Society, Miscellaneous Manuscripts, 1650–1679; A *Report of the Record Commissioners, Containing the Roxbury Land and Church Records*, p. 193; MCS, XXX, 695–97; 2 MHC, VI, 642–43; Cotton Mather, *Magnalia Christi Americana*, I, 491–92; Benjamin Thompson, *New-Englands Tears for Her Present Miseries.*

[16] MA, XXX, 201b; MCR, V, 86–87; Gookin, *op. cit.*, p. 517.

[17] CA, War I, 11c; CCR, II, 349, 400.

[18] Gookin, *op. cit.*, pp. 441–42.

[19] NCP, I, 39–40.

[20] MCR, V, 95.

[21] RIHC, X, 163.

[22] MA, LXVII, 220; Gookin, *op. cit.*, p. 462.

CHAPTER IX   A TIME OF TROUBLES (FEBRUARY–MAY, 1676)

[1] Daniel Gookin, *An Historical Account of the . . . Christian Indians of New England* (*Transactions and Collections of the American Antiquarian Society*, II), 486–89; CA, War I, 35c; 1 MHC, VI, 205–208; Cotton Papers, Part VII, 4.

[2] MA, XXX, 210a, 211, LXVIX, 105.

[3] Gookin, *op. cit.*, pp. 489–90; 4 MHC, V, 1–2.

[4] CSP, 1675–1676, pp. 350–51; Gookin, *op. cit.*, p. 490.

[5] *Narratives*, pp. 83–84, 113, 116, 118–22; Henry S. Nourse, ed., *The Early Records of Lancaster, Massachusetts*, pp. 104–106; NEHGR, L, 483–85.

[6] The Committee of Militia of Chelmsford to the Governor and Council, Feb. 15, 1675/6, Shattuck Papers; MA, LXVIII, 133b, 134a; William T. Davis, ed., *Records of the Town of Plymouth*, I, 146–47; Haverhill Town Records, II and III, 235.

[7] MA, LXVIII, 135.

[8] Curwin Papers, III, 9; A *True Account of the Most Considerable Occurrences; Narratives*, pp. 80–81, 127; MA, LXVIII, 139; Gookin, *op. cit.*, pp. 493–94.

[9] Gookin, *op. cit.*, p. 494.

[10] MCR, V, 71–72.

[11] Mather, p. 23; MA, LXVIII, 145a, 151; PCR, V, 185–87.

Notes

[13] CCR, II, 413; Franklin B. Dexter, ed., *Ancient Town Records* [New Haven], II, 349–51.

[13] PCR, X, 359; Winthrop Papers, XVII, 78; 1 MHP, XIII, 234–35; CCR, II, 409–10; *Narratives*, p. 81; Gookin, *op. cit.*, pp. 500–501.

[14] MA, LXVIII, 134, 152a; MCR, V, 74–75.

[15] Gookin, *op. cit.*, pp. 501–504; MA, XXX, 190a, 200.

[16] *Narratives*, p. 81.

[17] Gookin, *op. cit.*, pp. 505–506; Hubbard, p. 77; Mather, p. 23; *Narratives*, pp. 130–31.

[18] *Narratives*, pp. 81, 134–36; *A True Account of the Most Considerable Occurrences*; MA, LXVIII, 163, CCXLI, 279; 3 MHC, I, 68–70.

[19] George Sheldon, *A History of Deerfield, Massachusetts*, I, 138–41; George M. Bodge, *Soldiers in King Philip's War*, pp. 377–86.

[20] Above, pp. 149–50.

[21] *Narratives*, p. 82; Curwin Papers, III, 9; MA, LXVIII, 196.

[22] MA, LXVIII, 160.

[23] MA, LXVIII, 169a, 172a, 174, 175b, 176a, 179, 180, 183; NEHGR, XXIII, 328; Bodge, p. 214; Report of Middlesex Committee, March 28, 1676, Shattuck Papers.

[24] MA, LXVIII, 165a, 168a; *Narratives*, pp. 81–82, 84; PCR, V, 204–206; Increase Mather, *Diary*.

[25] MA, LXVIII, 189; *Narratives*, p. 85.

[26] MA, LXVIII, 180, 191; Bodge, pp. 98–99, 213; CA, War I, 61; CCR, II, 412, 423; Simsbury Town Records, I, 13.

[27] William Hubbard, *The Happiness of a People*, p. 60; 1 MHC, VI, 89; MA, LXVIII, 177, 191; CA, War I, 61; Curwin Papers, III, 8; Richard LeBaron Bowen, *Early Rehoboth*, III, 14–19; Bodge, pp. 98–99; *Narratives*, pp. 84–85; *A True Account of the Most Considerable Occurrences*; Philip Walker, *Captan Perse* (Bowen, III, 34–38). Bowen has advanced the theory that Pierce was to have been joined by Moseley's company, but that instead of waiting for their arrival he went into action with only his own small force.

[28] CA, War I, 61, 68; PCR, V, 192–93; Davis Papers, I, 93; John Davis, Appendix to Morton's *Memorial*, pp. 438–40; Curwin Papers, III, 8; Bowen, III, 15–23; CCR, II, 445–47; *Narratives*, pp. 86–87.

[29] Benjamin Thompson, *New-England's Crisis*.

[30] MA, X, 233; R.I. Historical Society Manuscripts, X, 103; RICR, II, 535–36; *The Early Records of the Town of Providence*, XV, 148.

[31] MA, LXVIII, 167, 181a, 194, 235a; CA, War I, 62a, 65, 66; CCR, II, 431; Westfield Miscellaneous Records, 1675–1694.

[32] Cotton Papers, Part VII, 6; Curwin Papers, III, 8; Bowen, III, 15–19; *Narratives*, p. 90; PCR, V, 193–94; 4 MHC, V, 2–8.

[33] CA, War I, 55, 60, 61; Winthrop Papers, XIX, 45; *Narratives*, p. 142; CCR, II, 425–26; NEHGR, LXXXV, 85; MA, LXVIII, 204; Cotton Papers, Part VII, 6; 4 MHC, V, 6–8.

[34] MA, LXVIII, 157, 196, 203a, 229, CCXLI, 279; Bodge, pp. 238–41; CA, War I, 45b, 60; 3 MHC, I, 69; CCR, II, 434–35; Gookin, *op. cit.*, p. 506.

³⁵ John Hull's Commonplace Book, I.

³⁶ For a delightful biographical sketch of Winthrop, see Samuel Eliot Morison, *Builders of the Bay Colony*, Chap. IX. Edward Randolph, a not unbiased observer, attempted to belittle the severity of the epidemic. CSP, 1675–1676, p. 494. See also Winthrop Papers, XIX, 45; CHC, XXI, 242–44; *Narratives*, p. 89; John Hull's Letter Book (Typescript copy), I, 305; John Hull's Diary, *Transactions and Collections of the American Antiquarian Society*, III, 241.

³⁷ CA, War I, 53, 54, 56, 133; CCR, II, 418.

³⁸ CA, War I, 58a, 65, 66; CCR, II, 430, 432; MA, LXVIII, 235a; *Narratives*, Pᵢ. 90–91.

³⁹ MA, LXVIII, 220, 233, 234; Bodge, p. 226; *Narratives*, pp. 94–95.

⁴⁰ *Narratives*, pp. 152–53. Many years ago there was a warm dispute among antiquarians as to whether the attack on Sudbury occurred on April 18th, the date which appears on the stone monument, or on April 21st. The evidence now available leaves no doubt that the latter is the correct date. See Gookin, *op. cit.*, pp. 510–12; *A True Account of the Most Considerable Occurrences*; *Narratives*, pp. 92–94; MA, XXX, 204b, 205, 205b, LXVIII, 220, 224, 234; Bodge, pp. 225–27; 5 MHC, V, 12; NEHGR, VII, 221–24, XX, 135–41, 341–52; Francis Baylies, *An Historical Memoir of the Colony of New Plymouth*, II, Part V, 56–64.

⁴¹ It has usually been assumed that this group was led by Captain Hugh Mason. There can be no doubt that the group was sent out by Mason's order, but since he himself was over seventy years old it seems doubtful that he would go with them. This conjecture is given some support by MA, LXVIII, 224; Bodge, p. 227.

⁴² Gookin, *op. cit.*, pp. 509–12; MA, XXX, 201, LXVIII, 211; *Narratives*, pp. 93–94; *Collections of the New Hampshire Historical Society*, III, 99.

⁴³ *Narratives*, p. 93.

⁴⁴ MA, LXVIII, 221, 222a.

⁴⁵ MA, LXVIII, 223; Bodge, p. 215; *Narratives*, p. 153.

⁴⁶ MA, LXVIII, 228, 228a, 231, 240, 247a, LXIX, 9, 259; CA, War I, 78; John Hull's Letter Book (Typescript copy), I, 303; *Narratives*, p. 94; *A True Account of the Most Considerable Occurrences*: MCR, V, 90, 96–97; 5 MHC, V, 13.

⁴⁷ MA, LXVIII, 17, 17a; CA, War I, 36, 41, 43a, 44, 44b; CCR, II, 350, 397–98, 404, 406–407; Winthrop Papers, XV, 154; *Documents Relative to the Colonial History of the State of New-York*, III, 254–57, 264–65; CHC, XXI, 226–27, 241–42; *Narratives*, pp. 88–89; Franklin B. Hough, ed., *A Narrative of the Causes Which Led to Philip's Indian War*, pp. 102–103, 146–47; Bodge, p. 242.

⁴⁸ CA, War I, 43b, 49, 63a, 65; CCR, II, 414, 419–20, 436.

⁴⁹ CA, War I, 40; CCR, II, 404–405; MA, LXVIII, 165, 189, 202, CCXLI, 269; Hough, *op. cit.*, p. 136.

⁵⁰ MA, LXVII, 247, LXVIII, 199, 200, 201, LXIX, 7; Deputy Governor Symonds to Sir Joseph Williamson, April 6, 1676, Plymouth Papers, I; CSP, 1675–1676, pp. 317–19; CSP, 1677–1680, pp. 233–34, 236, 244; *Documents*

Relative to the Colonial History of the State of New-York, III, 258–59; 4 MHC, II, 288.

⁵¹ Hough, *op. cit.*, pp. 137, 160–61; Daniel H. Carpenter, "Rhode Island Families Who Went to Long Island, 1676, During King Philip's War," *Rhode Island Historical Magazine*, VI, 213–16 (1885–1886).

⁵² 5 MHC, VIII, 175–77; Winthrop Papers, V, 140; CA, War I, 45b; MA, LXVIII, 157.

⁵³ CA, War I, 45b; MA, LXVIII, 157.

⁵⁴ CA, War I, 67a, 67b; CCR, II, 425, 438–40; CHC, XXI, 241–42.

⁵⁵ MA, LXVIII, 193, 228, CCXLI, 282; Nourse, *op. cit.*, pp. 110–12; *Narratives*, pp. 155–58, 161–62; Gookin, *op. cit.*, p. 508. The author of *A True Account of the Most Considerable Occurrences* reports that an insolent letter from the Indians was received by the colonial authorities on April 6th. No such document is now known, and I am inclined to believe that the letter referred to was in fact identical with the reply presented to the Council on April 12th.

⁵⁶ MCR, V, 82–83.

⁵⁷ MCR, V, 93, 97; MA, XXX, 279, LXIX, 11a; Nourse, *op. cit.*, pp. 113–14.

⁵⁸ CA, War I, 85; CCR, II, 450; Governor Leverett to Sir Joseph Williamson, June 15, 1676, Plymouth Papers, I; CSP, 1675–1676, pp. 405–406; *Narratives*, pp. 163–64; Mather Papers, I, 76; NEHGR, VII, 209–19; MA, XXX, 279.

⁵⁹ *Narratives*, p. 165.

⁶⁰ Gookin, *op. cit.*, p. 508; Mather Papers, I, 76; NEHGR, VII, 209–19; Increase Mather, *An Historical Discourse Concerning the Prevalency of Prayer*.

⁶¹ CA, War I, 65; MCR, V, 82–83.

CHAPTER X *THE SPIRIT OF ZION*

¹ MA, LXVII, 252, LXVIII, 151; MCR, V, 50; R.I. Historical Society Manuscripts, X, 152.

² MA, LXVIII, 59; George M. Bodge, *Soldiers in King Philip's War*, p. 328.

³ MA, LXVII, 252; MCR, V, 54. The difficulties experienced by Lieutenant John Ruddock, commander of the garrison at Marlborough, furnish a good example of the tensions that existed. See MA, LXVII, 279, LXVIII, 4, 31; Bodge, pp. 211–12.

⁴ MA, LXVII, 288, LXVIII, 48, 51, 168, 182.

⁵ MA, LXVII, 259.

⁶ Eastham Records, 1650–1705.

⁷ MA, LXVIII, 179a.

⁸ MA, LXVII, 270.

⁹ MA, LXVIII, 21, 71; NEHGR, XXIII, 327; CCR, II, 272–73.

¹⁰ MA, LXVIII, 106, 117; CA, War I, 115.

¹¹ MA, LXVIII, 203, 216a, 234a.

¹² MA, LXVIII, 231a; PCR, X, 461.

¹³ MA, LXVIII, 179, 227, 234; MCR, V, 79–80; NEHGR, XXIII, 328; Bodge,

pp. 214, 216; Billerica Records (Transcript), 1653–1685, p. 187. It was almost as hard to conscript a horse as a man. See MA, LXVII, 245, LXIX, 1; Connecticut Colonial Probate Records, III, County Court, 1663–1667, p. 151.

[14] Marshfield Records (Transcript), I, 137; *Town Records of Salem, Massachusetts*, II, 204–205; Billerica Records (Transcript), 1653–1685, p. 186.

[15] MCR, V, 64; 2 MHP, XII, 402.

[16] MA, LXVIII, 12; MCR, V, 48, 51; NEHGR, XXII, 462; PCR, V, 185–86; *The Early Records of the Town of Providence*, XV, 160; RICR, II, 533.

[17] 4 MHC, VII, 628.

[18] Franklin B. Hough, ed., *Papers Relating to the Island of Nantucket*, pp. 103–107; *Narratives*, pp. 86–87; Clarence S. Brigham, ed., *The Early Records of the Town of Portsmouth*, pp. 188–89; Daniel H. Carpenter, "Rhode Island Families Who Went to Long Island, 1676, During King Philip's War," *Rhode Island Historical Magazine*, VI, 213–16 (1885–1886).

[19] CA, War I, 68; CCR, II, 445–47; Richard LeBaron Bowen, *Early Rehoboth*, III, 20–23; MA, LXVIII, 202a. Roger Williams testified that Governor Coddington himself was a wartime profiteer. See "An Answer to a Letter Sent From Mr. Coddington," *Proceedings of the Rhode Island Historical Society*, 1875–1876.

[20] Hampshire County Court Record, I, 172.

[21] CA, War I, 92; CCR, II, 445, 454–55, 457; Curwin Papers, III, 7, 77; Cotton Papers, Part VII, 10; *Narratives*, pp. 36, 38, 41.

[22] MA, X, 291, LXVII, 255; 4 MHC, VIII, *passim*; Perry Miller, "Declension in a Bible Commonwealth," *Proceedings of the American Antiquarian Society*, LI, 37–94 (April, 1941). Probably a small minority of the people continued to doubt that the Indian War was a punishment for sin. Among them was Samuel Gorton of Warwick. See 4 MHC, VII, 630.

[23] Cotton Papers, Part VI, 24.

[24] CCR, II, 354–55.

[25] Increase Mather, *An Earnest Exhortation to the Inhabitants of New-England*.

[26] Bowen, III, 40–50.

[27] MCR, V, 59–64; CCR, II, 280–83.

[28] Cotton Papers, Part VI, 25, 26.

[29] William Edmundson, *Journal*, p. 298.

[30] MA, CCXLI, 284.

[31] 5 MHC, V, 15.

[32] [Edward Wharton], *New-England's Present Sufferings under Their Cruel Neighbouring Indians*, pp. 3–8.

[33] RICR, II, 495–99, 549, 553–55, 567–72; R.I. General Court of Trials, I, 1671–1724, p. 27; 3 MHP, II, 378–81; Edmundson, *Journal*, pp. 81–83.

[34] Edmundson, *Journal*, pp. 79–80.

[35] MA, LXVIII, 241; Bodge, p. 242.

[36] PCR, V, 207; CCR, II, 418.

[37] CA, War I, 46.

[38] Cotton Papers, Part VII, 10; MCS, XXII, 148–53.

CHAPTER XI   *THE WANING OF INDIAN STRENGTH*

[1] *Narratives,* pp. 154–57.

[2] CA, War I, 71a.

[3] Mather, pp. 29–31; Hubbard, pp. 87–89; A *True Account of the Most Considerable Occurrences;* MA, LXIX, 230; *Narratives,* pp. 95–96; Hadley Records (Transcript), pp. 91–92; Epaphras Hoyt, *Antiquarian Researches,* pp. 128–31.

[4] MA, LXIX, 26; CA, War I, 74; George Sheldon, A *History of Deerfield, Massachusetts,* I, 161–68.

[5] CA, War I, 76; CCR, II, 442–43.

[6] CA, War I, 74, 84a; CCR, II, 450; Winthrop Papers, XIX, 15; NEHGR, XXV, 72; Sheldon, *op. cit.,* I, 170–71; 5 MHC, V, 13–14.

[7] CA, War I, 75b, 78; MCR, V, 92–93, 96–97; MA, LXVIII, 36; 2 MHP, VIII, 65–67.

[8] CA, War I, 77, 79, 81, 82, 83, 84, 85, 86, 88, 90; CCR, II, 444, 447–49, 452–53; MA, LXIX, 16b.

[9] Cotton Papers, Part VII, 9; MA, LXIX, 17; Samuel G. Drake, ed., *The Old Indian Chronicle,* p. 264n.; A *True Account of the Most Considerable Occurrences; A Report of the Record Commissioners, Containing the Roxbury Land and Church Records,* p. 194.

[10] This may be the attack around which has grown the story of how William Goffe, one of the regicide judges, suddenly appeared and saved the town. The episode is legendary rather than historical.

[11] CA, War I, 96.

[12] The Council of Massachusetts to Henchman, June 26, 1676, Shattuck Papers; CCR, II, 455–56; George M. Bodge, *Soldiers in King Philip's War,* pp. 57–58.

[13] 4 MHC, V, 8–10; CA, War I, 78; MA, LXIX, 9; MCR, V, 96–97.

[14] PCR, V, 197; Church, pp. 20–21.

[15] It was at about this time also that Awashonks sent an emissary with a message to the governor and Council of Rhode Island. Whether this message had any relationship to the negotiations with Church is not clear. See RICR, II, 545.

[16] Church, p. 23.

[17] PCR, V, 201–203.

[18] Bradford's letter of June 30, 1676, Mass. Historical Society Photostats, XX.

[19] Curwin Papers, III, 16; MA, LXIX, 24, 25; Bodge, pp. 262–63; 5 MHC, V, 14.

[20] CA, War I, 97, 100; CCR, II, 455, 458–59, 461–62. The evidence bearing on this episode leaves some doubt as to the actual site. One contemporary writer placed it "near Pawtuxet" (A *True Account of the Most Considerable Occurrences*). The Connecticut Council interpreted Talcott's report to mean that the skirmish took place at Nipsachuck. Bradford, who had direct information from Talcott shortly after the event, said that it occurred above Cowesit, but was

clearly in error as to the date (Curwin Papers, III, 16). Sidney S. Rider has concluded that the skirmish took place on the south bank of the Pawtuxet River just below the present Natick (*The Lands of Rhode Island*, pp. 174–75), but fails to give reasons for his conclusion. I am inclined to favor Nipsachuck, but the matter is by no means settled.

²¹ CA, War I, 97; CCR, II, 458–59; Curwin Papers, III, 16; RICR, II, 548; RIHC, X.

²² Hubbard, Appendix, pp. xi-xii.

²³ MA, XXX, 202, 203, LXIX, 16b; CA, War I, 99; CCR, II, 465–66.

²⁴ MA, XXX, 204, 206; Bodge, p. 304.

²⁵ MA, XXX, 207, 216; 5 MHC, V, 14; Daniel Gookin, *An Historical Account of the . . . Christian Indians of New England* (*Transactions and Collections of the American Antiquarian Society*, II), 527–29.

²⁶ *A True Account of the Most Considerable Occurrences.*

²⁷ CA, War I, 98, 100, 101c; CCR, II, 461–64.

²⁸ CSP, 1675–1676, pp. 406–409; MA, CVI, 212, 213, 214; Thomas Hutchinson, ed., *Collection of Original Papers Relative to the History of the Colony of Massachusetts-Bay*, II, 241.

²⁹ 5 MHC, V, 14; Church (Dexter Edition), pp. 104–105n.

³⁰ Church (Dexter Edition), pp. 104–105n.; Curwin Papers, III, 17; Cotton Papers, Part VII, 10.

³¹ Cotton Papers, Part VII, 10; Church, pp. 31–33.

³² Cotton Papers, Part VII, 10; Bradford to Cotton, July 24, 1676, *Providence Journal*, Jan. 15, 1876.

CHAPTER XII *PHILIPUS EXIT*

¹ Hubbard, p. 100.

² MA, LXIX, 41a, 42a.

³ MA, LXIX, 43, 46.

⁴ *Narratives*, p. 105.

⁵ Hubbard, p. 101.

⁶ 5 MHC, V, 15.

⁷ 5 MHC, V, 17, 21–22, 24n.; Increase Mather, *Diary; Records of the Court of Assistants of the Colony of the Massachusetts Bay*, I, 76.

⁸ RICR, II, 586; R.I. General Court of Trials, I, 1671–1724, pp. 34–37; Franklin B. Hough, ed., *A Narrative of the Causes Which Led to Philip's Indian War*, pp. 173–90.

⁹ *The Early Records of the Town of Providence*, VIII, 13.

¹⁰ MA, XXX, 173; PCR, X, 451–53. See above, pp. 148, 150–51.

¹¹ CSP, 1675–1676, pp. 378–512 *passim*; 1 MHC, III, 182–83.

¹² PCR, V, 207; NEHGR, VIII, 271–73; MCS, XIX, 25–28; MA, XXX, 209; MCR, V, 136. The Chamberlain Manuscripts in the Boston Public Library contain a list of Indian children put out to service, together with the names of the families to which they were assigned.

[12] Winslow Papers, 103, 105; MA, LXIX, 95a; RICR, II, 548–50; RIHC, X, 178.

[14] *The Early Records of the Town of Providence*, VIII, 12–13, 15, XV, 154–58, 161–62; MA, LXIX, 91, 95a; *Further Letters on King Philip's War*, pp. 22–25; Elisha R. Potter, *The Early History of Narragansett*, pp. 219–20.

[15] CCR, II, 297–98, 308.

[16] *Magnalia Christi Americana*, II, 499.

[17] Church, pp. 30-31.

[18] 2 MHC, VII, 157–58.

[19] NCP, I, 118.

[20] Davis Papers, I, 95–96.

[21] Church, p. 42.

[22] Church, p. 43.

[23] There is little reason to believe the old story that Philip, having dreamed that very night that he would be seized by the English, was just telling the dream to his companions when the English sprang their trap. See Cotton Mather, *Magnalia Christi Americana*, II, 498.

[24] Church, p. 45.

[25] MA, LXIX, 46; 5 MHC, V, 17; Hubbard, p. 109.

[26] Hough, *op. cit.*, p. 171; CA, War I, 109, 112, 113; CCR, II, 469–70, 477–78.

[27] Church, p. 48.

[28] MCR, V, 130; NEHGR, II, 201.

[29] MA, XXX, 227, 233, 234; Church, pp. 53–54; Hubbard, pp. 111–13.

CHAPTER XIII *THE AFTERMATH*

[1] Ipswich Town Records, II (Transcript), 1674–1696, p. 50.

[2] Stevens Transcripts (John Carter Brown Library), 454; RICR, III, 64.

[3] MA, LXIX, 169; CA, War I, 128a, 128b, 128c, 130; CCR, II, 502–504; Davis Papers, I, 103.

[4] 1 MHC, III, 179; 2 MHC, VI, 636–37; CHC, XXI, 267–69; NEHGR, XXXVIII, 381–83; MA, III, 330; MCR, V, 162, 168; Samuel G. Drake, ed., *Tragedies of the Wilderness*, pp. 60–68.

[5] PCR, V, 203, 210, XI, 242–43, 252–55; CCR, II, 285–86, 440, III, 309–10; MCR, V, 136–37; RICR, II, 560–61, 577–78; NEHGR, VIII, 273; 1 MHP, X, 16–18; Conn. Colony Records of Deeds, III, 1671–1724, p. 314.

[6] Edward T. Fisher, tr., *Report of a French Protestant Refugee, in Boston, 1687*, p. 40.

[7] RICR, III, 60; MCR, V, 145–46, 482; Middleborough Early Records (Transcript); Wrentham Records, I (Transcript); Samuel A. Green, ed., *The Early Records of Groton, Massachusetts*, pp. 52–53; Henry S. Nourse, ed., *The Early Records of Lancaster, Massachusetts*, pp. 119–21; CCR, II, 328; MA, LXIX, 238; Cotton Mather, *Magnalia Christi Americana*, I, 83.

[8] *A Report of the Record Commissioners, Containing the Roxbury Land and*

Church Records, p. 195; MA, LXIX, 85, 90; CA, War I, 117; CCR, II, 483n.; NEHGR, II, 247, 249; *A Report of the Record Commissioners of the City of Boston, Containing the Boston Records from 1660 to 1701,* p. 107.

⁹ PCR, VI, 65. See also MA, LXIX, 230, 230a, 236a, LXX, 134; CA, War I, 135; MCR, V, 80, 189, 226–27; CCR, II, 288, 320; PCR, V, 239–40, 271, VI, 18, XI, 243; *Town Records of Salem, Massachusetts,* II, 318.

¹⁰ Winslow Papers, 106; Franklin B. Dexter, ed., *Ancient Town Records* [New Haven], II, 374, 390; Saybrook Town Acts, I (Transcript), 1667–1727, p. 75; Gloucester Town Records, I (Transcript), p. 149.

¹¹ George M. Bodge, *Soldiers in King Philip's War,* pp. 252–54, 406–46; MA, CXII, 398, CXIV, 610; MCR, V, 487; 2 MHP, I, 229–31; 3 MHP, V, 34; MCS, XXIV, 38; CA, War I, 149a.

¹² MA, II, 204a, CCXLI, 292; CA, Colonial Boundaries I, 104, 107, 111, 112, 117, 118, 124, 130; CA, Foreign Correspondence I, 15; CA, Trumbull Papers XXII, 86; CCR, II, 315–16, 473–74, 487, 589–90, III, 506–509; CHC, XXI, 275–76; NCP, VI, 385–86; PCR, X, 407–409; 1 MHC, V, 226–29; 3 MHC, I, 70; 5 MHC, IX, 100–101; RICR, II, 556–58, 573–74, 582–83, 595–97, III, 18, 40–42, 58–60, 143–44, 174–75, 179–80; RIHC, XXIX, 2; CSP, 1677–1680, pp. 270–71, 306–307, 309, 402–403, 409, 421–22; CSP, 1681–1685, pp. 494–95, 521–24, 743–45; James N. Arnold, ed., *The Records of the Proprietors of the Narragansett,* pp. 29–30; John Hull's Letter Book (Typescript copy), II, 335–36; Davis Papers, I, 109; Stevens Transcripts (John Carter Brown Library), 120, 126, 134, 135, 136, 140, 448, 449; R.I. General Court of Trials, I, 1671–1724, pp. 42, 44, 48; Daniel B. Updike, *Richard Smith,* p. 115; Clarence W. Bowen, *The Boundary Disputes of Connecticut,* p. 48.

¹³ Winslow Papers, 111; Stevens Transcripts (John Carter Brown Library), 129, 130, 131, 147, 451, 452, 453, 454, 456; CSP, 1677–1680, pp. 319, 320–22, 324–25, 328, 409, 435, 450, 466; MA, III, 26, 27; CA, Foreign Correspondence I, 13, 15; CCR, III, 269–72, 506–509; PCR, X, 407–409; RICR, III, 64–66; 1 MHC, V, 226–29; 4 MHC, V, 31–33.

Bibliography

The person who wants to explore the subject of King Philip's War has available a treasure of fascinating material. Unfortunately, the Indians themselves left no record of their experiences, so all of our primary sources reflect the English point of view. Hence the student must be constantly on guard against bias. Three important contemporary narrative accounts of the war are available; to read any one of them, but especially the first, is an exciting and enlightening experience. These are:

Church, Thomas, *Entertaining Passages Relating to Philip's War Which Began in the Month of June, 1675*. Boston, 1716. Thomas Church, the actual author of the narrative, was the son of Captain Benjamin Church who appears as the hero of the book. Although the account was written many years after the war, Captain Church verified his son's narrative before it went to the press. Thus it is probably as accurate as an old man's memory and self-esteem will permit. The second edition, of 1772, is notoriously inaccurate. In 1865 Henry Martyn Dexter carefully edited and published a reproduction of the first edition under the title *The History of King Philip's War*.

Hubbard, William, *A Narrative of the Troubles with the Indians in New-England*. Boston, 1677. Hubbard was a Massachusetts clergyman who probably never witnessed any of the battles about which he wrote, but based his account on whatever evidence was available at the time. The first edition was revised slightly and then published in London in the same year under the title *The Present State of New-England*. In 1865 Samuel G. Drake republished Hubbard's account under the title *The History of the Indian Wars in New England from the First Settlement to the Termination of the War with King Philip, in 1677*.

Mather, Increase, *A Brief History of the War with the Indians in New-England*. Boston and London, 1676. This account of the war, intended as a competitor to Hubbard's narrative, reflects the views of the government and Puritan clergy of Massachusetts. In 1862 it was edited and republished by Samuel G. Drake.

There are also other contemporary narratives, as follows:

A Brief and True Narration of the Late Wars Risen in New-England. London, 1675.

Easton, John, *A Relacion of the Indyan Warre* [1675] (published in Charles H. Lincoln, ed., *Narratives of the Indian Wars*). Easton was a Rhode Island Quaker, and his account reflects that colony's attitude toward the war.

Drake, Samuel G., *The Old Indian Chronicle*. Boston, 1836 (republished in 1867). This contains a number of contemporary accounts.

A Farther Brief and True Narration of the Late Wars Risen in New England. London, 1676. This letter, dated December 28, 1675, has been reproduced in facsimile by the Society of Colonial Wars in Rhode Island.

Gookin, Daniel, *An Historical Account of the Doings and Sufferings of the Christian Indians of New England* (published in the *Transactions and Collections of the American Antiquarian Society*, II [Cambridge, 1836], 423–534). This essay constitutes an eloquent defense of the Christian Indians.

Harris, William, Letter to Sir Joseph Williamson, August 12, 1676 (published in the *Collections of the Rhode Island Historical Society*, X [Providence, 1902], 162–79).

[Hutchinson, Richard], *The Warr in New-England Visibly Ended.* London, 1677 (republished in Charles H. Lincoln, ed., *Narratives of the Indian Wars*). Richard Hutchinson was a nephew of the famous Anne Hutchinson.

Lincoln, Charles H., ed., *Narratives of the Indian Wars*. New York, 1913. This useful volume, one of the *Original Narratives of Early American History* Series, contains a number of the important contemporary narratives.

Mather, Increase, *A Relation of the Troubles Which Have Hapned* [sic] *in New-England, By Reason of the Indians There*. Boston, 1677. This volume covers the period from 1614 to 1675. In 1864 it was edited and republished by Samuel G. Drake.

News from New-England, Being a True and Last Account of the Present Bloody Wars. London, 1676.

Rowlandson, Mary, *Narrative of the Captivity of Mrs. Mary Rowlandson*. Cambridge, 1682 (republished in Charles H. Lincoln, ed., *Narratives of the Indian Wars*). This is an exciting account of the hardships endured by a white woman who was captured by the Indians and later released.

[Saltonstall, Nathaniel], *A Continuation of the State of New-England*. London, 1676.

————, *A New and Further Narrative of the State of New-England.* London, 1676.

————, *The Present State of New-England with Respect to the Indian War.* London, 1675. This and the above two tracts have been republished in Charles H. Lincoln, ed., *Narratives of the Indian Wars.* They contain numerous inaccuracies.

Thompson, Benjamin, *New-England's Crisis.* Boston, 1676. There is also a London edition of 1676, bearing the title *New-Englands Tears for Her Present Miseries,* which varies from the Boston edition in some respects. In 1894 this interesting poem was republished at Boston by the Club of Odd Volumes.

A True Account of the Most Considerable Occurrences That Have Happened in the Warre between the English and the Indians in New-England. London, 1676.

[Wharton, Edward], *New-England's Present Sufferings under Their Cruel Neighbouring Indians.* London, 1675. Wharton was a Quaker, and his account displays strong feeling against the Puritans.

Wheeler, Thomas, *A True Narrative of the Lord's Providences in Various Dispensations towards Captain Edward Hutchinson of Boston and My Self, and Those That Went with Us into the Nipmuck Country.* First published in 1675, this interesting narrative has been republished in the *Collections of the New-Hampshire Historical Society,* II (Concord, 1827), 5–23, and in the Old South Leaflets, No. 7.

Public documents, both published and unpublished, add greatly to our knowledge of the war period. The two most important collections of official wartime documents are located in the Massachusetts State Archives at Boston and in the Connecticut State Library at Hartford. Public documents consulted for this study include the following:

The Empire

Acts of the Privy Council of England. Colonial Series (1613–1720). Hereford, 1908–1910.

Calendar of State Papers. Colonial Series. America and the West Indies (1661–1685). London, 1880–1898.

Connecticut

Connecticut Archives
Civil Officers, I, 1669–1680.
College and Schools, Series 1, Vol. I, 1661–1762.
Colonial Boundaries, I, 1662–1742.
II, 1662–1731.
III, 1670–1827.

Connecticut Colonial Probate Records, III, County Court, 1663–1677.

Connecticut Colonial Records, New England, 1659–1701.
> The first part of this volume contains records of the Commissioners of the United Colonies. The last part contains records of the Court of Assistants at Hartford.

Connecticut Colony Records of Deeds, III, 1671–1724.

Crimes and Misdemeanors, I, 1663–1706.

Ecclesiastical Affairs, I, 1658–1715.

Foreign Correspondence, I, 1663–1748.
> II, 1661–1732.

Indians, I, Part 1, 1647–*ca.* 1728.

Private Controversies, I,   –1682.

Towns and Lands, First Series, I,   –1695.

Trade and Maritime Affairs, Series 1, Vol. I, 1668–1751.

Trumbull Papers, XXII.
> These documents relate to affairs in the Narragansett country during the period from 1659 to 1699. Most of the papers have been published in the *Collections of the Massachusetts Historical Society*, Fifth Series, Vol. IX, or elsewhere, as indicated in the front of the volume.

New Haven County Court Records, I, 1666–1698.

New London County Court Records, II, 1668–1669.
> III, 1670–1681.

Talcott's Account Book, 1673–1712.
> John Talcott was the Treasurer of Connecticut during King Philip's War.

War Colonial, I.
> Most documents of a military nature, appertaining to Connecticut's role in King Philip's War, are contained in this volume.

Trumbull, J. Hammond, ed., *The Public Records of the Colony of Connecticut.* Vol. I (1636–1665), Hartford, 1850. Vol. II (1665–1678), Hartford, 1852. Vol. III (1678–1689), Hartford, 1859.

Massachusetts

The General Laws and Liberties of the Massachusetts Colony. Cambridge, 1672.

Hampshire County Court Records, I. This volume, which commences in 1677, is in the office of the Clerk of Courts at Northampton, Mass.

Hampshire County Court Record, I. This volume, covering the period from 1660 to about 1690, is in the Registry of Probate at Northampton, Mass.

John Hull's Journal. Hull was the War Treasurer of Massachusetts, and this is his account book for the war. It is in the possession of the New England Historic Genealogical Society at Boston. Also in the same library are three other volumes of Hull's accounts.

Massachusetts Archives
Most of the documents directly related to King Philip's War are to be found in Volumes XXX, LXVII, LXVIII, and LXIX.

Records of the Court of Assistants of the Colony of the Massachusetts Bay. Vol. I (1673–1692), Boston, 1901. Vol. III (1642–1673), Boston, 1928.

Records of the Suffolk County Court, 1671–1680 (Publications of the Colonial Society of Massachusetts, XXIX, XXX. Boston, 1933).

Shurtleff, Nathaniel B., ed., *Records of the Governor and Company of the Massachusetts Bay in New England.* Vol. III (1644–1657), Boston, 1854. Vol. IV (1650–1674), Boston, 1854. Vol. V (1674–1686), Boston, 1854.

New York

Documents Relative to the Colonial History of the State of New-York, III. Albany, 1853.

Hough, Franklin B., ed., *A Narrative of the Causes Which Led to Philip's Indian War . . . With Other Documents Concerning This Event in the Office of the Secretary of State of New York.* Albany, 1858.

————, ed., *Papers Relating to the Island of Nantucket.* Albany, 1856. At the time of King Philip's War, the islands of Nantucket and Martha's Vineyard belonged to New York.

Plymouth

Brigham, William, ed., *The Compact with the Charter and Laws of the Colony of New Plymouth.* Boston, 1836.

Records of the Colony of New Plymouth in New England.
Nathaniel B. Shurtleff, ed.
Vol. III, IV. Court Orders, 1651–1668. Boston, 1855.
Vol. V. Court Orders, 1668–1678. Boston, 1856.
Vol. VI. Court Orders, 1678–1691. Boston, 1856.
Vol. VII. Judicial Acts, 1636–1692. Boston, 1857.
Vol. VIII. Miscellaneous Records, 1633–1689. Boston, 1857.
David Pulsifer, ed.
Vol. X. Acts of the Commissioners of the United Colonies of New England, 1653–1679. Boston, 1859.
Vol. XI. Laws, 1623–1682. Boston, 1861.
Vol. XII. Book of Indian Records for Their Lands. Boston, 1861.

Rhode Island

Bartlett, John Russell, ed., *Records of the Colony of Rhode Island and Providence Plantations in New England*, II, III. Providence, 1857–1858.

General Court of Trials, Record 1, 1671–1724. This volume is in the custody of the Clerk of Superior Court, Newport, R.I.

Rhode Island Archives
    General Treasurer's Accounts, 1672–1711.
    Governor and Council Records, 1667–1753.

Rhode Island Court Records, I, II. Providence, 1920–1922.

Rhode Island Land Evidences, Abstracts, I (1648–1696). Providence, 1921.

Of all the available manuscript material relating to the period of King Philip's War, the town and other local records are the most difficult to reach. For this reason they have been neglected by historians of the war. In 1675 there were more than a hundred towns in the area directly affected by the Indian uprising, all of them keeping official records of some kind. Today the remains of those records, for the most part, are still held in the local town vaults. The historian who would consult them all must travel far and wide through southern New England, and will find himself spending considerable time in delightful little communities which still lie far off the beaten track. In some of the local records there are no entries during the war period, which indicates either that the town ceased to function as such, or that the inhabitants were too preoccupied to hold town meetings and keep records. In other cases the records continue during the war, but fail to mention the very event which was uppermost in men's minds. Apparently the clerks in these towns were interested in recording only routine matters of town business. In almost no town will there be found anything but the most casual and incidental references to the war, but these scattered bits of information, when pieced together with dozens of others from many towns, help to round out the picture of what was happening on the local level.

Unless otherwise indicated, unpublished volumes listed below are in the custody of the town or city clerk.

Connecticut

Branford Records, I, 1645–1679 (Transcript). The original is available for comparison.

Farmington Church Records, 1652–1698 (Transcript). State Library.

Farmington Town Records, I. The State Library has a transcript of this volume, entitled Farmington Town Votes, 1650 to 1699.

Farmington Land Records, I, 1645–1769 (Photostatic copy). The original is in the State Library.

Guilford Records, B. The State Library has a transcript.

Haddam Miscellaneous Records, 1666–1710.

Haddam Town Records, No. 1.

Hartford Town Votes, I. Charles J. Hoadly, ed. (*Collections of the Connecticut Historical Society,* VI. Hartford, 1897).

Killingworth Misc. Town Records, 1663–1747 (Transcript).

Killingworth Town Meetings, I. Marginal notes indicate which entries are included in the transcript above.

Killingworth Records, I. Marginal notes indicate which entries are included in the transcript above.

Lyme Land Records, I (Photostatic copy). The original is in the State Library. The period covered is 1672–1687.

Lyme Town Meeting Book, I.

Lyme Land Grants, I.

Middletown Land Records, I, 1654–1742 (Transcript). The original is in the State Library.

Middletown Town Votes and Proprietors Records, I, 1652–1735.

New Haven, *Ancient Town Records,* I, II. Franklin B. Dexter, ed. New Haven, 1917–1919.

Records of the New Haven Townsmen, 1665–1714 (Transcript). In the library of the New Haven Colony Historical Society. The original is in the City Clerk's Office.

New London Land Records, Court Records, IV, 1668–1707.

New London Land Records, V, 1675–1697. The period covered is actually much wider than is indicated by the title.

New London Miscellaneous Records.

New London Town Records, 1647–1666.

New London Town Records, 1661–1662.

New London Town Records, 1662–1664.

New London Town Records, 1665–1666.

New London Town Records, 1664–1703.

New London Town Records, 1667–1670.

Norwich Old Records, Book No. 1. State Library.

Saybrook Land Records, I (Transcript). In the office of the Town Clerk, Deep River, Conn. The State Library has an older transcript of the same volume.

Saybrook Town Acts, I, 1667–1727 (Transcript). State Library. The original is available for comparison.

Oyster River Quarter Records (Saybrook), 1666–1755 (Transcript). In the office of the Town Clerk, Deep River, Conn. The original is in the State Library.

Saybrook Proprietors' Records, Potapauge Quarter, 1670–1828. State Library.

Simsbury Town Records, I, 1660–1691 (Transcript).

Old Volume of Simsbury Land Records.

Stonington Records, No. 2, 1651–1714.

Stonington Town Votes, II. Entries begin in 1673.

Stonington Records (Transcript). Entries begin about 1664.

Suffield Town Records, I.

Wallingford Town Records, I, 1670–1692 (Transcript).

Wethersfield Town Votes, I, 1647–1717 (Transcript and photostatic copy). The original is in the State Library.

Wethersfield Land Records, II, 1660–1750. State Library.

Wethersfield Land Records, III, Part 1, 1677–1730. State Library. There are entries for earlier years.

Windsor Town Acts, 1650–1714. State Library.

Windsor Town Records, No. 1, 1640–1682. State Library.

Massachusetts

Amesbury Town Meetings, 1656–1717.

Andover Ancient Town Records.

Andover Old Tax and Record Book, 1670–1716.

Beverly Town Records (Transcript).

Billerica Records, 1653–1685 (Transcript). The original is available for comparison.

Billerica Book of Grants, II, 1678–1786.

A *Report of the Record Commissioners of the City of Boston, Containing the Boston Records from 1660 to 1701*. Boston, 1881.

A *Report of the Record Commissioners of the City of Boston, Containing Miscellaneous Papers*. Boston, 1886.

Records of the Town of Braintree. Samuel A. Bates, ed. Randolph, Mass., 1886.

Muddy River and Brookline Records, 1634–1838. n.p., 1875.

The Register Book of the Lands and Houses in the "New Towne" and the Town of Cambridge. Cambridge, 1896.

The Records of the Town of Cambridge, II. Cambridge, 1901.

Chelmsford Town Records, First and Second Book (Transcript). The original volume, entitled Proprietors' Records, is available for comparison.

Ancient Records of Concord, I (Transcript). The original records are available for comparison.

The Early Records of the Town of Dedham, Massachusetts. Don Gleason Hill, ed. Vol. IV (1659–1673), Dedham, 1894. Vol. V (1672–1706), Dedham, 1899.

Dedham Records, II (Transcript).

Records of the First Church at Dorchester in New England. Boston, 1891.

Dorchester Town Records. Boston, 1880.

Gloucester Town Records, I (Transcript).

The Early Records of Groton, Massachusetts. Samuel A. Green, ed. Groton, 1880.

Hadley Proprietors' Records (Transcript). The original is available for comparison.

Hadley Records (Transcript). The original is available for comparison.

Hatfield Records (Transcript). The original is available for comparison.

Haverhill Town Records, I, II and III (Transcript).

Hingham Records (Transcript). The original is available for comparison.

Hingham, Proprietors' Grants of Land.

Ipswich Town Records, I, 1634–1674 (Transcript), II, 1674–1696 (Transcript). The originals are available for comparison.

The Early Records of Lancaster, Massachusetts. Henry S. Nourse, ed. Lancaster, 1884.

Malden Town Proceedings, I, 1678–1764. Malden Public Library. Although these records are bound as Volume I, the real first volume, covering the period before 1678, is no longer extant.

Town Records of Manchester. Salem, 1889.

Marblehead General Records, I, 1649–1683, II, 1652–1710.

First Records of Marlborough, Massachusetts. Worcester, 1909.

Marlborough Old Records, 1666–1698. These are not the records referred to in the preceding entry.

Medfield Town Records, I, 1649–1742.

Medfield Records, I, 1649–1700 (Transcript). The original is available for comparison.

Medford Town Records, I (Transcript). Entries begin about 1674.

Annals of the Town of Mendon. John G. Metcalf, comp. Providence, 1880. Includes selections from the town records.

Mendon Town Records, I.

The Proprietors' Records of the Town of Mendon, Massachusetts. Boston, 1899.

Milton Town Records, 1662–1729. Milton, 1930.

Newbury Town Meeting Records, 1667–1680.

Northampton Proprietors' Records, 1650–1731 (Transcript). The original or an early transcript is available for comparison.

Northampton Proprietors' Records, 1653–1680 (Transcript). The original or an early transcript is available for comparison.

Northampton Records, I, 1654–1754 (Transcript). The original is available for comparison.

Reading Town Meetings, 1644–1773 (Transcript).

The Early Records of the Town of Rowley, Massachusetts, I, 1639–1672. Benjamin P. Mighill and George B. Blodgette, eds. Rowley, 1894.

Rowley Records, Book No. 1, 1660–1712.

Rowley Freeholders' Records, No. 1, 1643–1713.

A Report of the Record Commissioners, Containing the Roxbury Land and Church Records. Boston, 1881.

Town Records of Salem, Massachusetts, II. Salem, 1913.

Salisbury Miscellaneous Records, 1640–1730.

The First Century of the History of Springfield, I, II. Henry M. Burt, ed. Springfield, 1898–1899.

Town Records of Topsfield, Massachusetts, I, 1659–1739. Topsfield, 1917.

Watertown Records, I. Watertown, 1894.

Town Records of Wenham, I, 1642–1706 (Transcript). The original is available for comparison.

Westfield Miscellaneous Records, 1675–1694.

Westfield, Grants of Land at Worronoco.

Weymouth Town Meeting Records, 1643–1772.

Woburn Records, I. Woburn Public Library. This volume is a scrapbook containing clippings from the Woburn *Journal,* 1888–1889, which reproduces the first volume of Woburn records.

Woburn Records, II, 1674–1681 (Transcript). Woburn Public Library. This volume duplicates much of Vol. I as reproduced in the Woburn *Journal,* 1888–1889.

Records of the Proprietors of Worcester, Massachusetts. Franklin P. Rice, ed. Worcester, 1881.

Wrentham Book of Grants.

Wrentham Records, I (Transcript).

Plymouth

Barnstable Records, I. In the office of the Town Clerk, Hyannis, Mass. A transcript is also available.

Bridgewater Records, I, 1656–1702 (Transcript). The original records are available for comparison.

Copy of the Old Records of the Town of Duxbury, Mass. George Etheridge, ed. Plymouth, 1893. A "very few of the unimportant Town meetings have been omitted."

Eastham Records, 1650–1705. In the office of the Town Clerk, Orleans, Mass.

Little Compton, Proprietors' Records.

Marshfield Records, I, 1643–1778 (Transcript).

Middleborough Early Records (Transcript). The original is available for comparison.

Records of the Town of Plymouth, I. William T. Davis, ed. Plymouth, 1889.

Sandwich Records, 1651–1691 (Transcript). The original is available for comparison.

Sandwich Proprietors' Records (Transcript). The original is available for comparison.

Scituate Records, 1649–1707. Entries actually range from about 1636 to beyond 1740.

Scituate Records. The inside cover bears the designation Vol. II, 2nd Part.

Scituate Book of Accounts.

The Records of the Sowams Proprietary. Published in Thomas Williams Bicknell, ed., *Sowams, With Ancient Records of Sowams and Parts Adjacent.* New Haven, 1908. The site of Sowams is now within the boundaries of Barrington, R.I.

Taunton Proprietors' Records, No. 1, No. 2, No. 4.

Yarmouth Records [Town Meetings].

Yarmouth Records [Land].

Yarmouth Records, III.

Rhode Island

The Records of the Proprietors of the Narragansett, Otherwise Called the Fones Record. James N. Arnold, ed. Providence, 1894. These records relate mostly to the Atherton Company.

The Early Records of the Town of Portsmouth. Clarence S. Brigham, ed. Providence, 1901.

The Early Records of the Town of Providence, I–XXI. Providence, 1892–1915. Each volume is indexed, and Richard LeBaron Bowen has subsequently produced a master index for the entire set.

Copies of Records in Warwick With Some Original Deeds. In the library of the Rhode Island Historical Society at Providence.

The Early Records of the Town of Warwick. Howard M. Chapin, ed. Providence, 1926.

Records of the Court of Trials of the Town of Warwick, 1659–1674.
Helen Capwell, ed. Providence, 1922.

Warwick Records, Books A-1 and A-2 (Transcript by Marshall Morgan).
The originals are in the office of the Town Clerk at Apponaug, R.I.

Westerly Town Records, I, 1661–1707.

Scrapbook in Westerly Public Library. This volume contains documents relating to the early history of Westerly.

Many documents from the period of King Philip's War have been gathered into collections which are now in the custody of certain private or public organizations. These are listed below under the name of the custodial organization.

American Antiquarian Society, Worcester, Mass.

Curwin Papers.

John Hull's Letter Book, 1670–1685 (Transcript made under the direction of Samuel Eliot Morison). The original is available for comparison.

Boston Atheneum, Boston, Mass.

MSS. LI, Vols. I, III.

Boston Public Library, Boston, Mass.

Prince Collection.

Cotton Papers.

Mather Papers, I, II.

John Hull's Commonplace Book, I, III. These volumes contain his notes on sermons which he heard.

Connecticut Historical Society, Hartford, Conn.

Auwonecoo, Deed of . . . Concerning Sale of Indian Captive Boy to James Treat of Wethersfield. Jan. 9, 1676/7.

Letters of and about the Indians. Most of the letters in this mimeographed pamphlet are from the collections at the State Library.

Mohegan Indian Deeds. Part I. This is a mimeographed pamphlet.

Connecticut Valley Historical Museum (William Pynchon Memorial Building), Springfield, Mass.

John Pynchon's Account Books.

Pynchon Papers.

Essex Institute, Salem, Mass.

Curwen Papers, I–IV.

Military Manuscripts, 1630–1774.

John Carter Brown Library, Providence, R.I.

Stevens Transcripts, II, VI, VII. These are transcripts of documents in the British Public Record Office. Katharine Littlefield has made an annotated calendar of these transcripts.

Massachusetts Historical Society, Boston, Mass.
  Richard Baxter Papers (F. L. Gay Transcripts).
  Belknap Papers, 1637–1788.
  Davis Papers, I, 1627–1680.
  Miscellaneous, 1650–1679. A collection of unbound documents.
  Miscellaneous, II, III.
  Otis Papers, 1639–1714.
  Photostats. Many of these are from the State Archives.
  Plymouth Papers, I (F. L. Gay Transcripts).
  Trumbull Papers.
  Winslow Papers.
  Winthrop Papers.
New England Historic Genealogical Society, Boston, Mass.
  John Hull's Account Books.
  Shattuck Papers.
Old Colony Historical Society, Taunton, Mass.
  Old Documents, I, II.
Rhode Island Historical Society, Providence, R.I.
  MS. Vol. X.

The following personal diaries and journals deal with the period under consideration:

Bradstreet, Simon, Journal (1664–1683). Published in the *New England Historical and Genealogical Register*, IX (Boston, 1855), 43–51.

Edmundson, William, *Journal*. Dublin, 1715.

Hull, John, Diaries. Published in the *Transactions and Collections of the American Antiquarian Society*, III (Cambridge and Boston, 1857), 109–265.

Mather, Increase, *Diary by Increase Mather, March, 1675–December, 1676. Together with Extracts from Another Diary by Him, 1674–1687.* Samuel A. Green, ed., Cambridge, 1900.

Minor, Thomas, *Diary*. Sidney H. Miner and George D. Stanton, Jr., eds., New London, 1899.

Sewall, Samuel, Diary. Published in the *Collections of the Massachusetts Historical Society*, Fifth Series, Vol. V–VII (Boston, 1878–1882).

Additional primary sources which have been consulted include the following:

Bradford, William, *A Letter from Major William Bradford to the Reverend John Cotton Written at Mount Hope on July 21, 1675.* Providence, 1914.

————, Letter of July 24, 1676. Published in the Providence *Journal,* Jan. 15, 1876.

Brinley, Francis, "A Brief Narrative of That Part of New England Called the Nanhiganset Country" [*ca.* 1696]. Published in the *Publications of the Rhode Island Historical Society,* VIII (July, 1900). A version of the same work appears in the *Collections of the Massachusetts Historical Society,* Third Series, Vol. I (Boston, 1825), 209–28.

Cobbet, Thomas, "A Narrative of New England's Deliverances." Prince Collection, Boston Public Library. See also Massachusetts Archives, CCXLI, Docs. 288–89a. Published in the *New England Historical and Genealogical Register,* VII (Boston, 1853), 209–19.

Cooper, Simon, *A Letter Written by Dr. Simon Cooper of Newport . . . to the Governor and Council of the Connecticut Colony.* Providence, 1916.

Curtis, Ephraim, Report of July 16, 1675. Massachusetts Archives, LXVII, Doc. 214. Published in L. B. Chase, *The Bay Path and Along the Way.* Norwood, Mass., 1919, pp. 136–43.

————, Report of July 24, 1675. Massachusetts Archives, LXVII, Doc. 222. Published in L. B. Chase, *The Bay Path and Along the Way.* Norwood, Mass., 1919, pp. 150–53.

Eliot, John, Letter to Robert Boyle, April 22, 1684. Published in the *Old South Leaflets,* No. 21.

Fisher, Edward Thornton, tr., *Report of a French Protestant Refugee, in Boston, 1687.* Brooklyn, 1868.

Folger, Peter, *A Looking Glass for the Times* [*ca.* 1675–1676]. This poem was published in 1763, and has since been republished in *Rhode Island Historical Tracts,* No. 16, Providence, 1883.

Further Letters on King Philip's War. Providence, 1923. This volume consists of four letters from the Massachusetts Archives.

Gookin, Daniel, *Historical Collections of the Indians in New England* [1674]. Published in the *Collections of the Massachusetts Historical Society,* First Series, Vol. I (Boston, 1792), 141–232. The accuracy of this version has been questioned. See the *New England Historical and Genealogical Register,* XII, 163n.

Hubbard, William, *A General History of New England, from the Discovery to MDCLXXX.* First published in the *Collections of the Massachusetts Historical Society,* Second Series, Vols. V, VI (Cambridge, 1815).

————, *The Happiness of a People in the Wisdome of Their Rulers Directing and in the Obedience of Their Brethren Attending unto What Israel Ought to Do.* Boston, 1676.

Hutchinson, Thomas, ed., *Collection of Original Papers Relative to* the History of the Colony of Massachusetts-Bay. 2 vols. Albany, 1865. The original edition was published at Boston in 1769.

Josselyn, John, *An Account of Two Voyages to New-England*. London, 1675. Republished in the *Collections of the Massachusetts Historical Society*, Third Series, Vol. III (Cambridge, 1833), 211–354.

Mather, Cotton, *Magnalia Christi Americana*. 2d ed. Hartford, 1820. The first edition was published in London in 1702.

Mather, Increase, *An Earnest Exhortation to the Inhabitants of New-England, to Hearken to the Voice of God in His Late and Present Dispensations*. Boston, 1676. Published in the same cover with Mather's *A Brief History of the War with the Indians in New-England*.

————, *An Historical Discourse Concerning the Prevalency of Prayer*. Boston, 1677. Republished in Samuel G. Drake, ed., *Early History of New England*. Boston, 1864.

The Petition of Abigail Lay Relict of John Lay of Lyme to the General Court of Connecticut to Which Are Added Other Documents Relating to King Philip's War. Providence, 1920.

Richardson, J., *The Necessity of a Well Experienced Souldiery*. Cambridge, 1679. This sermon was delivered upon the occasion of an Artillery Election, June 10, 1675.

Some Further Papers Relating to King Philip's War. n.p., 1931.

Stockwell, Quentin, Narrative of his captivity. Originally published by Increase Mather in 1684, this account has been republished in Samuel G. Drake, ed., *Tragedies of the Wilderness*. Boston, 1846, and in *History and Proceedings of the Pocumtuck Valley Memorial Association*, II (Deerfield, 1898), 462–70.

Walker, Philip, *Captan Perse and His Coragios Company* [1676]. Published in Richard LeBaron Bowen, *Early Rehoboth*, III (Rehoboth, 1948), 34–38. The original is in the custody of the American Antiquarian Society.

————, *The Stragamen of the Indians* [1676]. Published in Richard LeBaron Bowen, *Early Rehoboth*, III (Rehoboth, 1948), 39-50. The original is in the custody of the American Antiquarian Society.

Williams, Roger, *A Key into the Language of America*. London, 1643. Republished in the *Collections of the Rhode Island Historical Society*, I (Providence, 1827), and in the *Publications of the Narragansett Club*, I (Providence, 1866).

————, *Letters and Papers of Roger Williams*. Boston, 1924. A photostatic edition of less than twenty copies.

Winthrop, Wait, *A Letter Written by Capt. Wait Winthrop from Mr. Smith's in Narragansett to Gov. John Winthrop of the Colony of Connecticut*. Providence, 1919.

————, *Some Meditations Concerning our Honourable Gentlemen and Fellow-Souldiers, in Pursuit of those Barbarous Natives in the Narragansit-Country; and Their Service there* [Dec. 28, 1675]. Republished at New London in 1721.

Publications of historical societies and certain other collected works contain a vast amount of pertinent material. The most important of these for the study of King Philip's War are the following:

The Colonial Society of Massachusetts
　Publications. Vols. I–XXXIV. Boston, 1895–1943.
The Connecticut Historical Society
　Collections. Vols. I–XXIV. Hartford, 1860–1932.
The Massachusetts Historical Society
　Collections. Vols. I–LXXIX. Boston and Cambridge, 1792–1941.
　Proceedings. Vols. I–LXVII. Boston, 1879–1945.
The Narragansett Club
　Publications. Vols. I–VI. Providence, 1866–1874. In these volumes are published most of the writings of Roger Williams.
The New England Historic Genealogical Society
　The New England Historical and Genealogical Register. Vols. I–CV. Boston, 1847–1951.
The New Hampshire Historical Society
　Collections. Vol. III. Concord, 1832 (reprinted at Manchester, 1870).
The Prince Society
　Publications. Vol. II (The Hutchinson Papers). Albany, 1865.
The Rhode Island Historical Society
　Collections. Vols. I–XXXIV. Providence, 1827–1941.
　Proceedings. Providence, 1872–1892, 1902–1914.
　Publications, New Series. Vols. I–VIII. Providence, 1893–1900.
　Rhode Island History. Vols. I–VII. Providence, 1942–1948.

Secondary Sources

The serious student of King Philip's War must use secondary sources with the greatest of caution. The war has been a favorite subject for the antiquarians and amateur historians of two centuries. Many of them did excellent work, but others produced only superficial accounts of the war, often teeming with errors. Most of the writers have based their accounts on Mather, Hubbard, and Church, without attempting to check the accuracy of those sources. They have given free rein to all kinds of unsupported folklore and tradition. Usually they reveal a decided bias either for or against the Indians. Nevertheless, the secondary accounts should not be ignored completely. If selected with care, and wisely used, they may serve to check our own conclusions and round out the facts which have been derived from primary sources. The following lists are selective rather than exhaustive.

Books

Baylies, Francis, *An Historical Memoir of the Colony of New Plymouth.* Samuel G. Drake, ed. 2 vols. Boston, 1866. This edition is a successor to the 1830 edition. Part III consists of a narrative history of King Philip's War based on the standard contemporary accounts.

Bodge, George Madison, *Soldiers in King Philip's War.* 3d ed. Boston, 1906. This book is indispensable for the student of the war. By diligent investigation, Bodge has reconstructed the rosters of the various Massachusetts companies. The book also includes many documents from the State Archives.

Bowen, Clarence Winthrop, *The Boundary Disputes of Connecticut.* Boston, 1882.

Bowen, Richard LeBaron, *Early Rehoboth,* III. Rehoboth, 1948. Many important documents are accurately reproduced in this volume. It is especially valuable for its penetrating analysis of the July campaign of 1675.

Brockunier, Samuel H., *The Irrepressible Democrat, Roger Williams.* New York, 1940.

Callender, John, *An Historical Discourse, on the Civil and Religious Affairs of the Colony of Rhode-Island.* Romeo Elton, ed. Rev. ed. Providence, 1838. The original edition was published in 1739.

Chamberlain, Daniel H., *Wheeler's Surprise, 1675: Where?* n.p., n.d. Originally this was a paper which was read before the Quaboag Historical Society on Sept. 12, 1899.

Chapin, Howard M., *Sachems of the Narragansetts.* Providence, 1931.

Chase, Levi Badger, *The Bay Path and Along the Way.* Norwood, Mass., 1919.

Collier, John, *The Indians of the Americas.* New York, 1947.

Davis, John, Appendix to Morton's *Memorial.* Boston, 1826.

DeForest, John W., *History of the Indians of Connecticut from the Earliest Known Period to 1850.* Hartford, 1851.

Douglas-Lithgow, Robert A., *Dictionary of American-Indian Place and Proper Names in New England.* Salem, 1909.

Drake, Samuel G., *The Book of the Indians.* 9th ed. Boston, 1845.

Ellis, George Edward, *The Red Man and the White Man in North America from Its Discovery to the Present Time.* Boston, 1882.

Ellis, George W., and John E. Morris, *King Philip's War.* New York, 1906.

The First Record Book of the Society of Colonial Wars in the State of Rhode Island and Providence Plantations. Providence, 1902. Included in this volume are several articles on King Philip's War.

Hoyt, Epaphras, *Antiquarian Researches*. Greenfield, Mass., 1824.

Hutchinson, Thomas, *The History of Massachusetts*, I. 3d ed. rev. Salem, 1795. The first edition was published in 1764. A modern edition, edited by Lawrence Shaw Mayo, appeared in 1936.

Morison, Samuel Eliot, *Builders of the Bay Colony*. Boston, 1930.

Osgood, Herbert Levi, *The American Colonies in the Seventeenth Century*, I. New York, 1904.

Palfrey, John Gorham, *History of New England*, III. Boston, 1892.

Parsons, Usher, *Indian Names of Places in Rhode Island*. Providence, 1861.

Pearce, Roy Harvey, *The Savages of America*. Baltimore, 1953.

Potter, Elisha R., *The Early History of Narragansett*. 2d ed. n.p., 1886. This edition is a reprint of the original 1835 edition, done by Potter's brother. It includes an after-section giving the various notes contained in Potter's own copy of the 1835 edition, and also a lengthy appendix in which are printed many documents relating to the Narragansett land controversies.

Rider, Sidney S., *The Lands of Rhode Island as They Were Known to Caunounicus and Miantunnomu When Roger Williams Came in 1636*. Providence, 1904.

Robinson, G. Frederick, and Albert H. Hall, comps., *Watertown Soldiers in the Colonial Wars and the American Revolution*. Watertown, 1939.

Sheldon, George, *A History of Deerfield, Massachusetts*. 2 vols. Deerfield, 1895.

Sutherland, Stella H., *Population Distribution in Colonial America*. New York, 1936.

Tompkins, Hamilton B., *The Great Swamp Fight*. n.p., 1906.

Trumbull, J. Hammond, *Indian Names of Places, etc., in and on the Borders of Connecticut*. Hartford, 1881.

Underhill, Ruth Murray, *Red Man's America: A History of Indians in the United States*. Chicago, 1953.

Updike, Daniel B., *Richard Smith*. Boston, 1937. The fourth section of this book contains some fifty letters written by Richard Smith, Jr.

Weeden, William B., *Economic and Social History of New England, 1620–1789*. 2 vols. Boston, 1890.

Willard, Joseph, *Willard Memoir; or, Life and Times of Major Simon Willard*. Boston, 1858.

Winsor, Justin, ed., *Narrative and Critical History of America*, III. Boston, 1884.

————, *The New-England Indians: A Bibliographical Survey, 1630–1700*. Cambridge, 1895. Reprinted from the *Proceedings of the Massachusetts Historical Society*, Second Series, Vol. X (Boston, 1896), 327–59.

Wissler, Clark, *Indians of the United States*. New York, 1940.

Articles

Arnold, James N., "Joshua Tefft," *Narragansett Historical Register*, III (1884–1885), 164–69.

Bennett, M. K., "The Food Economy of the New England Indians, 1605–75," *Journal of Political Economy*, Vol. LXIII, No. 5 (Oct., 1955), 369–97.

Brigham, Clarence S., "The Indians of Rhode Island," *The Apteryx*, Vol. I, No. 2 (April, 1905).

Carpenter, Daniel H., "Rhode Island Families Who Went to Long Island, 1676, During King Philip's War," *Rhode Island Historical Magazine*, VI (1885–1886), 213–16.

Crane, John C., "The Nipmucks and Their Country," *Proceedings of the Worcester Society of Antiquity*, XVI (Worcester, 1898).

Dorr, Henry C., "The Narragansetts," *Collections of the Rhode Island Historical Society*, VII (Providence, 1885), 133–237.

Eno, Joel N., "The Puritans and the Indian Lands," *Magazine of History*, Vol. IV, No. 5 (Nov., 1906), 274–81.

Greene, Welcome Arnold, "The Great Battle of the Narragansetts," *Narragansett Historical Register*, V (1886–1887), 331–43.

Hale, Edward E., "Boston in Philip's War," *The Memorial History of Boston*, ed. Justin Winsor, Vol. I (Boston, 1880), 311–28.

Leach, Douglas Edward, "The Military System of Plymouth Colony," *New England Quarterly*, Vol. XXIV, No. 3 (Sept., 1951), 342–64.

————, "A New View of the Declaration of War against the Narragansetts, November, 1675," *Rhode Island History*, Vol. XV, No. 2 (April, 1956), 33–41.

Miller, Perry, "Declension in a Bible Commonwealth," *Proceedings of the American Antiquarian Society*, LI (April, 1941), 37–94.

Paige, Lucius R., "Wheeler's Defeat, 1675: Where?" *Proceedings of the American Antiquarian Society*, New Series, Vol. V (1887–1888), 96–106.

————, "Wickaboag? Or Winnimisset?" *New England Historical and Genealogical Register*, XXXVIII (Oct., 1884), 395–400.

Reed, Samuel W., "Weymouth, Mass., During King Philip's War," *Magazine of New England History*, III (1893), 196–200.

Reynolds, Grindall, "King Philip's War; With Special Reference to the Attack on Brookfield in August, 1675," *Proceedings of the American Antiquarian Society*, New Series, Vol. V (1887–1888), 77–95.

Sheldon, George, "The Traditionary Story of the Attack upon Hadley and the Appearance of Gen. Goffe, Sept. 1, 1675," *New England Historical and Genealogical Register*, XXVIII (Boston, 1874), 379–91.

Washburn, Wilcomb E., "Governor Berkeley and King Philip's War," *New England Quarterly*, Vol. XXX, No. 3 (Sept., 1957), 363–77.

Index

Acushnet River, 217
Adams, Henry, 160
Agawam (in Plymouth Colony), 216
Albany, N. Y., 142, 176-177
Alequaomet, *see* Quinnapin
Alexander (Wamsutta), Wampanoag sachem, 23-24, 29, 248
Algonkins, see under various tribes
Andover, Mass., 166, 169, 186, 188
Andros, Edmund, Governor of New York, 34, 94; relations with New England, 59-60, 176-177, 236-237, 255; attempts to seize Connecticut territory, 59-60, 255; provides for defense of New York, 92; provides refuge for Rhode Islanders, 177; Governor of the Dominion of New England, 248, 249
Annawon, Wampanoag leader, 164, 235, 237-240
Apequinash, *see* Monoco
Appleton, Samuel, 84, 90; succeeds Pynchon as commander in chief, 96; operations in Connecticut Valley, 97-100; difficulties with Connecticut officers, 97, 99-100, 119; withdraws from Connecticut Valley, 101-102, 123; in campaign against Narragansetts, 123-124, 127; quoted, 97
Apprentices, *see* Indentured servants
Aquidneck Island, 54, 63, 64-65, 114, 125, 168, 208-209, 210, 232-233, 236, 237; as a place of refuge, 56, 168, 188, 246
Ashquoash (Quabaug Old Fort), 85

Assawompsett Pond, 30-31, 32, 33, 48, 207, 217
Atherton Company, 15, 16-17, 23
Attleboro, Mass., 47. *See also* Woodcock's Garrison House
Awashonks, squaw sachem of the Sakonnets, 5, 27, 63, 164, 216, 267; consults Church, 34-35; deserts Philip, 208-210

Barbados, 194, 226, 244
Barnstable, Mass., 194
Barrett, Stephen, 122
Barrow, Sam (Indian), 232
Bay Path, -8, 82, 207
Beers, Richard, 87, 95, 167
Belcher, John, 204
Belcher, Joseph, 52
Bermuda, 109
Beverly, Mass., 87, 92
Billerica, Mass., 165, 169, 174
Blackstone River, *see* Pawtucket River
Bloody Brook, 88, 202
Boston, Mass., 7, 9, 10, 27, 28, 37, 42, 44, 45, 46, 47, 53, 56, 69, 74, 76, 78, 102, 104, 106, 110, 115, 123, 142, 148-149, 150, 151, 158, 159, 160, 161, 162, 170, 172, 174, 179, 180, 186, 191, 211, 214, 215, 252-253; Commissioners of the United Colonies meet at, 9, 88-89, 115, 117-122, 123, 125; troops mobilized at, 45-47; as a supply center, 106, 107; Narragansetts sign treaty at, 115-116; Quaker demonstrations in,

57; activity in Pocasset country, 66-67, 68-69, 70; escape from Pocasset country, 72, 75-77, 78-80; in the Nipmuck country, 77, 84, 85, 101; sheltered by Narragansetts, 113, 114, 115-116, 126; in Plymouth Colony, 165, 216, 218, 219-220, 229-232; attacked by Church at Mount Hope, 233-236; finally subdued, 237-240. *See also* Pocassets; Sakonnets

Wampapaquan, Wampanoag Indian, 30, 32-33

Wamsutta, *see* Alexander

Wannalancet, Pennacook sachem, son of Passaconaway, 84-85, 213

Ware River, 78, 155

Warwick, R. I., 44, 117, 120, 122, 136, 188, 243, 266; Indians sighted at, 44; attacked, 166; abandoned, 188; Talcott overwhelms Indians at, 211-212

Warwick Neck, 211-212

Washaccum Pond, 206

Washington, George, 137

Watching and Warding, *see* Local defense

Watertown, Mass., 7, 45, 87, 162, 173

Watts, Thomas, 127

Waypoiset (Indian locality), 210

Weapons, of the English, 12-13, 68, 106, 123, 134, 160, 235; of the Indians, 5, 20, 25, 26, 27, 51, 172, 209, 219, 221, 238, 239

Weetamoo (Namumpum, Tatapanum), squaw sachem of the Pocassets, 5, 34, 35, 47, 50, 63, 68, 75, 164, 232; joins Philip, 55; at Nipsachuck, 76-77; takes refuge with the Narragansetts, 85, 113

Wells, Jonathan, 204

Wequogan, sachem of the Springfield Indians, 89, 90

Westerly, R. I., 146

Westfield, Mass., 90, 99, 169, 204, 236, 243

West Indies, 7, 148, 192, 226, 244

West Kingston, R. I., 128. *See also* Great Swamp

Wethersfield, Conn., 59, 97

Weymouth, Mass., 45, 160, 172, 185

Wheeler, Thomas, 78, 80-81, 84, 147, 256

Wickford, R. I., 42, 44, 107, 113, 114, 115, 117, 122, 124, 125, 126, 128, 131, 132, 133-134, 135, 137, 138, 140, 212, 243; Narragansetts sign treaty at, 57-59, 60-62; as a base, 120-122, 124, 126-127, 131-132, 135-136, 140-141, 142; Tefft executed at, 139-140; attacked, 166; abandoned, 188. *See also* Smith, Richard, garrison house of

Willard, Simon, 83-84, 170, 256

Willet, Hezekiah, 210

Willett, Thomas, 15

Williams, Roger, 11, 23, 44, 266; and the Harris Case, 18-19; missions to the Narragansetts, 41-42, 56, 58, 254; and the attack on Providence, 168; and Indian prisoners, 225, 227; quoted, 6, 231

Windsor, Conn., 59, 89, 96

Winslow, Job, 36

Winslow, Josiah, Governor of Plymouth Colony, 15, 45, 50, 51, 71, 92, 158, 161, 229, 260; entertains Alexander, 23; warned by Sassamon, 31; writes to Philip and Weetamoo, 34; receives Church's report of Indian hostility, 35; sends aid to Swansea, 37-38; corresponds with Gov. Leverett, 37-38, 40, 67; proposes reduction in size of army, 67, 69; commands expedition against the Narragansetts, 119, 123-144, 155; appraisal of as a commander, 133-134; agrees to Church's terms for the Sakonnets, 216; commissions Church, 217, 229; quoted, 37

Winthrop, Fitz-John, son of Gov. Winthrop, 44

Winthrop, John, Governor of Connecticut, 15, 28, 44-45, 118, 120, 170-171, 264; quoted, 59

Winthrop, Wait, son of Gov. Winthrop, 58-59, 60, 114, 118; quoted, 192

Woburn, Mass., 149, 169, 185

Wollomonuppoag, *see* Wrentham